# LOST IN CARE

To the late John Hamson

# LOST IN CARE

## The problems of maintaining links between children in care and their families

*Spencer Millham*
*Roger Bullock*
*Kenneth Hosie*
*Martin Haak*

Dartington Social Research Unit

Gower

Published by
Gower Publishing Company Limited
Gower House
Croft Road
Aldershot
Hants GU11 3HR
England

and

Gower Publishing Company
Old Post Road
Brookfield
Vermont 05036
USA

**British Library Cataloguing in Publication Data**

Lost in care: the problems of maintaining links
    between children in care and their families.
    1. Child welfare—England   2. Parent and child
    —England
    I. Millham, Spencer
    362.7'32        HV887.G52E5

**Library of Congress Cataloging-in-Publication Data**

Lost in care.
    1. Children—institutional care—Great Britain—
family relationships.   2. Problem children—Great
Britain—family relationships.   3. Social work
with children—Great Britain.

I. Millham, Spencer

HV866.G7L67        1986        362.7'32        85-27015

ISBN 0 566 00998 6

Typeset by Acorn Bookwork,
Salisbury, Wiltshire
Printed in Great Britain by
Blackmore Press, Shaftesbury, Dorset

# Contents

# List of tables

# Acknowledgements

The Dartington Social Research Unit gratefully acknowledges the help and cooperation of the numerous individuals, local authorities and institutions who have made this research possible. First, we should like to thank the staff and elected members in the five local authorities participating in this study. Social workers, care staff and administrative officers gave us much of their time and particular acknowledgement is given to D. Brown, K. Burrows, M. Cartwright, L. Challis, D. Davies, J. Davies, C. Doherty, G. Finn, A. Giller, J. Hamson, E. Hargreaves, A. Haynes, D. Hicks, C. Hookes, M. Jeans, J. Jillings, G. Lannin, J. MacLeod, J. Milford, O. Morgans, S. Park, E. Phillips, P. Pope, D. Rimmer, G. Royle, R. Shadwell, M. Sheehan, A. Shriever, J. Simpson, R. Stephens, H. Stephenson, P. Thistlethwaite, A. Tibbenham, J. Walker, S. Wallis, J. Yeomans and K. Young. We also express our gratitude to the many children, families, foster parents and other interested parties who contributed to the project. Needless to say, all names in this report have been changed to protect identities.

Secondly, we wish to acknowledge the help and advice received from our research and social work colleagues in various universities, colleges and institutes. Again a complete list would be far too long to include, but particular mention must be made of David Fanshel, Jill Farwell, David Fruin, Nicky Jacques, Steve Kelly, Ivis Lasson, Jean Packman, Roy Parker, Phyllida Parsloe, Howard Polsky, Michael Power, John Randall, Margaret Stacey and Jeni Vernon.

Thirdly, we are indebted to both the Department of Health and Social Security and to the Dartington Hall Trust for their support of the Unit while undertaking this study. At the DHSS, we would thank, on behalf of their many staff who have helped us, the Chief Scientists, Sir Douglas Black, Professor A. Buller and Sir Desmond Pond, the Under-Secretaries of the Children's Division, Mr J. Stacpoole, Mr N. Hardyman and Mrs J. Firth and the Director of Social Work Service, Mr W. Utting. We also acknowledge the particular assistance of Miss J. Gilbert and Mrs J. Griffin, the research liaison officers. At Dartington, we are grateful to the Trustees and to H. Williams and E. Cox for providing administrative help.

Many other people have also contributed in various ways and particular thanks are given to B. Bullock, R. Byden, J. Chant, A. Edwards, G. James and B. Kahan. The contribution of the professional organisations who provide the Research Unit with platforms for dissemination is also acknowledged.

Finally, we would thank members of the Research Unit who have helped so much: David Berridge, Margot Blake, Martin Johnson, Michael Kelly, Michael Little and Laurence Mitchell.

We are deeply grateful to them all.

# 1. Introduction

This chapter explores the reasons for mounting a study into the problems of maintaining links between parents and children absent in local authority care. It lays out our research intentions and suggests that in recent years concern has increased at the social isolation and limited family contacts of some children who stay long in care. Why do some children linger in care? How effective are our control and other child care strategies? Why in some cases do family links wither over time? In 1978 the DHSS was receiving conflicting messages on what constituted good practice in several aspects of child care and, as a result, set in motion a number of research initiatives to clarify issues and encourage relevant developments.

'To lose one parent, Mr Worthing, may be regarded as a misfortune, to lose both looks like carelessness,' thundered Lady Bracknell in the opening act of *The Importance of Being Ernest*. A late Victorian audience, more familiar with separations than ourselves and taught to view them with greater equanimity, would have rippled with uneasy laughter at both Ernest's embarrassment and the ironic element of truth in the aristocratic accusation. Separation from parents, either for a short or long period, is a distressing experience for most children, a cruel punishment for 'carelessness' and one which can have lasting consequences. This study looks at one small aspect of separation, the problems faced by parents in maintaining links with their children absent in local authority care. We shall demonstrate that maintaining contact between family and absent child is very important, for unlike the fictional Ernest whose substitute parenting was warm and life-enhancing, many children who stay in local authority care are not as lucky.

Maintaining links between parents and their children away in local authority care presents many difficulties. It is an issue which raises both ethical and practical concerns which the following study seeks to explore. Although there have been temptations to extend the boundaries of our investigation, particularly because the data generated have much wider implications for child care, the problems of contact between parents and absent child remain the prime concern of the pages which follow.

Our interest in the ways in which links between children and their parents are either encouraged, maintained or allowed to wither is of long standing. Much of our previous work, both practically and in research terms, has been into the residential care of young people

*1*

where we have been constantly reminded of the various functions fulfilled by parents' contact with their children.[1] For example, parental exhortation can be used to motivate the absent child, it can facilitate control and can offer unconditional love in contexts where approval is earned and the emotional climate is chilly. What was a continual surprise was the wide variation in the contacts parents and children enjoy with one another while in residential care. Several studies have suggested that similar variations in parental contact are common in foster care.[2]

In our studies of the boarding school system, we found that parents were omnipresent, exerting an influence on the policies and programmes of a wide range of schools.[3] Continuity of the school ethos was assured, sometimes even fossilised, by the expectations of parents and past pupils. Yet parents actually seldom visited the schools, access between parents and children was strictly limited; indeed, parents were frequently viewed by the institutions as nuisances created by the motor car. But if spontaneous parental visits were discouraged, in many other ways links were fostered and parents were used to reinforce the aims, strategies and control approaches of schools. We found that few boys and girls expressed concern over separation; indeed, more complained of the high level of parental scrutiny and the weight of parental expectations. It was also clear that parental involvement stimulated their children in a wide range of academic, sporting, social and even spiritual areas. This nurturing of parental interest was equally evident in the considerable sector of boarding school education provided by local education authorities, which was often meeting social needs that might easily have become the obligation of social services.[4]

The cherishing of links between child and parent in independent boarding schools is in strong contrast to our experience of residential child care and fostering. We shall note as this study develops that both implicitly and explicitly parents whose children are in local authority care face many barriers to maintaining contact, and are relatively powerless to change their situation. For example, in our studies of community homes with education, we found that while some parents continued to visit their children, parents and family were not incorporated into the care and control strategies of the institution.[5] They were occasional embarrassments, presented by the fitful arrivals of the omnibus or zealous social worker. In the same way, several studies of children in foster homes have highlighted how difficult the maintenance of parental contact can be and how stressful it is for children and foster parents. Because parents of children in care are unable to provide for their children, wider deviance often seems to be imputed and a contaminating influence accorded to them. Parental participation is not always ardently sought by alternative care-givers.

Unfortunately, it has been demonstrated that for many children who stay long in residential or foster care and for whom contact with their family is not deemed detrimental, links with home wither over time.[6] Children's isolation presents them with adjustment problems, both while in care and even more seriously on leaving care. Such young people are prone to social isolation, rootlessness, homelessness and shuffle from one bedsit to another, clutching their world in tired carrier bags. For example, we found in our studies of delinquent boys sheltered in community homes with education that two-thirds of the older boys, although initially returning to their parents, were not living with their families six months after leaving.[7] Similar problems present themselves with youths emerging from Borstal.[8] Homelessness correlated significantly with joblessness, poverty, social isolation and subsequent reconviction. Indeed, deep concern at the situation of adolescents, emerging from either residential care or foster homes, has recently prompted interventions, particularly in providing accommodation or sheltered employment. It has also led to some special efforts with those young people who spend several years in care.[9]

While a number of studies have urged earlier legal protection for the child and emphasised the damage of wrenching apart psychological bonds nurtured in substitute care, we shall note in this study that such situations affect only a small minority of the children in care.[10] Most children and young people enter care with ongoing relationships and well-forged links that they seek to maintain. While temporary separation might be necessary, it is to their family or neighbourhood that the majority of children will return. This justifies the focus in this study on the problems of maintaining links between children in care and their families, irrespective of the fact that for a few children, parental contact should be terminated and, for many, their brief stay in care may not raise problems of contact.

In addition, this study echoes the findings of other research in demonstrating that stable care situations, both residential and foster placements, are frequently difficult to maintain.[11] Thus, contact between absent children and their families should have higher priority both in the thinking and practice of social workers. Furthermore, links between absent children and their families not only bring benefits to the child, for parents and others are also fulfilled and supported by contact with children. The advantages of maintaining links between parent and child are not one-way.

On many criteria, therefore, it should be apparent that parents' access to their children is an important issue. Indeed, early in 1984, the government, anxious to clarify the situation, introduced legislation concerning access between children in local authority care and their parents.[12] They also provided a comprehensive code of practice concerning links between the child and the family.

**Reasons for the study**

In 1978, the DHSS was expressing increasing concern about the general child-care population. It was known that there were wide variations in local authority practice and in the rates of admission of children to care, but while policies varied, the reasons for decisions and their consequences for children and families remained unexplored.[13] The numbers of children staying long in local authority care were increasing, yet the factors influencing their length of stay were difficult to identify. It was known, however, that those who remained long in care experienced diminishing contact with their parents and considerable problems on leaving care in adolescence.[14] In the majority of cases, this was contrary to both the ideology and efforts of social workers. Yet, the reorganisation of social services as a consequence of the recommendations made by the Seebohm Committee should have provided the framework for a more comprehensive family service.[15] Clearly, there was a need to scrutinise what was happening, especially as public concern was growing over the alleged indifference of powerful statutory authorities such as social services and education to parents' and children's rights.[16]

Neither, during the decade, were juvenile delinquents gratefully and quietly enjoying their new status as waifs in need of care.[17] Far from hiding in the capacious bosom of social services, young offenders were increasingly evident and noticeable in a way that would have been quite unfamiliar before 1969. For example, the Expenditure Committee of the Social Services Sub-Committee (1975) concerned itself exclusively with the workings of the Children and Young Persons Act 1969.[18] It reviewed the fitful implementation of the legislation and looked at the role of social services with regard to the delinquent and the deprived. The report of the committee highlighted the need for more accurate information on a wide range of services for delinquents, on children's care careers and on the amount and quality of the input from social services. Acute concern was expressed over an increasing number of young people entering the penal system and at the growth of the use of maximum security in child care. The anxiety of the committee was mirrored by that of other influential groups, professional associations, magistrates, police and the youth services, all of whom expressed concern over the contribution and efficacy of social services in caring for and controlling the deprived and delinquent child.[19]

In 1979, the DHSS recognised the need to know more about the general child-care population, reflecting partly the concern within social services itself and partly the increased agitation outside. Improved child-care statistical returns to the Department were certainly providing a picture of what was happening at any given moment and a variety of longitudinal studies in health and education were demonstrating the value of looking, over time, at the careers of children.[20] Unfortunately, these national cohorts contained insufficient children entering and remaining in local authority care to provide an accurate, comprehensive, moving picture of social services child-care practice. Instead of snapshots, what was clearly needed was a movie, constantly changing yet sharply focused on the child-care population. These images would identify processes, problems and outcomes.

The Department was anxious not only to discover how children and their families were being looked after by social services departments but also to identify good child-care approaches as codes of practice and innovations in family care were to be developed. However, dispute rather than consensus raged on some key aspects of the care of separated children.[21] For example, the problems of children in long-stay hospitals were evident but ameliorative strategies were far less clear. Similarly, the increase in secure accommodation and demands for specialised treatment facilities for difficult children might not reflect actual need but might result from inadequacies within the child-care system and self-generated demand.[22] Particularly relevant to this study were the conflicting ideas on the significance of the blood-tie between parent and child, particularly in the light of the Maria Colwell tragedy and other scandals.[23]

## The research programme

The concerns just outlined led to a number of research initiatives from both the DHSS and the Economic and Social Research Council between 1978 and 1982.[24] In addition to looking at the factors influencing a child's entry to and length of stay in care, studies have recently been initiated into children's homes, into foster care, into children leaving care and the problems of long-stay care cases. Many of these studies are interrelated and, conscious of the need to link research to practice, they all seek to communicate and make accessible the findings in an appropriate form. Indeed, the communication and developmental aspects of the research have been increasingly stressed in recent years and some studies, including this one, have an obligation to stimulate and monitor experiment and innovation in the child-care services.

This study, which concerns itself with the problems of maintaining links between parents and children in local authority care, is closely associated with two other studies commissioned by the DHSS. David Fruin of the National Children's Bureau has looked at some of those factors which influence a child's stay in care, while Jean Packman of Exeter University has examined the processes of decision-making as children enter care.[25] Naturally, our research draws on these studies and upon other work completed at Dartington in recent years such as aspects of security in child care, issues of discipline and control in residential child care and the changing function and clientele of the smaller community home.[26]

Not only does evidence from a range of studies inform this work but our approach to the problem of maintaining links between parent and child in local authority care is similar to that which has already proved fruitful. We have always been interested in children's careers, be they unemployed adolescents or those in boarding schools, in reformatory institutions or maximum security. We have found it valuable to look at the sequence of events which change participants' definitions and perspectives of their own situation and of the outside world. Such an approach has yielded interesting material in our previous studies of the young unemployed and the rehabilitation of offenders and we adopt a 'career' focus in the following pages.[27]

## The aims of the study

This study seeks to explore what constitutes a link between parent and the child absent in local authority care. What sorts of links prevail among a characteristic population of children in care? How do these change over time and with what consequences, both for children and families? What are the problems that face linking between parent and child? It may be that links are discouraged by the child's family situation, by the placement which the absent child receives, or by social work policy and practice. A child's isolation in care may result from interaction between all of these factors. Indeed, we shall find that the link between parent and absent child is one facet of a complex child-care situation; parent–child contact is directly related to other factors such as the reasons for the child's admission to care, the legislation employed, and the hopes entertained by social workers for eventual outcome. So, the problems of maintaining links between parents and children in care cannot be viewed in isolation. It is important to bear this in mind throughout the study otherwise discussions of social workers' expectations and the legislation they employ might seem marginal to the links issue.

Because social services departments are known to vary widely in the child-care priorities they follow, we have looked at cohorts of children entering care (450 children in all) in five contrasting local authorities; rural, urban, suburban, and several decayed inner city areas. These have been selected to provide a representative national picture.

This study will concern itself with the problems of maintaining links with their families faced by *all* children entering care whatever their age, reasons for admission or length of stay. In addition, the focus of the research is the *problems* of maintaining links rather than the beneficial or other consequences of keeping in contact with parents. Inevitably, this gives the study which follows a 'problem' orientation. It is not disputed that, for a minority of children, it is in their best interests to discourage contact with home. Neither do we question the fact that only a few of the children who are able to leave care early suffer major difficulties in maintaining contact with parents. The study focuses on those children who are likely to stay some time in care and who, in spite of social work efforts, experience withering contacts with home. For these children, it will be shown that a decline in family contact means that they will stay in care and that their emotional and intellectual functioning will be impaired.

It is also important to stress that the study does not seek to advance the well-documented psychological and social consequences of separation for children. Neither does it investigate the criteria on which access and other contact decisions *should* be made.[28] It highlights the problems that social workers, children, families and care-givers face in managing links with home. It will be shown that links are part of the wider processes of social work intervention. They are a necessary, although not a sufficient, condition for return. The study provides guidance for social workers and seeks to show the ways in which many children are isolated as they remain in care and how this isolation has occurred.

Because the following report concerns itself with all children coming into care, whatever their age and reasons for admission, certain groups of children of particular interest are either insufficiently numerous in the sample or can only receive scant attention in what is a general picture of child-care processes. For example, many children are remanded to the care of local authorities because of delinquency, many enter care subsequent to a place of safety order, and many belong to ethnic minorities. These and other concerns are explored elsewhere.[29] In addition, the design and timing of the research means that certain issues have scarcely surfaced. For example, few care orders were revoked in the two years of the follow-up study, few adoptions had been finalised, and the legislation concerning wardship had only just been introduced.

We can now turn to look at the methodology in more detail, to examine some of the theoretical and practical problems faced by this study.

## Summary points

1. Much concern was expressed during the 1970s over the problems of maintaining links between parents and their children absent in local authority care.
2. The Expenditure Committee of the Social Services Sub-Committee (1975) highlighted deficiencies in and lack of information on chil-

dren's care careers, particularly the experience of delinquents and adolescents.

3. The DHSS was receiving conflicting messages from experts and pressure groups on what constitutes good child-care practice and, as a result, sought clarification of issues from research studies. They initiated several investigations to help them offer guidance to social workers.

# 2. Methodology

This chapter outlines our research design. It emphasises that the contractual approach to research adopted by government departments places limits on any investigation. It puts a premium on application, development and a concern with policy variables. We seek to justify a 'process' approach to the study of child care, an investigation which explores changes and revisions in participants' perspectives as well as outcomes over time. Here we attempt to clarify certain conceptual problems, such as what constitutes a family, what are links, and what problems are raised in the management of separation and parental access. We lay out the relationship between our *extensive* survey of 450 children entering care in five local authorities and our *intensive* study of the care experiences which is illustrated by four case studies.

A marked feature of British social research has been the desire to match theoretical ideas with empirical evidence. Ever since the early social surveys of Booth and Rowntree, there has been a concern to argue policy from a factual base, a procedure that contrasts sharply with many European traditions.[1] This wish to link the quantitative and qualitative in a way that seeks social improvement and delivers a policy message from research is manifest in the style of many government inquiries and the publications from academic institutes, and survey research companies.

This empirical tradition has naturally led to much criticism.[2] It is often claimed, for example, that micro-analysis does not contribute to macroscopic thinking and, thus, social theory is not advanced. Other observers stress that the approach is too inductive and that facts are often left to speak for themselves. For example, in this study one does not require much evidence beyond children's frequent movements while in care to account for their disrupted educational experience. But unquestioned faith in measurement and survey techniques avoids the deeper question of the values that are implicit in the questions asked, the data gathered and the methods of analysis.

In the 1970s, the criticisms of field-based research spread beyond these caveats. More searching questions were raised about the scientific and moral bases of data collection. The classic scientific procedure for examining hypotheses in the light of assembled evidence was complicated by debates about the very nature of social facts. A renewed emphasis was given to the 'meanings' intrinsic to action and this demanded a new definition of objectivity. It is clear that participants in social interaction will play their roles in the light of previous

experiences, they will interpret situations, choose actions and negotiate with others to achieve their ends. Prediction, one of the main
techniques of validation in the scientific method, is, therefore, made
more difficult in the social sciences as individuals can choose between
a range of strategies. Indeed, this lack of certainty and authority has
led to much discussion about the 'scientific' aspects of social research.[3]

Viewed in this light, research itself is a social process and, as such,
is subject to these same forces. Thus, links between research and
policy are rather more complicated than that suggested by the simple
perspectives of empiricism. As Rutter has commented:

Research is not primarily concerned with the collection of facts, nor even with
the derivation and testing of laws. Rather, it provides the means (or, more
accurately, many different means) of posing and answering questions.[4]

It will be seen that in the design of this research we have sought to
meet some of these criticisms. Various theoretical perspectives and
concepts have been explored in the hope that they will prove appropriate for understanding the problems of children in care. In addition,
the study is based on new evidence collected from two surveys. The
first is a two-year longitudinal scrutiny of 450 children coming into
care in five local authorities in England and Wales. This provides an
extensive picture across the country of broad processes and children's
care careers. The second study is an intensive examination of 30 of
these children, each from different families, which seeks to explore
the many negotiations which take place between child, family, social
workers and other professionals. Themes which emerge from this
exploration are illustrated in four case studies.

It is important to remember that from the outset this research has
sought to clarify policy issues. Questions of parental participation and
access to their children caused concern in social work in the late 1970s
and issues such as the conflict between the blood-tie and surrogate
parent, the problems of isolated 'children who wait' and the needs of
adolescents in care were much debated. In the 1980s, links between
children in care and their families remain a contentious issue and the
causes of many families have been taken up by pressure groups such as
the Family Rights Group, Children's Legal Centre and Justice for
Children.[5] Certain practices, such as the taking of place of safety
orders and the assumption of parental rights, have been widely criticised, and since 1984 the parents of children in care have had a legal
right to seek from a court an access order to their children if contact
has been terminated by a social worker. The DHSS has also issued a
code of good practice for local authorities in connection with parental
contact.[6]

**Methodological issues**
This study of the problems of maintaining links between the children in care and their families raises several of the issues just discussed and our research design has tried to meet the most significant of them. Inevitably, any research exercise has to be something of a compromise. In the study which follows, we attempt to link ideas on process, structure and function with people's perceptions of their situations. Not only is this extremely difficult, as our other studies have demonstrated, but the attempt is unlikely to satisfy those committed to a particular viewpoint, while, from the point of view of the research customer, such as policy-makers and social workers, such academic concerns are unlikely to be very interesting.

Our first task was to identify those theoretical perspectives which would best guide the investigation. Obviously, such selection would have to be somewhat arbitrary for certain perspectives emphasise order and stability in organisations at the expense of conflict and change. Fortunately, much previous work in child care coupled with an adequate pilot study helped our research orientation.

A decision on where to begin studying the links between children in care and their families was helped by the existence of the two other studies previously mentioned. Jean Packman has examined the decision-making processes surrounding children's admission to care and David Fruin has looked at the factors which affect the length of stay of children once in care.[7] Both of these studies provide new information about children admitted to care which means that in the pages which follow we can suspend concerns over why some children and their families surface for intervention and enter care, while others with similar problems do not. As these issues have been scrutinised by others, our starting point can be children as they come into care whatever the reasons and whatever the child's home circumstances. Once in care, our focus is the management of relationships between care-givers, social workers, parents and children, matters which we shall note have been shown by other research, such as that of Fanshel, Gambrill, Lasson and Thorpe, to be associated with length of stay and probabilities of rehabilitation.[8]

A number of theoretical perspectives were found to be useful in guiding this inquiry.

*Child care as a process*
First, there seemed to be considerable benefit in looking at the child-care system as a *social process*.[9] Our research into delinquency and our exploratory studies of children in care in one local authority have shown how children embark on a 'career' once they arrive in care.[10] This echoes many studies in the sociology of education, medicine,

deviance and in the psychology of organisations and mental health.[11] Several of our previous studies have used this perspective, for example in boarding education, in efforts to reform offenders or to provide for difficult children; indeed, even in research into social work training, we have found that a longitudinal perspective has been very fruitful.

Decisions on the placements of children in care, the legislation that has to be employed, and the caring potential of the child's family, have to be made regularly and each of these has important consequences, particularly for the contacts which children have with their families. We also need to know what happens to children when they are in care, how they progress and what are the possibilities at each stage. In a study of maximum security, for example, we were able, after examining large numbers of children passing through closed units, to identify the ways in which the child-care system both generates and then resolves failures of care.[12] Hence, to understand why some children linger in care and others emerge, and how parental contact is affected by wider social work decisions, a dynamic approach rather than a static analysis is needed. Children's responses to their placements, their emotional and educational progress and their ability to cope with new social roles are very much part of the care process and children's careers in care are shaped as much by their adaptations as by the resources at hand. Thus, it is important to monitor the 'career'.

*The care experience and separation*
The significance of early family experiences for the social and emotional development of the child has evolved out of extensive sociological, medical and psychological research.[13] The most publicised focus of separation theory has been the maternal deprivation hypothesis, which links the interference with early bonds between mother and child to subsequent development. Naturally, the medical and psychological literature surrounding this issue is extensive and will be reviewed in a subsequent chapter. Indeed, the original Bowlby hypothesis has been much revised. Writers such as Rutter and the Clarkes have questioned the biological basis of this explanation and have stressed the importance of other factors such as variations in the time and context of separation.[14]

Nevertheless, this perspective has clearly influenced the care of separated children. For example, the writings of Goldfarb, Bowlby and the Robertsons have contributed much to the 'humanising' of care provision for the very young, especially in residential nurseries and hospitals.[15] In addition, the unrestricted visiting of infants in some residential care, provision for mothers and babies and the development of special fostering services are all practical consequences springing from this theoretical stance. Indeed, the concept of 'psychological parenting' proposed by Goldstein, Freud and Solnit was influential in the drafting of the Children Act 1975.[16]

As our project is concerned with the more general problems of managing links between separated parents and children, we shall not seek to add to the micro-analysis of maternal deprivation. However, this study does raise some questions which are relevant to these issues, particularly the problems which families face in managing separation, the difficulties of return and the important, if neglected, contribution of the extended family. We also suggest that benefits may be gained if the fathers of children in care received greater scrutiny and encouragement.

Our findings should complement several other recent studies which have suggested that the break in the mother–child bond is not sufficient to explain the subsequent behaviour of children. Such a view seems too narrow in that it does not take account of the difficulties experienced by the older child who is removed from home, nor does it adequately explain the apparent normality of those socialised for the experience, such as children who go away to boarding schools at an early age.[17] It would appear that the manner in which children are prepared for leaving home is as important as the separation itself and the early psychological studies have been criticised for ignoring the influence of relationships which prevail in the child's family.

*Negotiations between individual and state*

The third theoretical view that has influenced our thinking is to view our system of care as a negotiation between the state and the individual.[18] The law demands only certain basic standards of parents; for example, that they should support their offspring, maintain their health and present them for education. Many other areas, such as a child's religious upbringing, diet, appearance and leisure activities are normally regarded as private. But, in cases where parents manifestly appear to fail in their task, the state assumes the authority to intervene and grants to its agents, such as police and social workers, a mandate to do so.

This assumption of parental rights by the state has been a very gradual process over the centuries and much that we take for granted today in child care has very considerable antecedents.[19] We shall briefly glance at the origins of care legislation for children because the present uneasy relationship between parent and child in care owes much to the Poor Law and to nineteenth-century infant and child rescue legislation. As in our other studies, such as those of boarding and reformatory institutions, it is difficult to understand the present without, at least, some glimpse of the past.

Today, the admission of a child to care is one solution to the problem of parents' inability or unwillingness to provide but, while the intervention is legitimate, the care options are negotiable. A child may be placed in any of a whole range of settings. This perspective leads us, therefore, to view care as a response to the problems of meeting the needs of vulnerable children. Such a view would ask why some children become visible to the authorities, why some are referred to social services, why some are admitted to care while others are not, how the care plan is constructed and why vulnerable children embark on different careers through health, education and social services.

Naturally, a study of the links beween parents and their children absent in care cannot hope to explore these questions but they need to be kept in mind as a research design is framed. Indeed, in the case of middle-class children or dislocations brought about for other reasons, such as divorce, the complementary question is raised as to why admission to state care is rarely entertained. Such a perspective also asks whether the state, through the local authority, is able to provide 'good enough' parenting.[20] Indeed, the study which follows offers some disquieting answers to these questions.

Because interference in parenting should only be justified if the state can be seen to provide a good alternative, such interventions should be evaluated. Much research indicates that long-term care itself creates many secondary adjustment problems for both child and family, such as social isolation, educational disadvantage or other problems of separation.[21] In addition, this perspective brings the role of the social worker under scrutiny, highlighting its varying legitimacy and intrinsic role conflict. For example, we shall see the omnipresent tension between care and control and between family support and child rescue. Indeed, we shall see that some of the families of children in care initially came to social services seeking help and advice, unaware of the full implications of their actions. Sometimes, quite unwittingly, they initiated a course of events which culminated in the removal of their child from home.

We have described three contrasting theoretical perspectives which have helped us to focus on some of the questions central to our research interests. Used in isolation, each perspective would act as a straitjacket on scrutiny rather than facilitate investigation. However, together they generate the concepts which will guide the research.

## Conceptual problems in this research

We have suggested that some methodological problems were eased in this study by the clear legal definitions of a child being in care. The population of our study has been mapped out for us by unambiguous legal and administrative categories. What is more, there are no 'grey' areas between those children 'in' and 'out' of care, although children at home 'on trial' are something of an intermediate category.[22] The initial problems of definition faced by much social research, such as that into delinquency or mental illness, are less severe in this study. But if our study population is clear, other aspects, such as children's social circumstances, are riddled with confusion and ambiguity. Several aspects of the child's social context require clarification.

### The child's family

Our preliminary studies quickly established that the family circumstances of children in care are very complex as often the family group has been dislocated and fragmented through death, illness or separation.[23] For example, we shall see that few of the children's natural parents were still living together at the time of our study. Family structures also change over time and reconstitution through cohabitations and remarriages are common. Frequently, even before the care intervention by social services, parents are not able to provide for their children, and relatives intervene.

We decided, therefore, that there was no simple way of classifying family structures.[24] So, for each child in our study cohorts, we recorded details of the *household* in which they were living – its location, who lived there, the occupation and ages of its members. This focus on the household overcomes problems presented by changing relationships in the family and sets out the physical and emotional bases in the child's life. If the child's mother or father is absent from this household, we then ask similar questions about their marital status and the households in which they live. We also note close relatives who are alive, and explore their contribution. This enables us to identify the extended family which may include step- and half-relatives as well as siblings, aunts, uncles and grandparents. Thus, complementary maps are built up of both the family structure and location.

In following up children as they remain in care, changes are carefully recorded. Modifications to the household, such as deaths, divorces and remarriage, are noted. Questions also explore changes in the employment, health and economic circumstances of each household, as well as in the quality of prevailing relationships. At six months, or earlier if the child leaves care, an assessment is made of the health problems, behavioural difficulties and economic circumstances faced by the child's family in addition to the quality of care experienced by the child in the early years. As these factors have implications for links between parents and the child in care, all such issues are explored even if their influence on relationships with the child is not immediately apparent.

This approach enables us to chart the emotional, geographical and physical features of the child's family and to monitor changes over time. It overcomes the danger of concentrating on one aspect at the expense of others and highlights the overall context in which links between home and the child take place. Indeed, family structures at the point of the child's admission to care may well be temporary and abnormal. Thus, our approach can highlight rapid family changes and the ways in which children in care fit into or are stranded by such vicissitudes.

*Links*

A second problematic concept has been the *links* between the children in care and their families. This is explored further in a subsequent chapter but the *Oxford Dictionary* defines a link as 'a thing or person that unites others'. It would have been a relatively easy task to record meetings between a child and relatives but a link includes much more than personal contact. There are other communications, by telephone, by letter or by mutual acquaintances, such as relatives attending the same school or social workers themselves. Our studies of other children in residential care have also shown that perceptions of contact are quite as important as the frequency.[25] Links have a symbolic dimension and those separated clasp mementoes, personalise space and jealously guard territory. Hence, in undertaking this study of links we had to consider not only distance between separated parties but also such things as access to telephone and public transport, the ability of participants to read and write and cultural perspectives entertained by children, parents and care-givers. Naturally, social worker contacts and the bridging role they pursued will be very significant as will the financial help available to families, the information that is made available, the differing styles of placements, such as fostering and residential care, and the constraints offered by access and other restrictions.

Links also have a power dimension. Actual contact may not be necessary when the participants have power to intervene and change a situation should the need arise. In our earlier work in preparatory schools, for example, we were often surprised by children's statements that they felt close to their parents in situations when they saw them infrequently, perhaps when parents were overseas.[26] It was clear that perceptions of links did not correspond with the frequency of contact and children felt close to absent parents who they knew would act in their interests as and when necessary. Lack of knowledge and the inability to initiate action puts a strain on links, particularly as parental ignorance can give advantage to social workers in managing the child's care career.

When a child is away from home it is the responsibility of a social worker to keep parents closely informed of the child's situation and to arrange, except in cases where severance of contact is deemed necessary, for parents and children to have access to one another. Travel can be subsidised, visitors escorted, meetings arranged, all at the social worker's discretion. Yet, we shall find that what might have been expected to be early, precise and explicit understandings between participants are rarely in evidence.

## Access

It should be noted that few parents are anxious to see the departure of their child to care and the majority seek access to their children and strive to make contact in other ways. However, depending on the family situation, social workers will decide what sorts of contact are advisable. As a result, some social workers' decisions on access will be explicit, such as those following non-accidental injury when a parent may be restrained from seeing their child. But such clearcut arrangements are rare, particularly in the early months of the child's stay in care. In fact, decisions on contact are rarely explicit and access arrangements tend to 'emerge'. They are often seen as and allowed to remain subsidiary to other issues deemed more important.

It will also be established in the following pages that a lack of official restriction on contact between family and absent child does not necessarily imply free and unimpeded access. Sometimes, restrictions on contact with the child are *specific* to individuals whereas in other cases, they are inherent in the placement, such as in the visiting regulations to residential institutions or in foster home arrangements. These *non-specific* barriers can be both severe and widespread, even encouraged by social workers to limit contact, such as when placing a child received into voluntary care with foster parents who have adoption aspirations. Therefore, we need to know a great deal more about decisions which ostensibly have little to do with access, for example, the placement of children in distant, controlling settings to discourage family contacts or using 'out of county' secure accommodation or remote community or foster homes.

The exploration of access is a salient feature of both our extensive and intensive studies. The extensive study of five local authorities provides a wealth of evidence on the sorts of links experienced by the children and their parents and explores the range of formal and informal access arrangements which influence such relationships. It should also elucidate important decisions which affect the wider social networks of the child in care, such as placement and access arrangements. This picture will be given depth by an intensive study of families in one area which looks in detail at the ways in which access is negotiated between parents and child, the perceptions participants have of satisfactory links and the bargaining that takes place. Particular note will be taken of visits to children by parents, highlighting the difficulties the participants face, the message conveyed in the interaction and the role taken up by social work staff. But we have to take care not to impose our own assumptions. For example, our interviews with children and parents suggest that anxieties about travel are often caused as much by unfamiliarity with new districts as by the vagaries of public transport. Similarly, regular access may actually generate stress in parents and children rather than reduce it, yet it should not be assumed that distress provides the most effective barometer of either the child's or the parent's psychological health or long-term well-being.

## Theoretical and conceptual problems: summary

We have now considered some of the theoretical perspectives which have guided our thinking about this project and examined some significant concepts. As we have suggested, any research design must stress certain values at the expense of others. However, this approach, we believe, is as objective as is possible in the circumstances. By using a range of methods, multidimensional concepts can be explored in the light of evidence gathered from a variety of sources. This would seem to us to be the best way to promote a scientific assessment of the problems of maintaining links and to highlight other aspects of family/ child relationships or care careers which merit further investigation. We accept Merton's view that objectivity is established over time by the institutional structure of science and the values permeating its practice rather than the absence of bias in value-free research designs.[27] Let us now turn to the details of the research design itself.

## Research design

The study of the problems of maintaining links between children in care and their families is divided into four parts. The first task was to identify those areas of concern which, as we have just noted, were relevant to this study. Naturally, a number of useful studies existed and, indeed, in some areas such as the family, separation/divorce/ bereavement and issues of social policy, the literature from both here and abroad is considerable. Of particular interest to us has been the work of Fanshel, Goldstein *et al.*, Gambrill, Tizard, Hall and Stacey, Lasson, Kellmer Pringle, Walton and Heyward, Anna Freud, Rowe and Lambert and Wallerstein and Kelly, all of whom have written about the family situation of client groups similar to our own.[28] There are, of course, numerous studies of other aspects of the problem, such as fostering, children in residential care and family disruption. It was from this literature, which is more fully described later in this study, that we were able to extract the key issues which we have just described.

Concurrent with this review of the literature and discussions with those who have mounted similar research programmes, a feasibility study for the project was undertaken in one local authority.[29] This preliminary investigation involved studying all children in the care of three areas of the county on a particular day. The case histories of every child (165 in all) were analysed from records and carefully discussed with the social workers concerned. It was from this and other knowledge gleaned from social work literature that the theoretical problems were approached and the following programme of research was planned.

## The extensive and intensive studies

In January 1980, a number of separate studies began: the first, a longitudinal, extensive study of large numbers of children coming into care in five different areas of the country, the second an intensive follow-up of 30 children in one of the areas (of which four provide our case studies) and the third, a more detailed study of important sub-groups of children or care situations. A cross-section of local authorities was required because there are wide variations in the child-care policies and populations of different areas.

### Selection of local authorities

For the extensive study, five contrasting local authorities were carefully selected. From the analysis of local authority characteristics published by the DHSS, census data and national child-care statistics, local authorities were classified according to the characteristics of their children in care, their general population profiles and their child-care policies and practices.[30] Using this classification of local authorities, we selected five contrasting areas which were representative of different types of child-care problems and national characteristics. Hence the areas are widely distributed geographically and include districts that are predominantly rural, urban, inner city and large housing estates. Some also contain ethnic minorities and have different occupational and social structures with wide variations in social services provision and policy.

### The extensive study

The extensive study monitors the progress of a large number of children coming into care and enables us to see where these children are placed, what decisions have to be made and the links between child and family that prevail. Hence, it offers a comparative view of child-care services and provides us with a picture of national trends and current social work thinking. This is important simply because very little information seems to be available on child-care populations, how they change over time and what provision is made for them. The weakness of any examination of the work of social service teams, particularly from the narrower perspective of links between parents and families, is that the evidence inevitably rests on social workers' case records, views, administrative decisions and policies. It can only look in very general terms at the negotiations between child, family and social services.

As statistical analysis is often hampered by small numbers, particularly when sub-groups need scrutiny, it was important that our survey should be sufficiently large for us to chart child-care processes satisfactorily. The feasibility study suggested that five cohorts of 100 children would be adequate in providing both sufficient numbers of long-term cases and a wide range of care situations.

The population for this extensive study, therefore, comprises the first 100 children in each of the five areas to come into care, for whatever reason, after 1 January 1980. In four of the participating local authorities, receptions were frequent so cohorts of children entering care were built up quickly. However, in the remaining local authority rates were slower and by the autumn of 1980, the cohort was closed with 50 children included, making the total study population 450.

Generally, all children entering care have been included, whatever their age and care status. However, when a child has been *remanded* to care, usually for persistent and serious delinquency, these situations have been studied separately.[31] This is because short-term remands do not raise immediate problems of maintaining links and in the city areas the high numbers of such cases would have dominated the study population. However, when those remanded to care subsequently receive care orders, they become part of the cohorts under study.

Place of safety orders are also included *ab initio* in this study although, legally, such children are not in care.[32] Our pilot study confirmed that in place of safety situations, social workers have to make urgent decisions about family links, usually removing children to child-care placements for safety, and seeking action that often has long-term consequences. Again, these orders are studied separately, even if they are not followed by care proceedings.

The social worker responsible for the child has been carefully and repeatedly interviewed from the moment the child enters care. This investigation includes items relevant to our theoretical perspectives on the care process and on the negotiations between social workers and parents as well as the aims and functions of social work intervention.

Information on family structure, parental contact and decision-making incorporates the dimensions previously described.

All children were followed up until either they left care or had remained in care for two years. The pilot study suggested that this was an optimum period for scrutiny as, by then, most of the important decisions had been made and the implications of these for family links would be clear. A longer follow-up might have yielded some benefits, such as making the study more comprehensive, but small gains were likely to be offset by the common risk inherent in all longitudinal work, namely the problems of ageing data which become out of tune with current thinking.

After six months, the child's social worker was again interviewed. Details of the child's family situation and placements were updated and the interview explored the relationship between the social work decisions, the patterns of links between parent and child that prevail and the child's adaptation to the care process; that is, the way that intellectual and emotional progress is perceived, any changes in his or her social life and the ability to respond to the roles demanded. This follow-up interview was repeated at 12 and 24 months if the child remained in care.

When the child left care, social workers were interviewed to assess the reasons for the patterns of family links that prevailed and assessments were made of the child's home and placement. There were also questions about the social worker's views of the situation, the social work team's perspective on the possibilities of a child's return to care and the long-term viability of the family.

When a child is readmitted to care, the precipitating circumstances are again recorded but the admission does not become a new entry to the cohort. This group of readmissions is important as it throws light on why some children are able to leave care quickly, how vulnerable they are and whether or not they are likely to be referred to social services on subsequent occasions.[33]

Although social workers have had the option not to participate in this research or to exclude certain problematic cases, there have been no refusals or omissions. Hence, there has been neither sampling nor exclusion in this research and the study cohort represents the complete population of the first 100 children coming into care in each area in 1980.

Nevertheless, such a longitudinal survey of a large number of children suffers from some of the criticisms of empiricism which we have described. Even though sampling problems are absent, there is still the danger that the survey design as well as the content of questions may reflect implicit assumptions on our part.

These criticisms may be quite valid but we would stress that this survey is only one part of a wider research programme. It is paralleled by other on-going studies which have adopted a different stance and by research both here and abroad which looks at identical issues. As designed, we feel that it is relevant to our understanding of care as a process and of the functions of social work for the wider society. It also explores the 'meaning' of structures as faced by social workers and the perceived options available at various times. We shall find as the study progresses that it echoes many other findings from research and thus builds up a consensus on what is appropriate regarding family contact.

### The intensive study

The extensive survey is supplemented by deeper research into one of the study cohorts. In one of the participating areas, the longitudinal study involves more intensive work with a group drawn from the 100 children coming into care. A sub-group of 30 children was selected and for these children, members of the research unit visited parents, care-givers and children soon after reception and at regular intervals to explore in greater detail the experiences and perceptions of all parties involved in the care situation.

From 30 children in this intensive study four families were selected for case studies which provide illustrations of important child-care processes. For example, the crisis nature of entry, the sense of shock experienced by the family and the difficulties of visiting and return. These situations will not be analysed statistically as this would mirror too much the extensive survey but will be used to explain the processes identified by the wider survey. In combination with the extensive study, the knowledge gained from the intensive work should enable us to generalise with greater confidence.

The intensive study will explore further some of the theoretical dimensions which have guided our extensive survey. We have noted how our interest in process and client careers has led us to consider changes over time in people's self-perceptions and the roles they adopt. While the extensive research will provide much that is relevant to these points, we see the intensive work as particularly important in understanding the perceptions of those involved in the care process and the changes in role that they adopt over time. Similarly, many issues surrounding separation will be explored in the intensive study.

While we accept that interviews have rather limited value in generating hard information, we believe that this approach is acceptable as long as interpretation of replies takes note of any independent indicators available. Often, grand intentions prove pretentious in the light of their poor results. In the present study, breakdowns or changes of placements, problem behaviour of children, variations in parental visiting, changes in social work strategy or significant changes in legislation all provide independent guides to the child's care career and the links enjoyed with the family. Nevertheless, great care must be taken not to assume that all these are negative indicators of the care situation. Children's distress, for example, attendant on a parental visit may be a positive sign. Similar problems of perception and interpretation arise when considering people's feelings about family relationships, a deep hatred may be as psychologically healthy as deep love. It has proved extremely difficult to use standardised tests in this research which involves such a heterogeneous group of children and setting of established tests in households had to be abandoned.

One further problem raised by the intensive study is that many children coming into care are very young and interview methods will not be appropriate to explore their perceptions. In such situations, there is no single alternative to questionnaires and here, one must look at indices of the child's adaptation. Evidence from parents, placement staff and social workers, as well as the health visitors and paediatricians who are usually involved, provide some indication and, once the child is in care, a check-list is used to coordinate information. Heads of residential homes in the local authority selected have also assisted us by making available their records of the child's behaviour. In foster placements, however, such records do not exist and we have had to rely on interviews with foster parents, social workers' reports, parents' replies and our own observations.

In the following chapters, we shall pay particular attention to four of the families studied. The families have been selected to illustrate the range of child-care problems facing social services departments and the ways that these are related to the difficulties in maintaining links between children and their families. Hence, one example focuses on a difficult adolescent, another on an unsupported mother with young children, and so on. The four case studies also seek to illustrate that within a single category, such as 'single parent', several child-care careers are possible and the role of contacts between parent and child can be quite different. They also seek to show that families are more vulnerable to disruption at some times than others and that the juxtaposition of different crises can be as significant as the individual crises themselves. For example, it is clear that the reconstitution of dislocated families is as likely to precipitate children into care and keep them there as much as are other deprivations and dislocations.

We have seen that while our extensive study lays out the processes and boundaries of the child-care system, this intensive inquiry seeks to explore further the actions involved and to explain the connections observed. Each study is limited without the other but in combination they tackle the nature, cause and consequence of the present problem at hand.

## Sub-studies

There are several weaknesses in the use of longitudinal cohort studies. One is that certain important categories may be little represented. Secondly, because there is a focus on changes over time, important micro-studies excite less interest. For example, in this study of children's care careers, certain age and legal categories may be uncommon and some important care situations will be unusual. Children in care as a result of matrimonial proceedings or offenders in secure accommodation are good examples. While they cause concern at a national level, they occur in insufficient numbers for study. Although the research design can highlight these groups, it does not lend itself to detailed studies of particular clients or issues. It has, therefore, been necessary to explore some of these problems in a series of sub-studies which complement the general study.[34]

## Conclusions

The methodology for this study of maintaining links between children in care and their families is complex. This arises from the need to consider a variety of theoretical perspectives and from the multi-dimensional nature of many concepts. It will be seen that a range of research techniques has been employed in the belief that some methods are more appropriate than others. In the extensive work, which charts processes and draws boundaries, we have used questionnaires, analysis of records and interviews with social workers. This approach has been supplemented in the intensive study by an exploration of the perceptions of all participants in the care experience, made by repeated, in-depth interviews. A degree of objectivity is ensured by the fact that the issues we are investigating are subject to wider research scrutiny and have independent criteria of outcome.

However, any preoccupation with some aspects of a methodology can easily distract us from other equally important issues. There are many forces influencing the construction of a methodology. Just like the clients, research workers are much influenced by their social situation.

The factors which influence a methodology are not only theoretical but, as we have illustrated, are also simply pragmatic. Indeed, fashioning the methodology is often less fraught an enterprise than gaining the cooperation of social workers, achieving access to clients and information or meeting the expectations of those who commission research. What is more, the longitudinal nature of this study means that people's commitment has to be maintained over time. The construction of the methodology is only a small part of the task and its sophistication is often greatly limited by the restricted time and involvement available to others. Setting a test of family relationships is difficult in competition with the TV, just as we have found sociometry breaks down with bored adolescents who would rather be playing football. Nevertheless, in this chapter, we have tried to describe the ways in which we have attempted to overcome research problems, both theoretical and pragmatic, and how we have tried to devise a methodology appropriate for the study of the problems of maintaining links between children in care and their families.

## Summary points

1. A 'process approach' will be adopted in this research, looking at children's careers over time. The *extensive* study of 450 children entering care in five local authorities and scrutinised over two years was supplemented by an *intensive* study of 30 families experiencing a care intervention from which our four case studies have been selected.
2. The study focuses on the management of separation by social workers, families and care-givers.
3. It clarifies what is meant by 'parents', 'wider family' and 'household'.
4. It distinguishes between 'family contacts', 'relationships' and the wider concept of 'parental links'.
5. Access to their absent children is important for most parents and we distinguish between *specific* restrictions on access, i.e. peculiar to individuals or location and duration of visits, and *non-specific* restrictions, those which are inherent in the child's placement, e.g. distance, routine and regulations.

# 3. Entry into care – the legislation and its antecedents

This chapter lays out the various ways in which children can be admitted to the care of local authorities. It explores some of the antecedents of present child-care legislation. Because poor parents, falling upon parish relief, were often considered to be a source of contamination to their children and because supplicants were to be discouraged from and punished for seeking support, children in state care were frequently separated from destitute parents for long periods. Consequently, in the past, the maintenance of family links received little consideration. However, recently, perspectives have changed, culminating in access legislation and the development of codes of good practice concerning parents' contacts with their separated children. We also suggest that while issues of control and the visibility of certain problems previously prompted legislative action concerning children, pressures have changed as the needs of both children and parents have come to be recognised.

Children can be admitted to the care of the local authority in a variety of ways.[1] Section 2 of the 1980 Child Care Act allows for any boy or girl under the age of seventeen to be 'received into care' of the local authority if he or she is abandoned or lost, has no parents or guardian or has parents or guardians who are prevented for some reason for caring for them. The arrangements for such receptions are voluntary in that the local authority provides temporary relief and parents can remove their child from care during the early stages at will. Indeed, the local authority has a specific responsibility to ensure that, if appropriate, the child is returned home as quickly as possible. However if the child has stayed in care for more than six months, parents must give the local authority notice of their intention to seek the return of their child.

However, we shall see that the family situation of children in care changes rapidly and fresh information comes to light concerning the child's problems as the care situation develops. As a result, under certain conditions, where substitute care is deemed preferable to the child's natural family, the social services committee of the local authority responsible for the child can pass a resolution in respect of a child already in care in order to assume full parental rights (Section 3 of the 1980 Act). In this case, the parents cannot ask for the automatic return of their child and, if their influence is thought to be detrimental, can even be denied access to their child.

The 1980 Child Care Act consolidates much previous legislation. For example, the 1948 Children Act distinguished between voluntary receptions and parental rights resolutions. It also set up a children's department in every local authority.[2] Although later Acts gave additional functions to these children's departments, for example, in the field of adoption, a predominantly rescue role continued to be the statutory function of the service until 1963 when further legislation empowered local authorities to develop preventive work, 'designed to reduce the need to receive children into care or to bring them before the court'.

Further protection was also given to children already in care and to foster parents by the 1975 Children Act which obliges social workers to consult the child about his or her wishes and restricts parents' freedom to take their child out of care unilaterally once six months have elapsed. New rights of appeal have also been made available to parents, including a procedure in the Health and Social Services and Social Security Adjudications Act 1983 for parents to appeal to a court for an 'access order' when contact with their child had been formally terminated by a social worker.

Children in need of care and protection or who are deemed to be beyond control can be committed to care by a juvenile court, if necessary against the wishes of parents. The 1933 Children and Young Persons Act allowed a court to order that a child who, for example, failed to attend school or who was considered to be 'at risk', be committed to care on a 'fit person order', with the local authority usually designated as the 'fit person'. Delinquents, however, were dealt with slightly differently. While some were cared for by children's departments under fit person orders, many of the more serious offenders received approved school orders and were the responsibility of the Home Office. It was not until 1969 that legislation embraced all children at risk under a single 'care order' and made them the responsibility of the local authorities.

Committals to care by courts are now governed by the 1969 Children and Young Persons Act. Seven grounds for care proceedings now exist and include, as before, the absence of adequate care, protection or control, neglect or ill-treatment, in which case the local authority, police or NSPCC may initiate care proceedings and, in some cases, seek a 'care order'. For dealing with young offenders, however, the old system has changed. Where appropriate, criminal proceedings against juveniles of ten years and over are heard in the juvenile court and care orders can be made.

Under both these procedures, the care order made by the court gives the local authority full parental rights. Care orders have no specific duration and can continue until the age of eighteen or even nineteen in some cases. However, the child, parents or local authority can apply at any time to the court for a discharge of the care order.

In non-criminal cases, the 1969 Act also includes provision for the court to make a renewable interim care order, usually for 28 days. This gives the local authority full control of the situation while further evidence accumulates. Such a measure may be followed by a full care order. In cases of criminal proceedings, however, a young person can also be remanded to the care of the local authority pending further court appearances or for the completion of social inquiry reports. Here again, the order can last up to 21 days and is often followed, if guilt is proven, by a sentence to a penal establishment or the imposition of a full care order.[3]

In care order cases, the local authority social worker, acting in *loco parentis*, can place the child wherever he or she thinks appropriate, including at home with parents. There is no statutory requirement for removal from home or for a residential placement. However, removal from home for a period of up to six months can be specified if the court, under the Criminal Justice Act 1982, adds such a condition to an existing care order. This provision can only apply to young people who offend while already in care for delinquency and, in such cases, a variety of placement options, including fostering, are possible.

In addition to these provisions, children sometimes come into care by other means, for example, as a result of wardship proceedings or where custody following divorce has not been resolved. Also, many children at risk require removal to a 'place of safety' for which an order for up to 28 days can be obtained from magistrates.[4] Such children are not legally in care but are the responsibility of social services who have to find an appropriate 'safe place'.

Naturally, with such a range of legislation at their disposal, social workers and local authorities will vary considerably in the use that they make of various legal provisions. There have also been significant changes in social work practice over time. For example, in the last decade, there has been a decline in voluntary admissions to care while wardship proceedings and place of safety orders have shown a marked increase.[5]

Our evidence would suggest that care orders are sought by social workers as the appropriate legislation when situations are explicit, where the need for intervention is clear and where the family is well known to social services.[6] Voluntary care may be used for short-term breakdowns in family support and where, although there are insufficient grounds for securing a care order, some intervention is deemed necessary. Place of safety orders, which are often followed by full care orders, enable social workers to ensure the child's safety, to help them to gain control rapidly, to facilitate investigation and, where appropriate, to consolidate their position in subsequent court hearings.[7] Naturally, in some situations, where care orders are taken for delinquency, neglect and school non-attendance or where children are remanded to care, the freedom accorded in law to social workers is circumscribed by the fact that such referrals usually come from powerful statutory agents outside social services. Nevertheless, even here, the existence of consultative procedures between police, education and social services enables some educational and delinquency problems to be subsumed under different care categories.

This flexibility adopted by social workers in their use of legislation is greatly facilitated by the complexity of many children's presenting problems. For example, difficulties at school, delinquency or being out of control may stem from deep-seated problems at home such as rejection, neglect or abuse.[8] Hence, the legislation sought by social workers to legitimise their intervention may reflect the problem in which they have the strongest case, such as school non-attendance and which will grant them rapid and sufficient authority. The order may not, in fact, reflect the child's most pressing problem. In addition, mindful of the stigma associated with certain categories of care order such as those for delinquency or moral danger, social workers may seek more 'cosmetic' categories for entry to care, such as 'being beyond control' or voluntary care. Indeed, one experienced social worker summed up the situation thus: 'I can hardly think of any case where the initial legislation used matched the exact requirements of the case.'

However, what may at first appear admirable flexibility and sensitivity in the use of legislation can have some unsatisfactory consequences. We shall find that it leads to frequent changes in legal status during the first few months of a child's care career, almost all in a more controlling direction. It encourages considerable confusion in the minds of social workers as to the implications and obligations attendant on different legislative categories and a rather cavalier attitude to the legal process as a whole. Indeed, much of the informality of juvenile court proceedings, as highlighted by Hilgendorf, encourages such perspectives, particularly the attempt to achieve a consensus and ratification of social work decisions.[9] Were parents in a stronger position, represented in court by solicitors who are well versed in child legislation, cognisant of provision and backed up by a wealth of case law, social workers would probably have to prepare their submissions more carefully and be more sensitive to the implications of the authority they seek. Certainly, recent legislation (1982) makes this a very probable future trend in criminal cases.

If legislation is confusing to social workers, the implications of various entries to care are even more obscure for parents. Indeed, social workers offer parents little guidance in legal niceties and, as the family is usually unsophisticated in legal matters, they view the courts more as agents of control and retribution than of protection.[10] We shall see how this confusion over the authority and scope of social services' intervention colours the negotiation of parents, care-givers and social workers as the child enters care, in some cases even voluntary care. Parents feel they are not kept fully informed and the implications of the care legislation are not made explicit. For example, restrictions on access can come as a surprise to parents, as does the need to negotiate a wide range of daily parental responsibilities through the social worker. Similarly, adolescents entering care can find themselves liberated on some criteria yet more restricted on others. Thus, the client rapidly finds that welfare has unexpected strings attached.

### Legislative antecedents

Scarcely a decade passes without some major revision in the law governing children and young persons and the family as a whole is continuously subject to legislative change because of its central position in society. As a result, social workers and administrators can be excused for taking a 'here and now' perspective on the legislation governing the provision of child welfare. Yet the wording of much legislation and the situations it seeks to control have considerable antecedents. For example, the late and unmourned 'sus' laws owed their origin to attempts to control vagrancy in the sixteenth century while the removal of a child from poor parents for neglect was first authorised by the Poor Law of 1536.[11] In the same way, the problems posed by unmotivated adolescents are not twentieth-century phenomena, they first attracted legislation in compulsory apprenticeship orders of 1572, the Tudor equivalent of our Youth Training Scheme.[12] Although the late nineteenth century saw the battle joined in earnest to protect children from various forms of exploitation and cruelty, the children of the poor had long been subject to controlling legislation through apprenticeship and vagrancy laws which pressed heavily on any destitute family.[13]

Inevitably, this lengthy pedigree gives much of today's child-care legislation a punitive aura and is administered by courts in an adversarial way. Many care decisions still involve parents and children attending a juvenile court which, in spite of conciliatory symbols, is not the best arena for engineering cooperation, shared care or joint preventative work with social services.[14] Recent developments in Scotland, particularly the children's hearings, have encouraged some to advocate the introduction of 'family courts' in England.

In the past, for the state to intervene in the family was seen as a violation not only of the property rights of the father but also irreligious, tampering with a unit ordained by God.[15] Thus, any intervention with children either by the parish authorities or by the philanthropic societies, many of which flowered in the eighteenth and nineteenth centuries, had to be carefully, even reluctantly, undertaken. Indeed, the struggle to legitimise interference was long fought out in Parliament and, ironically, it was the abject poor who received earlier, better and more consistent protection than did those children who were neglected or abused within their own families.[16] Many of these neglected children simply took to the streets and alleys of the rapidly growing cities where 'they hopped about like birds waiting for scraps from rich men's tables'.[17]

Poor and abandoned children were an omnipresent reproach, they could be dangerous and, through disease, prostitution and delinquency, offer a source of contamination to the respectable. Yet Lord Shaftesbury, no small reformer himself, in replying to a letter as late as 1871 which canvassed his support for legislation to protect children from family neglect and cruelty, hesitated with the words, 'The evils you state are enormous but of so private, internal and domestic a character as to be beyond the reach of legislation'.[18] Indeed, it was left to the NSPCC in 1882 to push Parliament to legislate on behalf of neglected and abused children. As a result, the child rescue societies came to share the views of those administering the Poor Law, that the parents of these children had largely forfeited any rights over their offspring apart from some residual claim of religious affiliation, although the obligation to pay, where possible, was exacted from parents and even today is expected.

Parents were viewed as a source of contamination and evil influence, their poverty and ignorance largely the just deserts of indolence and immorality. Thus, children who were removed from parents or lifted from the gutter were frequently boarded out in the depths of the countryside where child mortality was lower than in cities. Other children were incarcerated in institutions whose grand façades, high walls and intricate ironwork gates gave substance to the Christian compassion of the rich and a twinge of guilt to those who had not subscribed.[19] While there were considerable variations both geographically and over time in the separation of children from those parents who entered the workhouse, generally, infants were boarded out, older children were educated separately and rapidly put to service or apprenticed outside while mothers were set to work. In fact, parents and children were more likely to remain together in the casual wards of the workhouse where all laboured, a situation which excited the greatest criticism from reformers because of the risks of pauperisation.

Indeed, legislation in the eighteenth and nineteenth centuries remained largely indifferent to issues of parental contact and welfare practice usually sought to block links between poor parent and absent child, ostensibly to foil avaricious families from claiming back their children when they had reached an age or acquired a sufficient skill to work. Interestingly, this eventuality was still much bewailed in the old approved school system less than twenty years ago, a cherished myth in which boys brimming with technical skills would be torn from the care of loving trade instructors to keep profligate parents well supplied with beer and cigarettes.[20]

In these circumstances, maintaining links between children removed for asylum and their natural parents rarely entertained the conscience of those bent on reform and rescue. Parents were punished for their failures and the loss of their children offered a salutory example to others who might be negligent. Thus, the philosophy of exclusion of parents was explicit until very recently. Indeed, for half a millennium, while child legislation concerns itself with rescue and refuge, it fails entirely to mention contact and reciprocation between absent child and parents.

For example, in 1818, in a rare reference to parental contact, the Marine Society, which sent to sea 10,000 boys between 1756 and 1862, was asked by MPs what provision was made to maintain contact between sailor boy and parent.[21] After some hesitation, the Society gave the rather discouraging reply, 'None'. In the same way there was no obligation on those who offered or received children for apprenticeship or put others out to service, either here or abroad, to inform parents of their offsprings' welfare or whereabouts.

Thus, links between children in care and their families have not until very recently been the subject of legislation. While the various Acts concerning children in care have specified the circumstances in which children can be taken into care, when parental rights can be assumed by the local authority and when adoptions can be sought, access between the child in care and his natural family has received no specific focus. As far as the law is concerned, the links parents might enjoy with their absent children are consequent on other important decisions taken on the child's entry into care, rather than viewed as an issue in its own right.

This is in strong contrast to the considerable body of judgement and legislation concerning parental access in divorce cases. In the nineteenth century, disputes over access to children often involved ladies of quality and their agitation acted as the spearhead for women's and children's rights.[22] Yet, as children of the poor never figured in disputes over access, the courts were not asked to arbitrate between parent and parish authorities.

While the general principles of 'the child's best interests' and respect for 'the child's wishes' have been guiding principles in interpreting child-care legislation during the twentieth century, very few of these principles concern themselves with access and the maintenance of contact with the absentee child. Until recently there have been no enforceable rights available to children or parents concerning contact once their child has been received into care. The legacy of punishment and contamination continued to press hard.

Hence, for children in voluntary care, the implication is that children cannot be kept in care if parents seek their return, disagree with the care arrangements or if it is in the child's best interests to go home. In law, these parents have access when they wish, although we shall note that in practice, many voluntary care situations present considerable barriers to parents and children attempting to maintain contact.

In the case of children in care under Section 3 resolutions and care orders, both of which remove parental rights, the power to restrict or terminate access between natural parents and child is implicit. This is equally the case in the laws governing the use of remands to care and interim care orders although in these there is no provision for parental rights to remain with the local authority once the initial orders expire. In addition, the power granted to the courts to adjudicate on matrimonial supervision and guardianship can have important implications for the links between children in care and their families. Here the court can decide on the most appropriate form and locus of contact. In fact, this later option was recently used by a mother in Liverpool to challenge limitations on access to her child in local authority care. Her contact with the child had been reduced as part of the local authority's plan for adoption and the mother tried, unsuccessfully, to get the High Court to examine its wardship jurisdiction so that her access demands could be adjudicated.[23]

When the parental rights of children rest with the local authority, there has been, until recently, little that a dissatisfied parent could do other than to apply for a discharge of the care order. This is not, in most circumstances, a viable course of action. There has always been the possibility of contesting the procedures for making care decisions by seeking a judicial review in a divisional court of the Queen's Bench but this was both somewhat unrealistic and a very lengthy process. Therefore, the only way open for a parent was, until very recently, to negotiate and convince the social services of the legitimacy of their concern.

These limitations have aroused much criticism from lawyers and social workers for giving excessive powers to social services and providing scant opportunity for parents to contest important decisions about their children's future. The concern was particularly cogent in cases where parents could not adequately care for their child and did not seek a revocation of the care order or the return home for the child, but nevertheless wanted regular contact with their offspring. This situation is particularly common with children 'at risk' or 'beyond control' who, at any one time, form the majority of long-stay cases in care.

These views were argued by the Family Rights Group, a pressure group of social workers and lawyers set up in the 1970s to seek a fairer framework for negotiation between local authorities and the families of children in care. The Family Rights Group and others advocated that legislation should be introduced which would allow the parents of all children admitted to care, for whatever reason, to apply to a court for access to their children if this had been restricted by social workers.

A subsequent Private Member's Bill sought to implement these suggestions but failed to get through Parliament. Nevertheless, the government was sympathetic to the issue and it was agreed that provision for a parent to apply to a juvenile court for an access order would be incorporated into the Health and Social Services and Social Security (Adjudications) Act 1983. This enables parents to apply to the court for right of access if contact with their child has been completely and formally terminated by the local authority. The court has power to attach conditions to any access order it chooses to make and there is a right of appeal to a High Court by those disagreeing with judgements.

This safeguard for parents is less comprehensive than that originally advocated for it applies only when termination of access is complete; it also excludes children in voluntary care. Nevertheless, for the first time in many centuries of intervention on behalf of poor or neglected children, legislation has addressed itself to the complex issues raised by parental access. The government's position is that disputes over other decisions concerning access or the situation of children in care voluntarily should be resolved within local authorities which are themselves publicly accountable bodies.

In addition, a code of practice concerning the arrangements for managing links between children in care and their families has been produced by the DHSS.[24] Here, the emphasis is much wider than that of parental access. The code spells out in considerable detail the arrangements that local authorities should make to promote contact between children absent in care and their families. It also makes clear the procedures that should be adopted if contact is to be limited between parent and child or access terminated altogether. The code lays out not only the most suitable administrative arrangements, in terms of decision-making and the roles of senior social workers and elected members, but also indicates what, in the light of available knowledge, should be considered 'good practice'.

The code is both comprehensive and sensitive and has been generally welcomed. Indeed, it breaks new ground in that it seeks to provide clear guidance, at a very practical level, in an area of increasing concern to social workers and social services departments. While access and parental contact increasingly arouses anxiety in social workers, it is an area in which very little is being done by the local authorities themselves. Something of the essence of the DHSS code of practice can be learnt from the following extract:

> For the majority of children, however, there will be no doubt that their interests will be best served by efforts to *sustain links* with their natural families. Access, in the sense of personal meetings and visits, will generally be the most common and, for both parent and child, the most satisfactory way of maintaining their relationship. But other means which can help to keep family bonds alive should be borne in mind: letters, telephone calls, exchange of photographs. Such contacts – however occasional – may continue to have a value for the child even when access has ended and there is no question of returning to his family. These contacts can keep alive for a child a sense of his origins and may keep open the options for family relationships in later life.
>
> The first weeks in care are likely to be particularly crucial to the success of the relationship between the parent, the social worker and the child's carers and to the level of future contact between parent and child. It is at this time that patterns are set which it may be difficult to change. Parents should be involved in the admission process and wherever possible, in pre-reception planning. Emergency admissions – where they cannot be avoided – require special care if parents are to be reassured from the outset that they have a continuing role in their child's life. Early visits and meetings should be encouraged, even though parents may need help to enable them to cope with the child's distress – and their own. These considerations – subject to whatever safeguards are necessary for the child's protection – are equally important where children are not in care but subject to place of safety orders.

The code also frankly recognises the difficulties faced by care-givers, social workers, parents and children in maintaining contact while the child is in local authority care. It also makes a number of useful suggestions concerning the role of foster parents, residential care staff and, even, the elected members in helping to maintain links between parent and absent child.

Naturally, today, we know more than early legislators about the complex situations which prevent some poor families from providing consistent and adequate care for their children. Nevertheless, it is unlikely that the Curtis Report 1946 and ten years of Seebohm could entirely overcome more than half a millennium of mutual suspicion between those who give substitute care to children and their parents. Similar barriers to mutual participation between parents and professionals were highlighted by those innovators who in the 1960s and early 70s tried to involve parents in the schooling of their children.[25] It will be interesting to see the ways in which initiatives which seek to involve parents in the care task, the code of practice just illustrated and recent legislation on access actually lead to significant changes in the contact enjoyed between parent and absent child.

## Summary

We have seen that the development of protective legislation for children has been long and fitful and that care and compassion have always included strong elements of control. The pressing nature of children's problems, rather than those of the family as a whole, has been a very cogent influence on legislation. This means that not only do social workers find themselves unwilling agents of social control but that the legislation they are forced to employ in child-care situations gives an inappropriate adversarial stance to care proceedings.

We have suggested that much of our present welfare approach is based on the Poor Law and social work practice is still influenced by ideas of less eligibility, of parental inadequacy and contamination. The removal of children from parents, which was explicitly punitive in previous centuries, now is justified in terms of care, protection and control. But we shall see in the following chapters that parents feel the pain of separation quite as keenly as in the days when punishment was explicit. For generations, the parents of children who entered state care were largely seen as failures, it was not envisaged that they could support the absent child in any way or share in the care task. As a consequence, until recently, separation of children and their exclusion from the family have been the involuntary experience of most entering care. Anxiety over the problems of maintaining links between absent child and parent has until the post-war years had very little priority.

We shall also find that the recipients of state care have long remained the same: illegitimate, neglected, abused and handicapped children and adolescents 'at risk'. Nevertheless, while change in our welfare approaches to children is slow and some still remain coloured by their antecedents, yet generally improvement is sure and perceptible. Any reading of the Curtis Report would emphasise this.

As we turn to look at the ways our cohort of 450 children experience state care, it is important to keep the wider context of child care very much in mind. The isolation, which we shall see is the unfortunate experience of some children who stay long in local authority care, results as much from the operation of our welfare system as from the ideology, values and practices of the social work profession.

## Summary points

1. Child-care legislation allows considerable discretion to social workers in determining the legal status under which children enter care.
2. In care negotiations, parents remain in a weak position *vis-à-vis* the powerful social services bureaucracy, they are ill-informed and unversed in the consequences of particular legal decisions.
3. Because the parents of children who entered state care were long viewed as a contaminating influence, the historical antecedents of much child-care legislation has a punitive aura and is administered in an adversarial way. This further discourages parental participation in the care task.
4. Maintaining links between parent and child had, until recently, little priority, a situation which new legislation and codes of practice seek to rectify.
5. Social work has always responded to the control demands and visibility of problematic children, groups as defined by others. The clients of social services today differ little from those of the eighteenth and nineteenth centuries.
6. Adolescents particularly cause problems because of the inadequacy of the nuclear family to meet their demands and its increased propensity to change.

# 4. The study context

This chapter lays out the current situation regarding children in local authority care. It distinguishes between the picture that develops when the child-care population at any one moment is considered and the different picture that emerges when children are looked at over time. We examine the age distributions and the legal status of children entering care and explore the care placements they experience. We show that, increasingly, adolescents are becoming the responsibility of social services, that they tend to stay long in care, and are often placed in residential settings.

To elaborate complex methodologies in social research is to ask for trouble. Unlike rats in a cage or chemical reactions from a reeking test-tube, the objects of social investigation usually have considerable freedom of manoeuvre and they are reluctant to stand still. For example, longitudinal studies of children are quite likely to lose respondents over time, key figures either doing research or under investigation will move and, inevitably, interest in any project wanes. Local authorities, subject to oscillations in political fortunes, change their priorities. What social services viewed at the outset as significant research, promising important revelations, can become something of an incubus as the study grinds on. Thus, keeping the research programme going presents many more problems than fashioning a methodology or tracing themes and antecedents.

Yet we were fortunate in the unruffled progress of this study. The cohorts of children were built without difficulty and although some social workers have changed during two years, no child has been lost from the cohort. Bureaucracies may be reproached for many things but the careful procedures and the administrative caution of social services' departments have certainly assisted the successful completion of this longitudinal study over its two years. In the same way, the close scrutiny of 30 children and their families, that is our intensive study, was completed as planned.

Elaborate research designs have other problems, particularly longitudinal studies. As the programme unfolds, changes of emphasis and the emerging issues of concern are difficult to incorporate into the study. In addition, as data accumulate one finds that the report that is written is closely circumscribed by a research design that was framed to investigate the unknown.[1]

In this study, another major difficulty has been to link the intensive and extensive studies into a coherent whole. While data from the extensive study lack much without the intensive material, unifying the outpourings of our computer with those of a distraught mother has not been easy.

It would have been a comparatively straightforward task to provide the survey of 450 children going through care and then to have followed it with the intensive study of 30 children and their families, hopefully highlighting some of the issues raised by the preceding general survey. Unfortunately, this would make very dull reading; few surveys are particularly riveting and the wide gap between general findings and the more intimate perspectives of participants in care would blunt the impact of both studies.

We have, therefore, decided to follow our 450 children through the care experience over two years and, at the various stages of the process, illustrate the issues that emerge with material from the intensive study. At each stage in the care process we shall draw out the implications of the findings for managing the child's care experience and the maintenance of links between the child and family. Thus, we begin by describing the characteristics of children admitted to care and then highlight the breakdown in parents' ability to provide by reference to four deprived families. This will be followed by the crisis of admission to care and the initial placement of the child where, again, general data will be given additional meaning from the experience of families in our intensive study. This plan will be followed at intervals as the child moves through care.

We shall begin by setting the scene, by describing the role assumed by the local authorities in caring for children deprived of normal family life and suggest some of the enduring features of state intervention with deprived children and their families. This will be followed by a description of our cohort as they begin their careers in care.

## The current national situation

The latest available figures (1982) show that there are 93,200 children in the care of local authorities in England and Wales.[2] This is, however, a fluid situation with some 43,500 new arrivals and departures each year. The majority of children are able to leave care quickly as family crises are resolved, but for others, the stay in care will be long, continuing until the age of eighteen or even nineteen in some cases. This poses difficulties in any discussions of the child-care population. The juxtaposition of a rapidly changing population of short-term cases alongside a core of children who remain means that it is difficult to generalise about the characteristics of children in care. Neither will there be many common features in access arrangements and contact between child and parent.

Indeed, a different picture emerges depending on whether we consider those in care at a particular moment or those coming into care over a longer period of time. For example, of the 43,500 admissions in the 12 months prior to 31 March 1982, 68 per cent were voluntary receptions, while 32 per cent were remand, care and other court orders, mostly under the 1969 legislation.[3] But, for those in care on the final day of this period, care orders form a greater proportion of those children cared for by local authorities and the proportion changes to 24 per cent for voluntary admissions, 19 per cent for children for whom parental rights resolutions had been taken and just under 57 per cent on court orders. Eighty-seven per cent of the court orders were under the 1969 Act and 13 per cent arising from family legislation and guardianship. The impact of the long-stay group becomes very marked when those in care at any one time are considered.

A similar situation is found when we consider the ages of children in care. Admissions for the year include many more infants and young children than does the end-of-year census. While older adolescents do not come into care in large numbers, they nevertheless represent a quarter of children in care at any one time. We shall note as this study progresses that adolescents tend to stay in care, presenting many problems.

Table 4.1   Ages of children in care in England and Wales (1982)

| Age | Coming into care during 12 months prior to 31.3.82 | In care at 31.3.82 |
|---|---|---|
| Under 1 | 11% | 2% |
| 1–4 | 21% | 9% |
| 5–9 | 17% | 18% |
| 10–15 | 43% | 46% |
| 15+ | 8% | 26% |
| | (N = 43,500) | (N = 93,200) |

*Source:* DHSS/Welsh Office, *Children in Care in England and Wales,* March 1982.
*Note:* Throughout this report, all percentages have been rounded to the nearest whole number, totals may not, therefore, add up to 100 per cent.

Further scrutiny reveals that children in care are a very diverse group. Not only are there wide differences in age, legal status and reasons for entry but there are also variations in the demands made upon social workers. While 13 per cent of the 'in care' population have been in care for less than six months, 32 per cent have been there for more than five years.[4] Girls are likely to remain just as long as boys and this long-stay group is equally divided between those on court orders and those in care under the 1980 Act.

The placements arranged by social workers also vary, with 42 per cent of these children living in foster homes, 27 per cent in local authority residential care, 18 per cent at home or with relatives and the remainder (13 per cent) in voluntary homes, special schools, lodgings or other accommodation.[5] We shall notice as this study progresses that these placements are not always stable and that there is considerable movement between them. Some of these transfers will be planned and others the result of breakdowns and crises within the placement. We shall also note that placements are chosen and changed with little priority given to maintaining links between parent and child.

The national picture of children in care has changed markedly in the last decade. Since 1974, the numbers in care have remained constant but annual receptions have dropped significantly by 17 per cent.[6] While fewer children now come into care, they stay longer, suggesting that the 'secondary' problems of coping with the care experience will be more severe than before. Preventative strategies adopted by social services appear to have been effective with young children, especially those who would have been received into care voluntarily in earlier years. The proportions of voluntary admissions and younger children have clearly fallen while those on care orders and older children have increased.

Nevertheless, it is important to note that infants (that is, children under one year of age) are still disproportionately prone to enter care. In addition, it is clear from differences between the child-care populations of the five local authorities participating in this study, that changing child populations have led to a fall in the overall number of admissions in the inner cities but a longer stay in care for those entering; whereas in the outer suburbs and shire counties, there has been a rise in the number of admissions but a fall in the average length of stay.[7] Nevertheless, when overall rates of children in care per 1000 population are considered, the vulnerability of children in deprived inner city areas still remains very high, as great as 2 per cent in certain areas.

This increase in the proportion of older children and care order cases might imply a rise in demand for residential care because older children present greater difficulty in fostering or community supervision. However, no increase in the use of residential care is apparent. Indeed, national figures reveal a decline in the use of such settings, especially in CHEs (community homes with education on the premises), residential nurseries and homes provided by voluntary organ-

**Table 4.2   Age and legal status of children in care in England and Wales (1974/1982)**

| | % In care population at 31 March | | | % Annual admissions prior to 31 March | |
|---|---|---|---|---|---|
| *Age* | *1974* | *1982* | *Legislation* | *1974* | *1982* |
| 0–4 | 12 | 11 | Voluntary | 80 | 63 |
| 5–15 | 66 | 64 | Court order | 20 | 37 |
| 16–16+ | 21 | 26 | | | |
| | (N = 95,900) | (N = 93,200) | *Age* | % | % |
| | | | 0–4 | 38 | 32 |
| | | | 5–15 | 57 | 60 |
| | | | 16–16+ | 5 | 8 |
| | | | | (N = 52,700) | (N = 43,500) |

*Source:* As for Table 4.1 and figures for March 1974.

isations, and a clear swing towards fostering and placements with parents or relatives, again reflecting specific social work policies of the last few years.[8]

**Table 4.3   Placements of children in care in England and Wales**

|  | In care at 31 March | |
|---|---|---|
|  | 1974 | 1982 |
|  | % | % |
| Foster homes | 32 | 42 |
| Local authority residential care | 34 | 27 |
| Home/relatives | 17 | 18 |
| Other* | 16 | 13 |
|  | (N = 95,900) | (N = 93,200) |

* Includes lodgings, residential employment, boarding and special schools, voluntary homes, hostels and boarding homes and hostels for the handicapped.
*Source:* As for Table 4.1.

As numbers leaving care match those coming in, the overall total of children in care tends to remain constant over time. Of the 46,000 who left care in the 12 months ending 31 March 1982, most moved back home or went to live independently or with relatives, while a further 4 per cent were adopted, a proportion which has not changed in recent years.[9] Nevertheless, 18 per cent left care simply because they attained the age of 18 (or 19, as appropriate) and what happens to this group is not altogether clear. Many may be back with parents but this figure is still disturbing, particularly as the proportion of young people leaving care when they reach the limit of statutory responsibility is growing, from 14 per cent of leavers in 1974 to 18 per cent in 1982. So great has been the attention given to children coming into care that the experience of these 9000 annual leavers has, until recently, been unexplored.

From this initial glance at the characteristics of children in care and the strategies for dealing with them, it is clear that, as a group, young people in need of care are extremely heterogeneous. The criterion of 'permanently or temporarily deprived of a normal home life' appears to cover a multitude of situations, from depressed, lone mothers unable to provide care, to battered infants, to unruly adolescents in trouble with the police or at school. It seems unlikely, therefore, that any one set of social work strategies or care provisions could meet the needs of so diverse a group, particularly when the characteristics of the care population can be seen to have changed widely in less than a decade. Similarly, it seems sensible that admission to care should be only one of several possible solutions to the child's or family's problems. It is also apparent that maintaining links between parent and separated child will be complicated and that any guidance for social workers on access and contact can only be given at a general level.

In this chapter, we have noted the wide variety of children who enter care and the ways that patterns have changed over time. As a result of such heterogeneity, it is not surprising that the child rescue perspectives which preoccupied the practice of the children's department after 1948 and which we have seen have long antecedents were soon supplemented by a growing interest in preventative work and in the establishment of a wide range of community facilities. The Curtis Report (1946) had not been enamoured of the quality of residential provision and it added evidence and authority to that drift away from residential care which still continues.[10] The report advocated a range of alternative provision. This wish to forestall family problems and to prevent their manifestation in abuse or delinquency directed attention towards the need for a total 'family service' which, it was envisaged, would work with families in their own homes. As no one agency could possibly meet all the needs of a deprived family, this approach would demand close cooperation from education, health and other statutory agencies. This view inevitably led to administrative reorganisation and the Seebohm Report (1968), drawing on the proposals of earlier official inquiries, recommended a simplified structure in which one local authority department of social services would offer a 'community-based and family-oriented service'.[11]

This policy was implemented with some administrative complications in 1971 and during the last decade social work ideology has moved uneasily between contrasting viewpoints – the need for a general, comprehensive family service and the specialisms required to help individual client groups, be they the elderly, the mentally ill or children in need of care. Indeed, this conflict has still not been reconciled and both theoretically and in practice these differences are marked.[12] While it is usual to regard such deep philosophical divisions as detrimental to social work, some have viewed the debate as creative and stimulating to practice. In much the same way, the omnipresent conflicts between deterrence and rehabilitation can stimulate our approach to juvenile offenders.

But this conflict between specialist and general social work is ever present in child care. Damaged children remaining at home will always be exposed to further risk, whereas separated children face all the secondary problems of being in care, such as distress, affective deprivation, placement breakdowns and diminished academic achievement. In addition, there is the omnipresent risk that over time social isolation and even institutionalisation will develop. It is within these constraints that social workers have to make firm decisions about the frequency and style of contacts between the child and family.

In a profession that is new, where even its training and qualifications are subject to constant revision, it is unlikely that social workers are encouraged to look back. Indeed, many studies of child welfare take the Report of the Care of Children Committee of 1946 (the Curtis Report) as the origin of present child-care approaches, not unreasonably when the only duty at that time laid on local authorities, other than relief, were the Poor Law requirements 'to set children to work or put them out as apprentices'. At that time even the boarding-out of children, although widespread, was not specifically authorised. Indeed, it required the upheaval of war and the 'visibility' to the nation of evacuated children, animated parcels crying through train windows, to prompt the 1946 inquiry.[13]

But the Curtis Report is comparatively recent; it highlighted bad practice in order to add cogency to its demands for administrative unity. It hoped that a reorganisation of the fragmented, confused and chaotic child welfare system, which had largely been inherited from the nineteenth century, would create a comprehensive family service. It will be interesting to see, as we trace the careers of children entering care, how far a comprehensive family service is provided by social services. Have the child rescue, punitive and family contamination perspectives that preoccupied welfare interventions for so long been reconsidered? How much of a reality are the oft-voiced social work ideals of shared care? Let us now turn to the experience of the 450 children in our study cohort who entered care between January and October 1980.

## Summary points

1. Children in care are a heterogeneous group, the majority, usually young children, enter care and leave quickly, while some, usually older children and adolescents, tend to stay in care. Children in care vary in age, in presenting problems and in their length of stay. This heterogeneity makes any overall social work strategy difficult and maintaining links between parent and child will be dependent on many other factors.
2. The national picture has changed markedly in the last decade. While receptions into care have dropped, suggesting the success of some preventative measures, the numbers in care at any one time have remained constant. Such children stay longer and are less likely to be voluntary admissions or younger children.

3. There has been a slight decline in the use of residential care for children over the last decade. It now roughly equals the contribution made by foster care. However, older children and those with control problems remain more likely to enter residential care.

# 5. Coming into care

This chapter looks at the ways in which children are referred to social services for help and why they come into care. Our investigation indicates that the events surrounding a child's entry to care are important as they can colour much subsequent interaction between child, family and social workers. Initial decisions can have a considerable impact on the links parents maintain with their absent children. We begin to look at the care process by introducing four case studies: the experience of each of these families will be reviewed at subsequent points in the study.

Admitting a child to care is very much a social work decision. Rarely in our study cohort of 450 children did social workers report that the decision to admit a child to care was out of their hands; for example, as a result of court hearings or other situations. The precipitating crisis leading to a child's admission to care was usually expected and, in three-quarters of cases, social workers felt that the referral was certain to lead to a care admission. Both the type of case and the individual problems of children and their families encourage these perceptions.

Yet, despite such knowledge and power, the actual moment of the precipitating crisis seems to have come as something of a surprise to social workers and, in 35 per cent of cases, there was little interval between the notification of a problem to the local authority departments and the actual reception of the child into care. For example, 35 per cent of children were both referred and admitted on the same day and, for a further 20 per cent of children, there was a gap between referral and admission of less than seven days. For another 13 per cent the negotiations took less than one month. Thus, 68 per cent of children were taken into care less than one month after their most recent referral.

The antithesis between long previous awareness on the part of social services and crisis admissions to care is difficult to interpret. Packman in her study of children entering care also highlights this contradiction.[1] It hardly suggests that well-prepared strategies have been fashioned for coping with crises, despite social work claims to have extensive involvements and knowledge of the family situation. This is surprising given the stress on preventative work in current social work practice. Indeed, there seems to be a serious conflict between the wish to keep children out of the care system and the rather haphazard strategy employed when admission becomes necessary. Admittedly, measures intended to discourage a child's entry into care and reassure families in crisis cannot easily encompass preparations for reception into care, particularly if a child's removal from home is envisaged. The result is that the admission to care is rarely viewed therapeutically by social workers, indeed, it is often seen as a confirmation of the failure of preventative measures.

Such social work ambivalence and apparent lack of planning has other consequences. It can make the care experience, which usually involves removal from home, traumatic for the child. It poses difficulties for parents in trying to negotiate access and adopt a meaningful role. Such action leaves some families with a sense of violation and distrust, all of which subsequently colour negotiations with social services. This emerges clearly in the case studies which close this chapter.

Nevertheless, social workers' failure to inform or plan is highly functional for the administration of the social services in that it strengthens social work control.[2] Sharing information with the child and family diminishes the social worker's power to manage entry into care and to control the situation. This aspect of client management will subsequently be confirmed when we look at the child's care situation six months after reception. In a subsequent chapter, we shall note that by the time six months have elapsed other interested groups, such as police, school and neighbours will have long since surrendered their interests to social services. Nevertheless, some parents are more indefatigable and press their claims. Thus, some early departures of voluntary admissions to care generate considerable social work disquiet and reinforce the control preoccupations of social workers.

**Referral processes**
The situation leading to the child's admission to care comes to the attention of the social services in numerous ways. No fewer than 21 different agencies referred our study group of 450 children to the local authority departments; the principal source being the child's parents (36 per cent), with a further 8 per cent coming from neighbours, relatives or the child himself. Another 15 per cent of referrals came from the police, 11 per cent from schools and education, 10 per cent from doctors, hospitals and health visitors and 9 per cent from the social workers already involved with the family. Reasons for seeking help were equally varied with no single situation standing out. Neglect, abuse and parents' inability to care account for 44 per cent of referrals, the child's behaviour at home or outside 27 per cent and illness of parent 9 per cent. Naturally, these circumstances were usually compounded by additional problems of marital conflict and general inability to parent.

These differences in reasons for referral are important for understanding the patterns of future social work intervention. Indeed, one of the themes we shall be exploring in this study is how social workers perceive the source of the child's problems and the way in which this determines the focus of their actions.[3] That is, whether the child's problems are predominantly *child*-centred or *family*-centred.

However, it should be recognised that referrals to social services carry no legal requirement for action and it is difficult to know why only a small proportion of child-care referrals culminate in admission to care.[4] Nevertheless, for some children, admission to care is the decision social workers make and it is the subsequent experience of this group that forms the basis of our study.

## Admissions to care

The reasons for admitting a child to local authority care usually mirror those of the initial referral and, as before, we find a wide variety of situations. There are, however, some important differences between the crises that prompt a referral and the reasons for actually admitting a child to care. Emergencies such as parental desertion assume greater significance on admission, while problems such as school attendance, although a prime reason for referral, seem less likely to precipitate care proceedings. Again, factors combine to propel a child into care, for example, truancy accompanied by offending is common. In the same way we find parents' inability to care for their child or to exert control closely linked with possibilities of abuse or neglect. Such combinations shift social workers towards taking a child into care rather than exploring other possibilities such as supervision or preventative work. Frequently, a referral for one reason reveals other deep-seated problems within the family such as marital conflict or neglect. Thus care proceedings are frequently a response to revised assessments of the child's circumstances rather than duplicating the reasons for a child's referral.

Naturally, the primary reason for admission to care will be supplemented by other stresses on children. For example, neglect or abuse affected nearly half of our total study group and a third were assessed as being emotionally deprived.

## Who comes into care?

Whatever their individual situations, nearly all children coming into care experience a breakdown in family support. In the majority of cases, our evidence suggests that it is not that relatives are absent but more the failure of the extended family to offer help when the child's primary caretaker, usually the mother, can no longer provide. We find that relatives may be too far away to help or the child's parents may be shunned by their family, often because of past disputes. In some cases, the extended family may not wish to get involved or take sides in a marital dispute. Reconstituting families have been shown to pose special problems of intervention for wider kin.[5] Not infrequently, relatives and friends have helped in the past with children, only to find themselves taking on more than they expected. In a number of cases, they have literally found themselves holding the baby.

Thus, unless the child has specific needs which can be met by other agencies, such as physical or mental handicap, the care responsibility falls to local authority social services. The circumstances which necessitate entry into local authority care will vary. In England and Wales, 21 per cent of admissions to care are due to the short-term physical/psychiatric illness or confinement of mother while in some cases (8 per cent), the child has actually been deserted.[6] A further 14 per cent of children come into care primarily because of unsatisfactory home circumstances. Remands and interim care orders made by courts account for a further 21 per cent of entries to care while full care orders make up another 10 per cent (4 per cent because of delinquency, 2 per cent because of school problems, 2 per cent because of neglect and 2 per cent for moral danger and being beyond control).

Our study of 450 children coming into the care of five local authorities would confirm this national picture as Table 5.1 shows.

**Table 5.1   Primary reason for admission to care**

|  | *Coming into care* |
|---|---|
|  | % |
| Breakdown in family care | 69 |
| Due to: mental illness of parent | 10 |
| physical illness of parent | 11 |
| neglect or abuse | 23 |
| abandoned/deserted | 7 |
| unwilling/unable to care | 18 |
| Behaviour of child | 25 |
| Other reasons | 6 |
|  | (N = 450) |

We have seen in this chapter that children are referred by a wide variety of agencies and that many young people have long been clients of social workers. We shall see that three-quarters of our study group were said to be 'already known to the local authority social services departments'. In some cases, this knowledge was very superficial, arising from other involvements with the child's family, but for other children, such as those who had been in care previously (29 per cent), there was already an extensive personal file. Most referrals came from parents seeking help, but health visitors, doctors, hospitals, police, juvenile courts and, increasingly in recent years, schools and the children themselves are significant. We have noted, however, that not all referrals lead to care, that some referrals have more cogency than others, such as those from police and education, and that admission to care usually has a crisis dimension.

It is also clear that many children who come into care will have experienced severe family dislocations. Their family structures are fragile, with frequent marital conflicts, cohabitations and changes of accommodation. Many are families in which there have been significant and recent changes brought about by divorce, separation and co-habitation. For many families, it is the actual process of reconstituting a nuclear family that precipitates the crisis.

These characteristics are reflected in the fact that a third of the children in our study were illegitimate and in only 41 per cent of cases was the child's natural father living in the household at the time of the child's reception into care. Indeed, in one-third of cases, the whereabouts of the child's natural father was not known to social services, despite the fact that for almost all of the children, both natural parents were alive. Forty-five per cent of the young people in our study population were in single-parent families at the time of their reception into care and 65 per cent of the households from which they came relied totally for their income on supplementary benefits. In only a minority of cases (27 per cent) were the child's natural parents still married to one another and 30 per cent of our cohort had at least one half-sibling.

We shall see that family situations are constantly changing, key roles are in the process of negotiation and redefinition. Thus, the family unit is unstable so that when illness strikes or the electricity is cut off, there is little resource on which to fall back. Indeed, although it is usual to highlight these issues as 'child-care' problems, it is clearly a family situation which accounts for the breakdown in child support and their entry into local authority care. In fact, 45 per cent of the children we have studied came into care with a sibling and many other family members had or were receiving support from health and social services.

Nevertheless, social workers usually perceived these problems in their wider context. For example, despite the high number of difficult adolescents coming into care, in only 37 per cent of cases was the child viewed as the client most in need of attention and in as few as 17 per cent was the emphasis solely on the child's family. Social workers clearly prefer a perspective which emphasises the interaction between the child and his or her environment, stressing the quality of relationships between the young person, his or her family, peers and other members of the community. Thus, the crude categories used to record both care admissions and referrals should not be allowed to conceal the complexity of many children's actual situations. Unfortunately, we shall find that external referral agencies such as the police or schools can find their expectations of a particular course of action greatly disappointed by social workers. This is because they largely remain unaware of the complexities of a situation and do not share social work perspectives on how to deal with it.

Children react to these family stresses in a variety of ways and some, including adolescents, find themselves at risk of injury or neglect while others are disruptive and become delinquent or beyond control. In addition, some children may pose a variety of school problems. For all, admission to care is seen by social workers as necessitating important decisions which have to be made quickly. We shall see that these have important implications for the child's future career in care.

We can already see that complex family difficulties precipitate the majority of children into care. In addition, a quarter of these will be adolescents. In spite of previous and/or ongoing involvements with children's families, social workers find that a crisis crystallises or precipitates situations and that rapid, sometimes hasty, care decisions are thrust upon them. Often the difficulties facing children on entry to care are considerable and unappreciated by those who refer so that expectations are disappointed. This disappointment can affect parents and children quite as much as teachers, policemen and doctors.

If we now turn to look at four typical families selected from those in the 'intensive' study, we can explore their similarity with all families at risk and how they understand their child's referral and admission to care. Such perceptions are likely to influence the links parents have with their children during their stay in care.

## Sally and David March

The first of our four families consists of Sally March and her 12-month-old son, David. Sally is 21, but looks older. She is attractive, with a ready smile but is usually described in reports as 'disorganised, depressed and not very bright'. Mother and child both live in a small, shabby council flat on the fringes of a large city. They are poor, they survive on social security and reel from one financial crisis to another.

Sally was married at 17 but her husband left her after only a year. Although he was her first love (the couple had met at school and they were engaged at 15) rapture cooled quickly and life together was turbulent and unsatisfactory. Since his departure, Sally has lived with a series of co-habitees. These relationships, with the exception of the most recent, were short-lived, punctuated by rows, desertions and financial crises. Joe, Sally's last co-habitee was, however, different, she became pregnant and had a baby. Their first year together was a success. Joe had a labouring job and Sally cleaned in the nearby social club two mornings a week. There was talk of marriage for, by now, Sally had divorced her husband. But the plans did not materialise. About three months after the baby's birth, the couple's relationship began to crumble. Joe distanced himself from the baby, found the responsibilities irksome, and did not like staying in at night. He spent an increasing amount of time away from home and Sally became depressed, disillusioned and a frequent visitor to the doctor. Joe rapidly lost interest in Sally and left for the consolations of another girl he had met while visiting the local launderette. Sally was greatly upset by Joe's departure. She does not know where he is living but she has seen him once or twice at a distance in the town.

Although Sally's mother lives nearby, and two of her three sisters live just outside the city, Sally is isolated and lonely. Since the disintegration of her marriage and her succession of co-habitees, she has seen little of her mother; she sees even less of her sisters, both of whom, according to Sally, have done well. Sally's father is dead, having committed suicide many years ago after losing his job. There are other relatives in the city but she sees little of them either, apart from the occasional nod of recognition when they pass her in the street. Sally says her mum softened a little when David was born but avoided visiting because of Joe whom she disliked intensely. However, the relationship does not seem close. As Sally comments, 'She thinks I'm a slut and prefers Maureen, my sister, because she can boss her about.' Sally has no contact with the family of either her ex-husband or David's father.

Sally's relationship with social services has been long and eventful and dates back to her schooldays when she used to truant and be disruptive in class. The records suggest that her behaviour was related to the suicide of her father, but she said she was just bored at school. Since then, there has always been a social worker hovering in the background, but contact has been sporadic, usually associated with crises of accommodation or unpaid bills.

During her turbulent marriage, Sally saw little of social workers, but after it collapsed and a subsequent incident with some pills that worried her local doctor, requests for help were frequent. A theft inquiry that fortunately did not lead to prosecution re-established close relations with social services and these ticked over quite steadily until the birth of David.

David has been in voluntary care twice in the past. The first occasion was shortly after he was born. Sally had a gynaecological problem and had to go into hospital for a few days. She hoped Joe would look after the child but he failed to do so. Sally's mum refused to help, somewhat discouraged by Joe's frequent references to 'that interfering old cow'. Everyone else was conspicuous by their absence. Consequently, the health visitor was worried about the whole situation. The father seemed indifferent and the wider family absent, thus, social services took David into care where he was looked after by a foster parent for two weeks. Joe did not visit the child and he visited Sally in hospital only once.

David's subsequent reception into care occurred not long after Sally's return home from hospital and the circumstances were identical. As the relationship between Sally and Joe deteriorated so did the fragile, domestic framework surrounding David; bills went unpaid, the flat was cold and uncared for. The health visitor became increasingly worried over the child's physical and emotional well-being. As a result, he was returned to care for a short period and placed in a different foster home. A case conference was held as there were suspicions that David could be the victim of some abuse. Some bruises had been discovered and social services were concerned. However, these marks were accounted for by Sally who, despite her depression and inadequacy, obviously loved the child. Social services were worried not only by Sally's inability to care for her baby but also by Joe's total indifference.

Joe's sudden departure one Sunday morning, irresistibly drawn towards the launderette, accelerated the family's disintegration. Sally became increasingly depressed and, according to the social worker, seemed to lose interest in everything. Her appearance deteriorated and she failed to meet the baby's needs. In Sally's words:

'I was just left in the lurch. I had no one when Joe left me. I was on the social but it took ages for me to sort things out. He was supposed to be paying the rent but he wasn't, and I ended up owing them a bloody fortune. The electricity were going to cut me off as well. Sometimes I went days without a penny to my name and no one would help at all. David just cried and cried.'

This time there was, in fact, a small army of people fluttering around Sally and attempting to meet her problems, but the efforts seemed rather uncoordinated. Although evidence of gross neglect was lacking, everyone entertained general but increasing concern about Sally's deteriorating domestic situation.

Sally's social worker remembers the period immediately before the child's present reception to care as a time fraught with many difficulties:

'She was very elusive at that time. I tried to see her as much as I could. Sometimes I called as many as three times a week at her flat but I often didn't get a reply. Basically, what I was trying to do was to help her organise herself. You see, she's not very bright and breaks down fairly easily under stress.

Before David came into care I was organising some home help for her but events overtook things.'

Sally was very aware that people were trying to help her at this time and she grew quite fond of her social worker:

'Yes, he used to come and see me quite a lot. Sometimes with Miss G. the clinic lady to see how the baby was. She was ever so nice. They understood all about the problems I'd been having with Joe. It's all very well though, but I was in a terrible state. I had to get out of the flat and see people. It was really getting me down. I needed company.'

Sally's need for companionship and oblivion took her down town, hovering around the discos and other hostelries. She began drinking quite heavily and with her friend, June, a girl much younger than herself, they became familiar with every nightspot. When she went out, sometimes she would leave the baby with her friend's mother, one of the reasons why her social worker had such difficulty in contacting her but, occasionally, Sally had a young neighbour to baby-sit for her.

The social worker was concerned at Sally's drinking, at her neon-lit whirl of a social life and was becoming increasingly worried about the whereabouts of the baby and his welfare at night. However, Sally always had a convincing explanation for her absence and managed to persuade the social worker that his anxieties were misplaced.

It is interesting to note that during this period of impending crisis, the social worker had no contact with Sally's mother or sisters. His focus was on Sally and the child and his hopes were largely pinned on the chimera of a home help. At this time, Sally also had very little contact with her family. The rift caused by her previous co-habitation and by Joe's dislike of her mother still yawned. Occasionally, Sally did have a meal with her mother when she ran out of money, but they never discussed her general plight.

The crisis that brought David into care for the third time came one wet Saturday night in January when Sally hurried off to a date with her friend June and two Dutch sailors. It seems that the previous night had not been a success for June's mother who, when seeing the lights on, had called in to find both young women enjoying the traditional sailor's return on the hearth-rug while the baby screamed nearby.

According to Sally, she had to see the Dutch sailor at the Anchor, a noisy emporium full of the visiting Dutch fleet, as it was his last run ashore and she wanted to talk things over. As Sally said, 'The social worker always said when you have a problem you must talk about it, so I did.' But her account of the events of that Saturday night are a little cloudy.

'As I said, I had to see him and June's mum wasn't having David. I wasn't going out for long, I just wanted to explain things and say goodbye. Little Angela who usually sits in for me wasn't about, so I asked Mrs Douglas across the landing to keep popping in the door to see if David was all right. He was asleep, you see. I fed him and he was tucked up. I wasn't going to be long. Any rate, the next thing I know is I come home and there's a bloody policeman telling me they've taken David away from me.'

The recollections of any Saturday night in dockside are likely to be confused but it seems that the police were telephoned by Mrs Douglas at midnight who said that the baby next door to her had been abandoned. The police went to investigate as there was insufficient emergency social work service available that weekend because of industrial action. On arrival at Sally's flat, they found Mrs Douglas attempting, somewhat unsuccessfully, to pacify a screaming David. The police report to social services states:

The flat was dirty, smelling of urine and human faeces. There was no heating and the place was extremely cold. The baby was lying in a cot and although adequately clothed was in some distress because of an unchanged nappy. There was no other occupant in the flat and the mother had obviously been away some time.

Mrs Douglas said that Sally never asked her to look after David and that she was distressed by his continuous crying. Sally, on the other hand, maintains that she did ask Mrs Douglas to keep an eye on the baby, and is sure that her neighbour called the police out of malice. However, the social worker tends to believe Mrs Douglas's story and that Sally did leave her child unattended. And Sally, in fact, admitted to being in a very distressed state during the days prior to the place of safety order and not really in control of events.

This first case study highlights some of those family situations that we have seen precipitate children into care. Sally March is a young, single parent, who has experienced disrupted relationships and considerable insecurity, both in her childhood and in her brief, unsuccessful marriage. Like the majority of the children in our study she was born locally, as were her two older sisters and mother, all of whom still live close by. Geographical mobility is not a characteristic of these families, although frequent moves within a locality are. Thus an extended family exists, but Sally is something of a scapegoat within it. Her unsuccessful marriage and subsequent liaisons earned her sisters' disapproval, both of whom are married, successful and aspirant. In addition, her dominating and concerned mother swiftly clashes with any male who lingers long with Sally. Neither is the father or his family in contact with Sally and, as a result, the young mother and her baby experience considerable isolation. They are poor and vulnerable to crises such as Sally's periodic illness and depression. This vulnerability is increased by the wider family keeping their distance, mainly to show their disapproval.

Sally has been long known to social services, although on this occasion they were not in regular contact with her until alerted by the health visitor. The child had been in care on two previous occasions, ostensibly to help Sally during her stay in hospital, a social services intervention for which she was deeply grateful. Yet neglect and non-accidental injury were never far from the social worker's mind, anxieties which were crystallised by the reports of the health visitor and the crisis of the unattended child. As a result, both workers have come to view David as highly likely to spend a long period in care. Nevertheless, firm evidence remains elusive and the social worker's team leader has reservations that an application for a care order would be successful, that removal from home is the best course of action, or that Sally March is unable to care in the long term. It is noticeable that in the rather uncoordinated preventative work with the mother and child, no attempt was made to involve the wider family.

The crisis which precipitated the removal of David under a place of safety order was unexpected and little contingency planning seems to have been made. The incident raised considerable anxiety among the social workers because of the age of the child, the intervention of the police and health authorities, the visibility of the case and the ever-present risk of accusation of inertia and negligence. It was unfortunate that the crisis occurred during an industrial dispute and at the weekend, when emergency social services were insufficient. In less pressing circumstances the place of safety order which, as we shall see, proved so violating to Sally March and her wider family could have been avoided by the use of other strategies. Nevertheless, social workers did act and moved quickly in a fraught and difficult situation.

Sally March lacks social skills and in her care of David she fails to meet the expectations of health visitors and social workers. She is not child-minded, partly because of her own childhood experiences, partly because of her poverty, isolation and depression, and partly because she is still young enough to want a social and sexual life of her own. Yet her love of the child is unquestioned as her subsequent behaviour will show. Thus, from the social worker's viewpoint, such cases present considerable problems in contingency planning. We shall also see that for a variety of reasons, the grounds have now been laid for David to spend a difficult and ambiguous period in care when negotiations will be fought over long-term responsibility and access.

## The Denbow family

The second of our four families comprises Mrs Doreen Denbow and her two children, Adam aged 6, and Lisa aged 5. Mrs Denbow is 40 and lives in a council flat adjacent to the city centre. She has been separated from her husband for two years. Since her divorce, she has lived alone. Doreen also has an 18-year-old son, Paul, who now lives with his father in Gateshead. She has not seen Paul for a year. Doreen is a slim, gaunt figure with large nervous eyes and twitching hands, forever touching her hair, flicking cigarette ash, or adjusting her dress.

Doreen met her husband, John, a marine, in the north-east of England while he was on leave. They married after a short courtship and eventually moved to our study area when he was posted there as an instructor for the Royal Marines. Doreen, almost from the outset, found marriage difficult. John was either on duty, away, or continued his gregarious social life. Life as a services wife depressed Doreen intensely, she knew very few people and was constantly on the move. Despite these difficulties both she and her husband created a home for Paul, their first child, and they stumbled on in what appeared to be a normal marriage. But problems accumulated, Doreen became mentally ill, suffering from a combination of depressive and neurotic disorders which her doctor suggested stemmed from a very deprived childhood.

Apparently, both Doreen's mother and father had histories of mental illness and this had led to a difficult childhood for Doreen, who spent four years in the care of Gateshead children's department living in a children's home which she remembers with some fondness. At this time, Doreen also attended a school for the maladjusted which she recalls with distaste as she says they used the cane a great deal. She also maintains that while there she lost her virginity to one of its staff who 'took advantage of her in the laundry'.

Although Doreen's relationship with her husband slowly deteriorated almost from the day she married, things brightened a little when John left the services and took a job as a security officer in a local factory. It was during this period that the two younger children were born. Both of them were unplanned and unwanted. The two young babies put additional strain on a cheerless marriage. Doreen's mental health began to deteriorate again and her husband embarked on a series of affairs that made for a tense domestic life. Doreen had few friends, no family nearby, and no one to turn to except her doctor. Eventually, she broke down and was admitted to hospital after being found by the local police in a distressed state in a public toilet.

She stayed in hospital for three weeks during which time John Denbow looked after the children with the aid of a home help. A week after Doreen returned, her husband left, stating he was fed up with marriage, and went to live with his brother in the north-east. Doreen coped remarkably well with her husband's departure and her mental health improved considerably. She busied herself with the task of looking after her children.

Social services first learned of Doreen's general predicament from the police as a result of the toilet incident. During her stay in hospital, it was social services that arranged the home help for her husband. The social worker at the time knew the marriage was shaky and that Doreen had a history of mental illness but was unaware of its antecedents and her general family background, although this was clear in earlier medical reports. When John Denbow left, some concern was felt about his wife's ability to cope with the children but these worries were allayed by Doreen's apparent determination to make a new life. Social workers gradually withdrew and Doreen was left to cope alone.

Paul, the oldest child, was unhappy. The departure of his father hurt him deeply as he identified with the tough, straight, no-messing-about marine. Paul blamed his mother for the breakdown of the marriage and called her 'mad'. He was increasingly difficult at school and at 16 promptly departed to live with his father. For Doreen, his departure was a blow for, despite his antagonism towards her, he was her only male friend. Although the two younger children, Adam and Lisa, were still with her, she felt abandoned, alone and began again to turn in on herself.

The circumstances under which Adam and Lisa came into care were in strong contrast to those of David March, in our previous case study. After the departure of Paul, her first and favourite child, Doreen sank into deep depression but she struggled on for six months before her doctor became aware of her condition. During this period, Doreen seemed to have lived an almost robotic existence, getting the two children up, feeding them, getting them off to school, working, shopping and washing. She felt lonely and abandoned:

'I just felt like a machine, trying to do my best for the two little ones but yes, I did miss my eldest [Paul] a lot but it was John's fault him going, he turned him away from me with his letters and big plans. He was always full of plans. Paul believed him, though, and nothing I could say would stop him.'

Although Doreen never made her ambivalent feelings for her two youngest children explicit, she often spoke with some regret about their birth and laid considerable blame for her mental and physical illnesses on them. Her social worker remembers an early conversation with her:

'She was a strange woman, you know, her eyes used to wander. You were never quite sure if she was talking to you or someone else. I remember one talk we had with her when she rambled on about Lisa and Adam and how they were the root of her problems. Apparently, they were quite difficult when they were babies, used to cry a lot and would never sleep. Lisa was also a difficult birth.'

Shortly after Doreen began treatment for her depression, a bomb-shell dropped. The nagging medical problem that had dogged her for years needed radical surgery; the consultant had decided that a full hysterectomy was now unavoidable. In two weeks she had to go into hospital. Delay would make things worse. Doreen was devastated and shocked:

'I has enough on my plate with one thing and another but when the doctor told me about my condition I felt terrible. It was like someone had switched out the lights, everything was black. The doctor told me to ring social services so I did. Mr Downes, the social worker came down to see me. He was very kind and said he would arrange for Lisa and Adam to be fostered while I was away.'

The social worker remembers Doreen at that time as being very shaky, bemused and disoriented:

'She seemed a very sad soul, everything had piled up on her and she obviously needed help. She seemed isolated, almost friendless, there was no immediate family in the city so voluntary reception of the children into care seemed appropriate for the period she was in hospital. I think I also discussed keeping the children for perhaps three weeks after she had left hospital to give her a chance to convalesce.'

Doreen liked her social worker and referred to him as 'her young man' – 'He was nice and understanding. I don't know what I would have done without him.'

This case study once more reminds us of the family situation of children who enter care, features which should already be familiar, such as the impoverished and chequered childhood experiences of the mother and disrupted marriages. In this case, the mother herself had been in the care of the local authority as a child. While many experts have rightly called into question the idea of a cycle of deprivation, a concept which has haunted social reformers for centuries, the families of children who enter care do, nevertheless, show long and recurring deprivation. While mothers can cope with several disadvantages such as ill-health, poor accommodation and family tensions, a series of crises in rapid succession, which are usually interrelated, put children at risk of separation from their parents.

Here, the social isolation of mother and the two younger children which followed the successive departures of husband and eldest son was intensified by the absence of any wider family in the area. Armed services families have many characteristics which make them vulnerable both while the husband is serving and in the period immediately following the conclusion of his service engagement. There are problems associated with the frequent geographic mobility of families, young mothers are isolated in tied accommodation, in which young families are reared with no sense of belonging. In addition, parents have to adapt to frequent separations which perpetuate the insecurities and adjustment difficulties of courtship and early marriage.

The crisis of mother's entry to hospital has been easier to manage for social workers as there was a breathing space of several weeks in which a suitable short-term foster home could be organised, the children prepared for separation and the mother's anxieties allayed. Nevertheless, it is noticeable that there was no contact between the family at risk and the foster parents prior to reception into care, no exploratory visits and little thought given to maintaining contact, mainly because limitations on access were not in question. Entry to care of the children was voluntary, welcomed by mother and engendered none of the resultant sense of betrayal, guilt and mourning that characterised our previous case study.

Yet acceptance of the situation by a participant does not necessarily imply a more optimistic care outcome. The isolation of the children while in care is likely to be considerable since, although placed together, there are no wider family or friends to act as intermediaries, the children are too young to communicate themselves and they will have to rely, at least initially, on the efforts of social worker and foster parents. The long-term prognosis of the social worker is not very encouraging as mother's recurring mental illness means, at best, that the children are likely to move in and out of care, a pattern that will increase their anxiety and insecurity. In addition, the mother's ambivalent attitude towards the children, springing from their unwelcome and difficult births and mother's subsequent related illnesses, adds an ominous reservation to any optimistic forecast of a swift and happy family reunion.

### The James family

The third family consists of Rose and Ted James and their three children, Andrew, June and Frances, aged 3, 5 and 7, respectively. Mr and Mrs James have been married for one year. All three children were born from Mrs James's previous marriage which came to a stormy end four years ago. Rose is 37 and Ted is 38. The family live in a rundown part of an inner city in a three-bedroomed council flat. It is sparsely furnished and rather cheerless, enjoying an unlovely view over disused railway sidings.

Rose is a small, tubby woman who looks old, tired and worn. Her first marriage, she says, was a disaster. She was apparently subjected to a great deal of violence by her ex-husband who had a drink problem. Despite the recurrent violence, the marriage held together for seven years, although Rose often left home for periods after a particularly severe attack by her husband. This turbulent relationship went on for many years for, in Rose's own words, 'Although he was a terrible man, John was like a little boy and when he'd come begging me to go back, I couldn't refuse.' Eventually, however, Rose did leave for good after receiving a broken arm and losing most of her front teeth. As she put it, it was 'a night to remember'.

After a short period of recovery in hospital during which all three children were received into care, Rose went to live with her aged mother but eventually plucked up courage to return to her flat. Her husband had vanished taking much of the furniture with him and she has not seen him since. For six months after this Rose lived alone supported by social security and social workers. It was at this time that she met Ted, a divorcee like herself.

Ted's background is rather obscure. No one seems to be too clear about his origins, least of all Ted. He was brought up by an aunt and he spoke about his past with great bitterness, disliking the aunt who bullied him as a child and hating his ex-wife who, he says, 'was a slag'. The circumstances surrounding the collapse of Ted's first marriage are also obscure, but apparently it was sufficiently traumatic never to be mentioned. Because of Ted's hostility to his first wife, he has not seen his son of that marriage since his divorce. Ted is a large, morose man who, according to Rose, is given to fits of depression and feelings of paranoia. He is a plumber by trade but has not worked for years.

As soon as Rose's divorce was granted she married Ted 'on the rebound'. Their relationship, however, has not been successful. It was full of brooding resentment and dissatisfaction brought to it from previously failed relationships. Despite, or because of this, Ted, rather than growing away from Rose and his marriage to her, withdrew into it. He never left the house and became obsessive about routine and control of both Rose and the three children. He demanded absolute obedience from everyone and punished the slightest infringement of his arbitrary rules. As punishments, the older children were often locked in their bedroom or made to stand in the corner with their hands on their heads for minor misdemeanours. If Rose was late back from the shops, she was interrogated and subjected to often bizarre acts of appeasement and submission. Ted kept a hammer in the spare room which he often threatened to use on the family and had a noose permanently hanging in the loft for himself.

Not surprisingly, life in the James's household was quietly horrific, and Rose never breathed a word to anyone, not even her GP, who provided her with a regular supply of tranquilisers. The older child's attendance at the primary school, although spasmodic, was never viewed as unusual and, apart from being a rather quiet, secretive child, she never gave anyone reason to suspect that she was being ill-treated. Consequently, social services knew nothing of this brooding situation although Rose had had occasional visits from social workers ever since the time all three children were briefly in care.

The routine horror of the household continued uninterrupted except for a period when Ted worked away for a friend down the road. During those two blissful months when 'he' was out of the house, life eased slightly. The paranoia, the obsession with discipline, the constant threat of violence, suicide and death receded. As Rose James said,

'He was lifted sort of, you see. [The work] seemed to take his mind off us and his stupid worries. He almost became human. You know, it was like some weight had been lifted off us all.'

But why did Rose put up with him? What was it that stopped her from walking out, or from seeking help before disaster struck? Rose looks beyond Ted to her first husband and even to her own childhood in answering this question.

'I don't really know. You just sort of get used to someone don't you? I mean, he wasn't all bad – I wouldn't have gone with him in the first place if he'd been *all* bad. Ted was a bit like John, my first husband, in that respect. I suppose I'm a fool, but I've always been a soft touch. I'm too soft, a bit like my mum in that way. She was always going to leave the old man but she didn't.'

The three children, Andrew, June and Frances, had always been a worry to Mrs Hurst, the health visitor, because of the disrupted parenting that had characterised their childhood to date. The concerns were not allayed when Rose remarried because Andrew and June, the two youngest, were not developing in the way that they should: 'They were crushed kids, frightened about everything,' said Mrs Hurst.

However, the last occasion on which Mrs Hurst called, the situation crystallised. Ted came into the room while she was chatting with Rose and the two younger children, something he had never done before: previously, he had always avoided seeing her. His effect on Rose and the children was immediate. The level of tension increased. Rose just stopped talking and the two little ones, both of whom were on the floor at their mother's feet, were obviously terrified of him and backed away to cling to their mother. Mrs Hurst commented later,

'I found that very worrying and decided there and then to have a word with Mr Arkwright who I knew was Rose's social worker. I told him of my fears and that there was something amiss in the family. I said I had no positive evidence of abuse but I was fairly sure that the two young ones were being ill-treated in some way.'

Mr Arkwright had not seen Rose for some time, having called perhaps twice to see her. Until the telephone call he felt nothing was amiss in the family. On the afternoon of Mrs Hurst's call, he went to see Rose on the pretext that he was passing and thought he would drop in for a chat to see how she was getting on:

'I had a good look at all three kids and they seemed fine to me. They were a bit bedraggled, but there were no obvious signs of abuse. I talked to Rose about life generally and about her new marriage but she didn't seem to pick up any leads I gave her that might have enabled her to talk about what was going on in the family. Finally, I put it to her that I had had a word with Mrs Hurst and that she was concerned about the children – that they seemed unwell and frightened of her husband. When I said that I could sense something was wrong she was very defensive but admitted nothing. I must admit I was worried by her response.'

Mr Arkwright talked things over with his senior the following morning and they decided that social work visits should be increased. They both knew the health visitor well and thought highly of her judgement. The social worker called again to see Rose on the Friday of that week and he also contacted the primary school which Frances attended and, although he learned very little from the teachers there, they promised to exercise additional scrutiny of the child. In the meantime, life for Rose and the three children began to hot up for, as Rose remembers,

'After the two visits from Mr Arkwright, Ted went potty. He kept threatening me. He locked all the doors and wouldn't let us out all weekend. He said if I spoke to anyone he'd kill me. He said he'd chop the kids' arms off and hang himself. He said the most terrible things. He got the hammer down from the loft and kept it beside the settee.
After Mr Arkwright's visit on Monday, he went mad and he punched me. You can imagine what it was like. He kept hitting Frances as well. The next day was his signing-on day so I decided to phone my social worker. I was terrified.'

Mr Arkwright had already talked over with his senior the possibility of a place of safety order being taken out for the three James children. He was in the process of arranging a meeting with the health visitor when Rose phoned and told him she was terrified that her husband was going to kill them all. She also said that she had kept Frances away from school because Ted had hurt the child's arm. After telling his senior of the situation and the possibility that a place of safety order might be needed that day, the social worker set off to the James's house.

When he arrived, Rose poured out her anxieties in a torrent of half-sentences interspersed with tears and pleas for help. Frances's arm was bruised and limp, the hammer was visible in the hall and the noose hung threateningly in the attic.

'I decided there and then that I was dealing with a nutter, so I phoned my senior from a neighbour's house and told him I was taking all the family to hospital and that a place of safety order should be obtained immediately. I also said that the police should be informed as the whole business was very heavy.'

When the police arrived, the social worker took Rose, Andrew, June and Frances from their home to the local hospital where they were carefully examined by doctors. Frances's arm was broken. Her mother explained,

'It was like some nightmare. I was terrified he was going to come back before the social worker could get us away. When the policemen arrived, I felt a bit happier and we left for the hospital. I was so ashamed of it all and kept wanting to be sick.'

On his return home from the social security office, the police arrested Ted and took him into custody. He wept as he sat between two burly policemen in the Panda car saying everything was his fault.

The hospital doctor decided that he wanted to keep all three children for a day or so to examine them thoroughly. Rose stayed at the hospital comforting her children until they finally fell asleep at 10.00 p.m. She then went to stay with friends. Rose's social worker says,

'It was a memorable day. I didn't know whether I was coming or going. I had to get the kids to hospital, to get the magistrate to sign the place of safety order, to see the police who wanted a statement from me and try to get a placement organised.'

What fresh features are highlighted by our third family case study? Here it is not so much family disintegration or turbulent reconstitution that precipitated the children into care; indeed, they are not neglected but live under constant threat of violence. Their mother and father are trapped in yet another unsatisfactory relationship, one that engenders fear and aggression, particularly in the husband. Indeed, as in so many wife-battering cases, the social pathology of initial, violent episodes is reproduced in subsequent relationships. Neither parent enjoys a wide, local, extended family network and friends are discouraged by the husband's paranoia and unpredictability.

Again, we can see the significance of agents such as the health visitor in referral and the involvement of both primary school and police in the initial stages of the crisis. Once more the social services, while on the scene, are overtaken by swift and unpredictable events. Indeed, in this case the sudden, uncharacteristic and frequent visiting by the social worker actually helped to precipitate the crisis. This illustrates how fraught the presenting situations can be, particularly those involving non-accidental injury. It also illustrates that suspicion, when met by parental denial, evasion and non-cooperation, provides insufficient reason for earlier intervention and makes support for the family extremely difficult. While this study will suggest that social workers are seen as, and become agents of, social control for some of our society's more vulnerable members, welfare interventions are not gratuitous. The problem, as we shall come to see it, is that once caught up in the welfare system, many families get more than they bargained for and find escape from scrutiny difficult. In this case, as in so many, non-intervention would, in retrospect, look grossly negligent. Yet, to have acted on suspicion before Mrs Hurst's phone call and if the concern had been unsubstantiated, would have looked like a high-handed invasion of privacy and the violation of the rights of a vulnerable family.

It would be unrealistic in this case to reproach social workers for a failure in contingency planning. Yet the sudden arrival of these children into care does not necessarily mean that the crisis will be easily resolved. Indeed, the social worker entertains a prognosis that these children will stay long in care and their return home will largely depend on the sentence the father receives from the Crown Court. As this is unlikely to involve his long absence from home, family reunion will need careful and prolonged scrutiny. It is also clear that the relationship between husband and wife, if it is renewed after this crisis, will require some case work. The father will be denied access for the foreseeable future, and barriers to mother's contact with the children could be posed by a distant and/or unwelcoming placement. Indeed, finding a foster home anxious to take on the burden of three young children will be difficult. Yet residential care, if it lasts for a considerable time, is clearly unsuitable for very young children. Short of a miracle, social workers will find it very difficult to locate a good, accessible, nearby placement. It is a case where many of the variables in operation encourage social workers to forecast a long stay in care for the children, yet make the fashioning of a coherent, satisfactory care plan very difficult.

**The Barton family**

Mrs Brenda Barton is 50, she looks older but has a resilient, almost defiant, air. She is severely incapacitated by short sight and deafness. Brenda is a stubborn and determined woman, a Mother Courage who dominates a household of rapidly fluctuating membership, unified by kinship or acquaintance. Her home is a refuge for those avoiding violent husbands, pressing debt collectors or those unable to reach their homes from nearby pubs at night. Everyone that comes and goes seems to be related either in law, liaison or suspicion and, as the family has lived in the same town for generations, the permutations in relationships are inexhaustible. They provide mum with a perpetual feast of recollection, resentment and speculation. Naturally, Brenda's reminiscences are both frequent and indiscreet as she is unable to see or hear the omnipresent television or clearly identify her visitors. Thus communication is impressed upon the unwary, and visiting social workers understandably do not stay long; neither are their calls particularly memorable.

Brenda holds court in the cavernous living-room of a large, top-floor, post-war flat that enjoys magnificent views across the town on one side and over the open-air market on the other. But interest lies within its walls, not outside. The endless, rich, funny, tragic saga of the huge extended family is played out each morning as a procession of visitors comes and goes, for the flat is strategically placed for the shops, support agencies, schools and pubs. As Brenda says, 'This is the best café in town, everyone uses it and pays nowt. I use five bottles of milk and 50 tea bags every day.' Yet the gossip, the excitement, who's been pinched by the police, who's died, who's left home, who's hit whom, who's diddling the social, each titbit provides the family with endless delight. Whenever one visits, there is a babble of conversation, punctuated by shrieks of derision and shouts of ineffectual control over the younger children who, crusts in one hand, torment the dog and each other. No one is ever lonely.

Brenda's husband, Derek, is 47. He is an ex-sailor, ex-mental hospital patient, ex-long sentence man of charm, intelligence and unpredictable violence. They have been married ten years. Brenda's first husband, Syd, also from the RN, died after 14 years of marriage while moving a wardrobe – 'I knew it would happen if he didn't take the clothes out,' volunteered Brenda. 'Nice man, never lifted a finger to me in all our years together.' But her first marriage, now wrapped in a haze of Fairy Liquid and blissful domesticity, was not uneventful. Her more incautious revelations, after several vodkas and lime, have suggested that Syd, on occasions, left for a quieter life.

Brenda has had many children – at least ten – but her recollections are rather imprecise. However, five have memorably survived. There is Sandra, aged 25, who married Colin, a car-sprayer. She has social pretensions, rarely visits and in Brenda's words, '. . . thinks she is a bloody duchess, she even dusts my three-piece with her hanky every time she sits down.' There is also Doris, 24, married with two children and now divorced. She seems quietly defeated by life and twitches her attractiveness away in psychosomatic illness.

There is John, 18, a quiet, furtive, model youth, elegantly dressed, who now works in a department store. He is seldom at home and seems to have spent most of his childhood hovering around the open-air market. He is an inscrutable youth and has defied the best efforts of a wide variety of social workers, teachers and others to find out anything about him. As Brenda says, 'He's just like his father, a loner. He only drank half-pints and never said a word, never heard him swear although he was in the Navy twelve years.' John is obviously an enigma. 'I just can't get through to him,' volunteered an earnest social worker – which is probably just as well as Dean, his 16-year-old brother, shy, handsome and delightfully devious, thinks his brother is a poof. Dean is under supervision for failure to attend school and for under-age drinking.

Finally there is Gloria, 15, a vivacious, pretty and manipulative young woman. She is an accomplished liar whose sexual exploits, if known, would leave most incredulous and a few deeply jealous. She and Dean have a close relationship in which they fit each other up with promising partners culled from community centres and markets. Both have a wide network of friends who hover on the margins of either care or custody, and much time is spent in borrowing money, drinking, playing pool, exchanging stolen goods and making raiding forays to the supermarket. Both Dean and Gloria seem to enjoy the *Sturm und Drang* of adolescence to the full.

Both of these two should attend St Paul's, a local secondary school which strives hard to care for the deprived and deliquent and other social casualties of the area. Run as a community school, within its cloisters everyone seems enriched. Membership is almost voluntary and suspension only comes to the violent. Each day is busy with the comings and goings of police, health visitors, social workers, services recruiting sergeants and youth workers who seem disappointed when four o'clock comes round and the teapot is put away. Gloria likes school, attends regularly and is popular, while Dean was moved to St Paul's from the local high school, a selective secondary school where expectations were higher – 'They all wore a bloody uniform, black jackets like some funeral, so I never went much.' Affectionately known to all as the DHSS, the high school was not sorry to lose Dean who was disruptive and uncooperative, although bright and an athlete of considerable promise. It was the school's agitation that led to transfer and their hostile court reports assisted social services in gaining supervision over the boy.

However, still waters run deep, according to Brenda, and the apparently happy, rumbustious family circle is periodically riven by crises. Derek drinks, has other women, is violent and manifestly prefers the children of a family he abandoned seven years ago to those he has inherited. Derek's children frequently visit, uninvited, unwelcomed and are generally disruptive. He is, in turn, frozen out by Brenda's children who act much of the time as if he is not there. The only periods of family harmony are offered by his regular visits to prison for non-payment of maintenance. In crises, Brenda talks endlessly of wanting to get away from it all and putting her hat and coat on, but, in fact, she seems to enjoy every minute of it and journeys only as far as the pub, the market and the doctor's, all of which seem to get daily visits. In each of these locations, similar coteries gather and discuss the health, indiscretions, appetites and possessions of those who have just left.

In spite of Seebohm, the family seems to enjoy a variety of social workers, there are two for Brenda (one for her sight and one for her deafness problems), Dean is occasionally visited by a Mr Hooker as well as by the school welfare officer. Not that contact with the statutory agencies is difficult, for the staircases for these heaven-reaching flats are constantly thronged with a procession of caring and controlling faces. As Brenda says, 'The nabs is always about when you don't want them, like when something has fallen off a lorry and they're never in when you do want them.'

The crisis that precipitated Gloria into care occurred one Tuesday evening. Returning somewhat unexpectedly from the Lord Raglan, Brenda discovered Gloria and two St Paul's boys busily furthering their education. Although short-sighted, her imagination quite adequately filled in the gaps in this little cameo. With a scream which suggested more a concern for her newly recovered eiderdown than her daughter's virtue, Brenda expelled the novitiates from Eden. But nemesis was quick to come. Brimming with disappointment and humiliation, Gloria gave an artfully staged and tearful performance at the nearby youth club, suggesting that Derek, her stepfather, also had a thirst for knowledge. As a result, Gloria was whisked to a place of safety in a police car and that very evening found herself in the glades of Sunnylands, an assessment centre, suitably located in a gin-and-tonic suburb of the town where she could offer extra-mural tuition to the local public school.

Naturally the next day, back at the flat, the conversation increased in volume, Brenda used more milk and tea bags, and enjoyed the excitement, particularly the prospect of Derek's forthcoming prosecution. Husband and wife spent the moments, while hunting for 50p to keep the television going, discussing what she should wear in court and how long he would get. Brenda did not seem particularly upset at Gloria's departure or scandalised at her husband's behaviour; indeed, she evinced a sense of relief. As she often commented, when the meters were full, she was housebound and now she only had Dean to worry about.

Commenting on the evening, Dean said, 'It was a right laugh, there was the fuzz, the social, half the staircase was involved. There was Gloria all innocent and Mum throwing things at Derek saying it was all lies. Which was stupid because we'd all known about it for years.'

Here again, we can see that a large extended family exists. However, it fails to function in crises. We have already noted that close relatives may have been previously involved in family crises and learned their lesson. Not infrequently, mothers actually conceal their children's departure to care, making the participation of wider kin difficult. Although visitors to the home often suspect the truth, an elaborate charade is often played out and much needed support is not forthcoming. It is also true that adolescents are viewed by the wider family rather differently from younger children. Although adolescents may have severe difficulties, they are expected to show independence, particularly boys, and delinquency and recalcitrant behaviour is frequently condoned. In addition, the endless control problems that adolescents present in inner-city areas encourage considerable ambivalence on the part of parents. The violation of parental rules on coming in at night, on dress and associates, on drinking and sexual behaviour leads to more stringent parental exactions and more aggressive responses from the youngsters. Thus, the disappearance of the child, at least in the short run, causes few tears but some guilt on the part of the mothers.

In this case study, some of the more familiar features of delinquency studies appear. The role of the school and neighbourhood in generating and identifying deviance is highlighted. In addition, the problems that social workers face in the community supervision of adolescents without parental support also emerge. As we have already seen, social services are alerted by others, in this case the police and the youth service. Contingency plans could hardly be expected and the whisking of the girl away to a cooperative assessment centre is highly characteristic of social workers' approach to difficult but not necessarily criminal adolescents.

While Gloria, and subsequently her brother Dean, present problems no different from many other adolescents in inner city areas, they should excite concern because they teeter on the edge of serious trouble and community support and supervision are insufficient. The social workers feel that Gloria is likely to remain in care until the age of 18 and that access of step-father to the girl should be denied. We also know that mother, because of her physical incapacities, will find contact difficult. Thus, links with home will wither unless the girl is placed very locally and the wider family is involved. As a result, social workers and placements should have family links high on their priority. As the girl is likely to be in a residential home, hostel or sheltered accommodation, control will remain an issue and her rescue from moral danger is likely to be something of a fiction.

## Conclusions

We shall return to these families at intervals during this study but already the complexity of the issues that bring children into care should be apparent. While heterogeneity may be a characteristic of the children, ranging from babes to 'bovver boys' and their stays in care very varied, yet their problems are very much a part of wider family problems. Thus, entry to care with siblings is very common and this complicates care arrangements and access conditions.

While families may have been long known to social workers, a social services department is reactive rather than proactive; it intervenes largely on the problems as defined by others. Thus, precipitating crises are difficult to foresee and contingency planning is easier to advocate the further one is from the crisis. Indeed, with such mercurial and changing family patterns, planning in the early stages of a child's care career lies in keeping options open.

Nevertheless, the entry of children into care is often ineptly managed, preventative work is patchy, and the ideas of participation in decision-making and shared care are little developed. Already, some issues are manifest which will have considerable relevance for the future links enjoyed between parents and children in care. The families feel they need more information from the very outset of the care negotiations. It may be, of course, that parents are told by social workers of the implications of entry to care and the alternatives and possibilities of social services intervention, all of which are expunged in the anxieties generated by crisis and separation. Nevertheless, none of our local authorities provided parents with a guide to the implications of care. In addition, where forewarning was available to social workers, there seems very little attempt to prepare children and parents for separation. The care potential of the extended family, if it does exist, is little exploited and the possible contribution of fathers quite ignored.

Let us now look at entry to care from another perspective, and explore the ways in which social workers define the task on reception of the child to care and the ways in which parents and children react to separation.

**Summary points**
1. Although the majority of families had been long known to social services, the crises precipitating children into care usually took social workers by surprise. This raises concern about the levels of preventative work enjoyed by families and the paucity of contingency planning.
2. A wide variety of agencies refer children to social services for help, but only a minority of these lead to entry to care and the reasons for admission are usually wider and more complex than the crises which initially attracted attention. This leads to conflict between the expectations of referrers and subsequent social work action.

3. Most children entering care experience a breakdown in family support. This may be because of parental illness, neglect, abuse or parental unwillingness or inability to care. Nevertheless, a quarter of children enter care due to their behavioural difficulties. The extended family often exists close by, but fails to support the child at risk when the crisis occurs, usually because of hostility or previous discouragements. The contribution of the wider family is seldom considered by social workers.

4. Children who enter care have disrupted, turbulent families, key members of which will be scattered through different households. Rapid and major changes in family membership, roles and location remain salient characteristics of children's home life, greatly complicating return and discouraging links between absent child and parents.

5. Nearly a half of the children under study entered care with one or more siblings; this considerably restricts social workers' placement options.

6. The case studies highlight the difficulties of easing children's entry to care and the fraught nature of most separations.

7. We shall see that these initial experiences colour subsequent negotiations between parents, care-givers, social workers and child.

# 6. Entry to care – the social work task

This chapter looks at the decisions social workers have to face when a child comes into care: what should be done and how long their help is likely to be required. Decisions are influenced by social workers' perceptions of the nature and duration of the child's problems and their previous knowledge of the family. These considerations influence the legislation under which the child enters and remains in care, the placements selected by social workers and the contacts which are deemed appropriate between the family and separated child. We suggest that barriers to parental contact with their children can be *specific*, that is, the restricting of access to children by an individual, or *non-specific*, that is, where barriers to contact are inherent in children's placements, for example, distance, routine and regulations.

We have suggested that the circumstances surrounding the child's admission to care will influence subsequent events, particularly the links that develop between absent children and parents. It is clear from interviews with parents, children and care-givers that the participants will have their perspectives coloured by initial negotiations. Where entry to care has been negotiated between parents and social workers, subsequent arrangements over access and maintaining contact with the absentee child are likely to be less fraught than where place of safety orders have been taken or where neglect or abuse have precipitated a child's entry to care. Our case studies have already suggested that the departure of an adolescent may be viewed rather differently by families from the separation of young children.

The admission of a child to care poses immediate problems for social workers. They have to decide what to do and the length of time the intervention is likely to take. Arrangements then have to be made about contacts with parents during the period the child is away. These will be influenced by all the other decisions taken and whether the child is perceived as a short- or long-term care case.[1]

Initially, the social worker has to decide the nature of the child's problem. For example, while the child may be beyond control, there could be a variety of reasons for this disruptive behaviour: conflict in the family, unsuitable schooling, physical or emotional factors. The social worker then has to devise a strategy of intervention and to fashion a care plan. It should already be obvious that planning in such circumstances is not easy. At the outset, it lies as much in keeping options open and continually revising ideas rather than in adhering to a fixed programme.

Our research would suggest that two factors influence social workers in making decisions. The first of these is previous knowledge of the child's family, and the second is how long the care experience is likely to last. These will have implications for the child's future and the links with home that will develop. Subsequent decisions, such as legislation, will often crystallise these initial social work perceptions, emphasising certain options while closing others, and placements will also be selected with these issues in mind.

Let us look at this process in greater detail.

### Previous knowledge of the child and his or her family

Many children have been involved both formally and informally with social services long before the issue of their reception into care presents itself. As we have noted, 76 per cent of our study population were said to be known already to social services – indeed, more than half of our study population had been known to social workers for more than a year. Some had already been the subject of child-care legislation. For example, 16 per cent of our study group had been on supervision orders and a further 29 per cent had been in care before, whilst, for 10 per cent there had been more than one care experience, and two children had been in care no fewer than ten times previously!

Nevertheless, most of these previous admissions to care were short stays due to the temporary breakdown in family care following illness, desertion or mother's general inability to cope. Usually, the children involved in these admissions were very young. For example, over 80 per cent were under the age of five. Simultaneously, groups of siblings had usually been involved; two-thirds of those children who had been in care before had been taken into care with a brother or sister. In addition, the evidence would suggest that these early separations from family had been traumatic. While in care, only a few had remained with parents or relatives and, in spite of the fact that they were infants, they had been placed in residential care or foster homes in equal proportions.

Prior knowledge of children's situations accumulates and comes to influence social work decisions. We have already noted that the family life of children who enter care tends to be turbulent, their households are punctuated by crises and break-ups. At each event, social work perceptions are revised and uncomplimentary views reinforced, ultimately justifying the use of legislation which restricts parental rights. This eventuality has been noted by Packman in her research into decisions surrounding admission to care.[2] She found that given similar precipitating situations, one of the principal features which distinguished children taken into care from those not admitted was not so much the gravity of the crisis, but whether or not the children (or their mothers) had been in care before. We find in interviewing social workers that previous knowledge of the child and family is an important feature influencing their perceptions of the care situation.

Social workers interpret presenting crises very much in the light of what has gone before, and are continually redefining the situation in the light of accumulated evidence and, far from staying their hand, we shall see that this leads to longer care episodes for those children that repeatedly surface for scrutiny.[3] Although the intention of this study is to chart the progress through care of groups of children, it is clear that the processes of care and the care careers of children are already ongoing, even before the episode examined in this study.

For the remainder of our study group, it is difficult to assess the extent of social services' previous involvement. In 41 per cent of cases, social workers claim to have undertaken measures to prevent entry of the child into care and usually described their attempts in terms of family case work. However, both from our scrutiny of the 450 children in the extensive study, coupled with that of the 30 families in the intensive study, the impression is one of rather superficial social work preventative efforts. Frequently, from the child's point of view, 'known to social services' implies little more than a record of their name in a file. What interventions there are do not appear to be either systematic or coordinated – a point made very forcibly by Jane Rowe in her study of long-term foster care.[4] However, in fairness to social workers, our case studies do illustrate that in many situations systematic and coordinated preventative work is very difficult. It may also be the frustrations engendered by working with these families and the difficulties of working in the community that makes social workers more controlling when care decisions are made and when they finally find themselves in a powerful position.

On a child's admission to care, the social worker has to make up his or her mind as to the child's likely duration in care. While there are the immediate needs for support and shelter of the child, long-term concerns about the child's best interests have to be considered. Some problems quickly pass as mothers recover from illness or housing problems are resolved but, in other cases, the future looks less certain and may depend on the efforts of other agencies, such as the education authority or upon decisions made by the courts.

Most difficult of all for social workers are decisions in situations which question the ability of the mother to care for her child in the long term. Such decisions are particularly fraught if the child is at risk of abuse or neglect. In these situations, there are no straightforward solutions. Children who stay long in care, who are left in uncertainty, whose needs are inadequately or temporarily met, are unlikely to thrive. Yet, premature return to home can lead to neglect or even injury. Already several of our case studies have illustrated the fraught situations social workers face. Unfortunately, as we shall see, many local authority care situations present numerous secondary dangers, those of frequent transfers between and breakdowns in placements and of long periods in care.

Even at the time of reception, social workers perceive children entering care as falling into clear categories: cases seem to divide themselves into long and short stay.[5] In all, 43 per cent of the 450 children we studied were expected by social workers to stay in care for only a short time, 22 per cent less than one month and a further 21 per cent for less than six months. For the remainder, 23 per cent were seen as likely to stay for up to two years, but for a smaller group of 13 per cent, their duration in care was envisaged as much longer, exceeding five years. In addition, the uncertainty of the child's situation meant that in a further 13 per cent of cases, the social worker was unable to offer any prediction. We shall find that many of these children are likely to remain long in care. Table 6.1 indicates social workers' views on children's likely length of stay in care.

**Table 6.1   Social workers' expectations, on admission, of the child's length of stay in care**

|  | % |
| --- | --- |
| Less than 1 month | 22 |
| 1–3 months | 14 |
| 4–6 months | 7 |
| 7–12 months | 5 |
| 1–2 years | 18 |
| 3 or more years | 21 |
| Don't know | 13 |
|  | (N = 450) |

When we look at social workers' expectations of children's likely placements, however, it can be seen that half of the children on admission were viewed as having a strong probability of being back home within six months and, for a further 12 per cent, the odds of returning home were 'moderate'. Seventeen per cent of all the children were said by social workers to have no hope at all of returning home within six months, and 19 per cent only a slight chance. However, it is surprising to note that when social workers are asked to predict the situation of children in two years' time, how little change there is. It might have been expected that the number envisaged as long-stay cases by then would have fallen, yet only 54 per cent were given strong probability of returning home even after two years in care and 27 per cent were seen as having very little chance of ever going back to their parents. It is evident, then, that social workers have very clear ideas on children's expected length of stay in care on arrival, and in an accompanying paper which deals with children's length of stay in care, we find that these estimates are very accurate.[6] However, their views on the duration of particular placements, such as foster homes, residential care or living at home 'on trial' within that time-scale are more varied. Social workers predict extensive use of both fostering and residential settings and that these will be closely interrelated and not mutually exclusive.

**Table 6.2  Probability of returning home to parents/ natural family** (social workers' prognosis at time of child's admission to care)

|  | Within 6 months | Within 2 years |
|---|---|---|
|  | % | % |
| Strong | 50 | 54 |
| Moderate | 12 | 15 |
| Slight | 19 | 19 |
| None | 17 | 8 |
| Don't know | 2 | 4 |
|  | (N = 450) | (N = 450) |

It is also important to note that possibilities of other options for the children are insignificant at this stage. Adoption is rarely entertained by social workers, even for the very young, neither are independent homes considered for the older adolescent. Without jumping to conclusions, such a finding has considerable implications for practice. First, it means that, for the foreseeable future, while substitute care is being provided, this will not necessarily be in a substitute family. Thus, even at this early stage, social workers should give serious consideration to the role and contribution of the child's natural family. Secondly, the management of links with home will be an important element of this strategy for we shall see that contact with the natural family greatly influences the duration of the child's stay in care and chance of returning home.

## Legislation
The next task facing social workers who take a child into care is to decide which legislation is most appropriate or provides sufficient

authority for an action. These are not necessarily the same thing. We have described the Acts of Parliament governing these decisions and the ways in which voluntary admission under Section 2 of the 1980 Child Care Act differ from committals and care orders and how each of these differs from place of safety orders. We shall shortly note that the legislation chosen not only influences children's placements but also the links that parents enjoy with their children. The initial legislation under which our study population of children came into care was as seen in Table 6.3.

**Table 6.3   Legal status of children entering care\***

|  | N | % |
|---|---|---|
| Voluntary care | 285 | 63 |
| Care orders: | | |
|     care/protection | 10 | 2 |
|     offending | 25 | 6 |
|     full-time education | 15 | 3 |
|     other care/interim orders | 17 | 4 |
| Place of safety orders | 97 | 22 |
| Other legislation | 1 | 0 |

\* We have previously explained that these figures have been compiled in a slightly different way from the child-care statistics for England and Wales published annually by the DHSS and Welsh Office. Our population includes place of safety orders and omits remands to care. Nevertheless, the observed balance between voluntary admissions and committals to care is still close to the national figures and is even closer if we adjust our categories to match exactly those used by the government department.

We were surprised to encounter such frequent use of place of safety orders. They are used for a wide range of contrasting situations and their use is increasing.[7] Overall 97 (22 per cent) of our 450 cases came into care under this order. Half of this group of children were girls (51 per cent) yet only 18 per cent were under the age of two, the group most likely to be envisaged as in immediate danger when neglected or deserted. Unexpectedly, more than a third of the 97 children were over 12 years of age; 13 of the 97 orders lapsed after the time-limit had expired, and 61 of them were subsequently followed by full care orders. We shall note that children entering care via this route generally have greater problems in maintaining links with their families, and that they tend to stay long in care.

Social workers seem quite content with the range of legislation available. They seem able to employ legislation which meets the problem as they, rather than anyone else, define it. In only 8 per cent of cases did social workers express unease about the legislation used for a child's entry to care, the most common anxieties being unexpected court judgments or where place of safety orders had to be arranged by a night or weekend duty team. It does not seem from our evidence that legislation is imposed on social workers or that local authority departmental regulations restrict their freedom of manoeuvre. It is also clear that as the child moves through care, social workers increasingly seek control over their clients and the families, replicating exactly the stance of the eighteenth- and nineteenth-century welfare authorities.

It is not surprising to find that the initial legislation employed to take the child into care is closely tied to other aspects of the care process. For example, the majority of care orders (79 per cent) arise because of the behaviour presented by the child, and 61 per cent of place of safety orders follow abuse or neglect by parents. Voluntary receptions, in contrast, tend to be used to deal with breakdowns in family care and 49 per cent of these admissions followed mother's illness or inability to cope. It seems to be the case that, in voluntary receptions, social workers have a predominantly family focus, whereas with care orders the child is seen to be the prime concern and in need of protection, counselling or therapy. For voluntary receptions, the child is likely to come into care with siblings, whereas in care order situations they more frequently come alone. Place of safety orders, however, do not mirror either of these patterns. While the urgency, often following a referral from police, necessitates child rescue, the precipitating crisis usually involves siblings and obliges social workers to adopt a family-oriented focus, albeit a rather controlling one.[8]

As a consequence, several other characteristics of the children such as age and sex are associated with the legislation initially selected by social workers. For example, there is little difference in the number of boys and girls voluntarily received into care or subject to place of safety orders. However, for the care order group, boys predominate in the ratio of 2:1 on reception, although this pattern rapidly changes in the direction of parity as a consequence of subsequent legislation. The age of the child also seems to influence social workers in their selection of appropriate legislation. Voluntary receptions and place of safety orders are applied to children of all ages, whereas care orders were initially applied to older children and three-quarters of the orders were applied to children over the age of 11.

The legislation selected is also influenced by social workers' perceptions of the child's duration in care. While care orders are rarely viewed as suitable for short-stay cases, there is considerable variation with place of safety orders and, perhaps surprisingly, voluntary admissions to care. A quarter of this voluntary group, for instance, are envisaged as staying for longer than two years. Curiously, the quality of relationships within the child's home, as perceived by social workers, does not influence their choice of legislation.

## First placements

Once the child has been admitted to care, shelter must be found. In a few cases (3 per cent) the child remains at home under close supervision, but the great majority are placed in various types of foster homes or residential settings. Table 6.4 indicates the range of placements initially selected by social workers.

**Table 6.4    First placement experienced by child**

|  | N | % |
|---|---|---|
| Remain at home | 14 | 3 |
| Foster care | | |
| foster home* | 189 | 42 |
| fostered with relatives | 14 | 3 |
| Residential | | |
| children's home | 102 | 23 |
| O and A centre | 94 | 21 |
| residential nursery | 5 | 1 |
| CHE | 0 | 0 |
| special school | 4 | 1 |
| hostel | 2 | 0 |
| hospital | 23 | 5 |
| Other | 3 | 1 |
|  | (N = 450) | |

* In this table, the term foster care includes all types of foster care with varied functions, e.g. short-stay or long-stay, pre-adoption and bridging arrangements, and different styles, such as inclusive, exclusive and contract. These will be more fully explored in subsequent chapters.

These are the initial placements of children immediately following their entry to care and many children will soon move elsewhere. However, it is significant that residential care is very widely employed in the early days of a child's care career, for observation and assessment (O and A) centres and the small community home emerge as having important reception functions. Hospitals, too, play an important role; for example, 23 children in our study went to hospital as their first placement in care. It appears that the residential sector has important reception functions in times of crisis, both when the child enters care and, as we shall see, after any subsequent breakdown of placement.

Selecting a placement is a difficult task for the social worker as freedom of manoeuvre is often circumscribed by limited resources and local authority policies. Social workers expressed greater disquiet about the placement decisions they have to make than they did about the admission of the child to care or the choice of legislation. While in 80 per cent of the cases social workers said that they were successful in getting the desired *category* of placement – that is, whether the child should be fostered or placed in a particular type of residential home – in only half of the 450 cases was the social worker able to place the child in the *specific* setting that they deemed most suitable. Indeed, in a quarter of the cases, social workers expressed considerable reservations about the actual placement chosen.

Frequently, social workers were hindered by lack of resource and this clearly affected a third of the initial placements. In a few cases (6 per cent), local authority policies and the decisions of other professionals, such as paediatricians, restricted placement options. However, a major constraint on social workers' freedom of action regarding placements was the laudable wish to keep siblings together. Indeed, nearly half of the children that entered care found that their placement possibilities were restricted by an accompanying sibling and, of course, this is even more pressing with younger children.

In seeking placements, social workers had a number of priorities which, obviously, are not mutually exclusive. In 55 per cent of the cases, they sought to alleviate the child's immediate situation, in three-quarters of situations they hoped to offer the child stable, long-term care, and for 31 per cent it was hoped that the whole family would be helped by the care intervention. The need for control greatly influenced the choice of a fifth of placements and in another quarter of placements more information on the child was seen to be essential. In both of these situations O and A centres were preferred. In 27 per cent of all cases, the child was viewed as having special difficulties which could be helped by other resources available, such as remedial teaching or medical care.

Considerations of access and other contacts between the family and the separated child, which might have been expected to be a factor of importance for all children coming into care, only emerged as an issue in the choice of 29 per cent of the initial placements. This failure to consider the family links of children entering care is significant because, as we shall see, the choice of placement has numerous hidden implications for any future contact between parent and child. Indeed, the propensity of many placements to frustrate links between parent and child often passes quite unrecognised by social workers.

Fosterings are clearly preferred for groups of siblings facing breakdowns in family care, especially if their expected stay in care is short.

We have seen from our case studies that foster care was readily provided for the Denbow children. Residential settings are favoured when behaviour problems are apparent or when neglect or abuse is present. Indeed, residential care is often preferred for and by adolescents. It will be recollected that Gloria Barton had been placed initially in an O and A centre where her situation could be more calmly explored. The quality of the child's relationships with parents is also important in influencing the placements selected, especially the child's feelings for mother. Our evidence suggests that fosterings are clearly selected for a first placement when the relationship between the child and parents is accepting; however, when children are hostile to parents, they are more likely to be placed in residential settings.

Another major factor which affects all placement decisions is the social worker's expectations of the child's length of stay in care and subsequent destinations. Although it is clear that a large number of children are initially placed in residential care, this is because social workers believe that they will move out quickly. For example, more than half of the children entering residential care on reception were viewed as likely to be home within six months, and a further quarter of them were seen as potential foster cases. Yet, of the 203 children placed initially in foster homes, 138 (68 per cent) were expected by social workers to be at home within six months, while only 9 per cent were expected to move into residential settings during this period. It is interesting to note how frequently residential care is viewed as the chilly anteroom to a warm foster family or to a return home while the reverse situation is hardly ever entertained. It will be interesting as the study progresses to see how far these perceptions on the suitability of certain placements for children by social workers and the effects of such perceptions on the links experienced between absent child and parents are realised.

## Links between children in care and their families

Implicit in many of the decisions made by social workers will be ideas on what sorts of contact families should have with their children in care. We have already seen that the members of a child's closest family may be scattered among several households, that the child may have been sheltered by grandparents or others before reception, and that some siblings may accompany a child into care while others remain elsewhere. We shall note that occasionally, in spite of social work efforts, siblings are separated, both at the time of entry to care and over time. Thus, a network of relationships has to be scrutinised by social workers during the first few days a child is in care and decisions have to be made either to encourage contact between children in care and their parents or to limit the links between children and various family members.

Although the child's family is often dispersed among several households, all children coming into care have a considerable number of living relatives. Of our 450 children who entered care, 97 per cent of the children's mothers and 90 per cent of their fathers were known to be alive. What is more, their grandparents are usually living, often locally, and half the children have a natural sibling alive while a third have at least one half-brother or sister. In all, only 11 per cent of our study population had no half-, step- or natural siblings. Over three-quarters (79 per cent) of the children were actually living with their mothers before their reception into care and, at that time, a third were said to be seeing a grandparent at least once a week. At the moment of entry to care, in only a small number of cases was the natural mother or father not the main provider of physical and emotional support for the child. Indeed, only a very small minority (11 per cent) of children had little contact with their mother before entering care, usually being looked after by a close relative. Thus, it should be apparent that a preoccupation with parental contact could easily displace consideration of many other significant individuals in a child's life.

We have already noted that severe family dislocations are common, with 45 per cent of the children coming from single-parent households, and there is likely to be financial and emotional hardship. This vulnerability of families is emphasised by the fact that only one-third of parents were still married to each other at the time of the child's entry to care and half of the children's households had youngsters under the age of five living in them. Similarly, although only 41 per cent of natural fathers were living in the child's home at the time of reception into care, the majority (60 per cent) had some sort of contact with their children.

For parents, having their children in care was often only one episode in a lifetime of difficulties. The stereotype of young, feckless girls asking the state to shoulder responsibility for their children is quite unsubstantiatied.[9] Indeed, 17 per cent of the mothers and 19 per cent of the fathers were over the age of 40 at the time of their child's reception into care, and only 6 per cent of mothers and 1 per cent of fathers were under the age of 20.

Nevertheless, the turbulence of children's family life, the coming and going of co-habitees, often accompanied by their children, and the fitful participation of wider kin and friends in their lives lead to many tensions and rejections between parents, children and the wider family. Thus, a third of the children were described by social workers as having rejecting, ambivalent or indifferent feelings for their mothers. Indeed, in 12 per cent of all children the rejection was severe and these feelings tended to be mutual. Thus, in considering links between children and their families, we shall see that a few children, particularly adolescents, have no desire to see their parents and that some parents have to be encouraged by social workers to visit, often with little success.

Maintaining contact between a family and its absent members is a complex process. It is part of the wider pattern of belonging which has instrumental and expressive dimensions. We shall explore these aspects of links between children and their families more fully in the next chapter but in this brief glance at the task facing social workers on a child's reception into care, some mention of access arrangements is appropriate. We shall see that access arrangements made at the outset have a tendency to persist and can influence the style of subsequent contacts between parent and child.[10]

On admission of a child into care, the social workers have to make up their mind what sort of access members of the child's family should enjoy, both in the short term and over the longer period. We have already seen from our case studies that contact is not always desirable, that some children and parents will shun any relationship, and that the stability and satisfactions of certain placements could be threatened by frequent visiting. It is also important to realise that to maintain frequent and regular contact between parent and child demands considerable social worker time, energy and skill. Thus, decisions on access should not be taken lightly.

It is useful to distinguish initially between two kinds of restrictions imposed on a family's contact with a child in care. First there are *specific restrictions*; that is, where access is denied between the child and a particular person or persons. At the time of reception to care, 36 per cent of admissions had a specific restriction of this kind placed on family members, generally on a natural or step-parent. In 63 per cent of specific restrictions, it was the natural mother who experienced the restriction, in 56 per cent of cases the father was restricted, while 15 per cent of restrictions affected siblings, 14 per cent step-fathers and 8 per cent step-mothers. In 61 per cent of specific restrictions, all contact was denied between the child and certain family members, but in the remainder limitations were less severe. Parental visiting was allowed but was carefully regulated in its frequency and length or in the meeting-place. Generally, it was the social workers who decided on these limitations of contact (81 per cent) but placements (25 per cent), courts (6 per cent), children themselves (13 per cent) and other members of the families (13 per cent) also sought to impose controls.

The reasons for discouraging or limiting family contact largely arose from a fear of endangering the child or upsetting the placement. For example, in over half (56 per cent) of the cases where restrictions were applied the risk of abuse or neglect was viewed as strong, in 38 per cent there was mutual rejection between parent and child, in 28 per cent of cases parents had disrupted, or were thought likely to disrupt, placements, and in 9 per cent of cases parents were seen as a bad moral influence on the child, and likely to encourage absconding (3 per cent) or offending (9 per cent).

Nevertheless, many barriers to contact between children in care and their parents are not deliberately constructed, but are peculiar to the placements selected or in the continuing incapacity of parents to visit. These *non-specific restrictions* are not simple reflections of the explicit barriers to contact that we have just described. Not only are they more widespread but they also are an inherent part of the separation experience and are also less subject to control by social workers.

In all, 66 per cent of children coming into care experienced these non-specific restrictions at the time of their admission. This arose largely from rules governing visits (75 per cent) which are frequently imposed on parents and children by residential and foster placements without consultation with the child's social worker. These limitations are usually compounded by other difficulties facing parents seeking to maintain contact, for example, distance of the child's placement (33 per cent), transport problems (16 per cent), unwelcoming attitudes at the placement (12 per cent) and health or handicap problems faced by parents (19 per cent). Financial problems and difficulties, such as those faced by parents on shift-work, can also be important. In many cases parents were unaware that financial assistance was available under Section 26 of the 1980 Act to assist visiting. Generally, it was the child's parents rather than the wider family members or siblings who were most likely to experience these sorts of restrictions. Conversely, the wider family or siblings were not sought out or encouraged to visit, neither were funds readily available for the journey or to pay for child-minders.

As with specific restrictions on access, these non-specific limitations on contact were more likely to be severe following place of safety orders and for children judged by social workers to be long-stay cases, rather than to affect voluntary receptions. But, unlike restrictions on access, the impact of non-specific restrictions was largely independent of factors in the child's family. Such barriers pressed as heavily on children whose parents were ill as on those children who were neglected. These non-specific restrictions were quite as onerous in residential situations as in foster homes. However, in both sectors, residential and fostering, some placements showed great flexibility in accommodating parental interests and some were very discouraging. The nature of the barriers to parental visits varied. In foster homes it is a question of role conflict and the deskilling of visiting parents, whereas in residential settings it is more a problem of fitting in with routine and bureaucratic constraints. For a quarter of children, the initial placement raised something of a dilemma as those children whom social workers seek to discourage from links with home are more likely than others to be placed in locations in which non-specific restrictions are far less pressing. Even at the point of reception into care, therefore, there seems to be a conflict between policy and outcome with regard to links between children in care and their families.

Let us now see how our four families perceived the removal from home and subsequent admission of their children into care. We have seen how David March was removed from Sally on a place of safety order and that the events surrounding the departure of the James children were similarly fraught. On the other hand, the move of the Denbow children into care could be more planned and was less immediately upsetting. Finally, we have seen how Gloria Barton found herself in an assessment centre, the focus of scandal and interest. Few tears were shed in the family at Gloria's dramatic departure and visits were not high on anyone's list of priorities.

### The March family

What happened to David March when the police wrapped him in a cot blanket and removed him in their care to a nursery? What were Sally March's reactions to this situation on returning home in the early hours of Sunday morning from a short tour of the local clubs? We saw Sally a few days after David had been taken into care and asked her.

'It was terrible. It was just bloody terrible. I went numb and just wanted my baby back. I kept thinking, they've stolen my baby – over and over again – they've stolen my baby. I really didn't know what was going on. It just seemed unreal. I really thought David had been kidnapped or murdered or something.'

The sense of panic and unreality that Sally described is typical of mothers in our intensive study experiencing the loss of their children. The shock is similar whether the separation is precipitate and fraught or expected and planned. In general, mothers find it difficult to comprehend what is going on. Sally was no exception. She was very confused and her mind was flooded with a variety of emotions. As a result, she was quite unable to make much sense of events:

'I just sort of went mad. There was this policeman and he kept saying things, asking me questions. There was another man there – there was two other men as well. I can't even remember who was there, let alone what they said or what I said to them.'

For Sally, the first 24 hours after David was removed were a blur of people, feelings, events and places. Her recollections of the night when viewed in the light of other evidence were clearly untrue or misinterpreted. Indeed, she could not recollect whether she was told where David had been taken or even if she had asked where he was.

Sally was eventually taken by the police to her mother's house where, according to her mother, she went straight to bed and slept through until 11.00 a.m. next morning. Mother was, in fact, welcoming to her daughter and deeply concerned about the whereabouts and safety of her grandson. Already, at the moment of David's reception into care, Sally's mother decided to adopt a belligerent stance towards the intervention by social services, an anger which we shall see amply fuelled her subsequent efforts to get the child back with mother. As she volunteered to us several days later, mainly to strengthen her daughter's sagging resolve,

'The social are always picking on them that can't fight back, stopping your money. Why didn't they bring David to me if they're so worried? No, they do it to keep themselves in a job, pretending to look after kids. I brought up three and went to work at the same time.'

The police officer who took charge of David that night, although deeply concerned about the child's distress and appalled by the physical state of the flat, was fairly sure that the child had not been injured in any way:

'We are trained to recognise the obvious signs of abuse and I felt sure that the little mite hadn't been subjected to any real injury. He was howling like a banshee for a start and he looked quite bonny although his clothes and his cot were in a terrible state. The smell was horrible. The PC I was with said he was nearly sick.

'Yes, well, I felt the best thing to do in the circumstances, and in the absence of a social worker, was to take the child to the children's home. PC Hindley contacted HQ who phoned through to the home to tell them that we were on our way.

'No, I didn't think it appropriate to wait for the child's mother to return. I had no idea when she would come back and Saturday night is one of our busy nights. He needed attending to, he was in a filthy condition – obviously neglected. No, the whole situation needed a social worker to look after it, if I could find one.'

The night staff at the children's home busied themselves after the phone call from the police. A cot was prepared and some milk warmed in a pan. They remembered hearing David's shrieks of protest as the car turned into their drive. Mrs Morgeson, head of the home, recalling the child's arrival, said,

'This flushed policewoman came in with a grubby bundle of noise . . . I remember thinking, there's nothing wrong with your lungs, my boy. That's always a healthy sign. I get most concerned when I get little silent packages – they are the ones that worry me most.

'I made a quick examination of the child to establish there were no obvious injuries requiring medical treatment. I did that as I removed his nappy which was in a terrible state and obviously hadn't been changed for many hours. He had a very bad nappy rash that extended down his thighs and over a good deal of the lower part of his body. There were no bruises, no deformities, no scars, he was a good weight and bright-eyed.'

David kept the children's home awake for much of that night with his howling, and eventually fell asleep at 4.00 a.m.

On the Sunday morning, as the now-forgotten Dutch fleet wallowed off the breakwater, Sally sat in the front room of her mother's house feeling forlorn and lost. A deep sense of helplessness engulfed her, feelings which encouraged in her mother a surge of protection. That afternoon, even her two sisters arrived, feeling that Sally's nemesis had amply borne out all their forebodings. Over cups of tea everyone assuaged their guilt by castigating Sally's ex-husband, the meddling neighbour, the police and, above all, the harassed social worker.

Entry into care for David March was a rapid and difficult process involving unfamiliar faces and places. What he felt about the event remains open to question. Whether removal from home by the police was preferable to a few more hours in a wet nappy cannot be known. However, the children's home staff maintained that David's distress and behaviour during the first hours of his removal from home were due more to the pain of separation from his mother than the nappy rash from which he suffered. Sally was also very upset by David's removal from her flat, thrust into the role of a neglectful parent with little information or awareness of what was happening. Sally's already poor self-esteem suffered an even greater setback. The place of safety order also violated the trust built up between her and the social worker, thus suspicion and silence came to characterise their contacts, in contrast to the trust and openness of previous months.

For the social worker, the events precipitating the place of safety order strengthened his suspicions about Sally's abilities as a mother and forced him to make rapid decisions and assessments. For example, we shall see that little or no consideration went into encouraging Sally's maternal role or her participation in caring for David in the children's home. Also, although it was decided very early on that all Sally's visits to her son should be closely supervised because non-accidental injury was suspected, little effort was made initially to involve other members of Sally's family.

## The Denbow family
Doreen Denbow had no relatives in the locality; all her family had either disappeared or died. As a consequence, her social worker, Mr Platt, explored the possibility of neighbours looking after the children

while she was in hospital. The search was fruitless, however, for Doreen's few friends were either too old to take on the care of Lisa and Adam, or were unwilling to volunteer.

We asked Doreen and her social worker if they had considered contacting her ex-husband and telling him of her plight. Doreen had dismissed the idea out of hand, and Mr Platt said he tried to persuade her to get in touch with her ex-husband if for no other reason than to let him know she was ill. But,

'Doreen was adamant that he wasn't to know what was going on and I was powerless to do anything and besides, I doubt if the husband would have helped very much anyway. According to Doreen, he was always pretty indifferent to Lisa and Adam. Paul was his favourite.'

Mr Platt at this stage was increasingly uneasy about Lisa and Adam and the relationships they enjoyed with their mother.

'I remember in my conversations with Doreen I kept getting conflicting messages about the children. On the one hand, she'd be saying how concerned she was about them and how she didn't want them to be looked after by this or that person because they weren't good enough, yet, on the other hand, she was obviously rather ambivalent about her feelings for the children. On numerous occasions she told me how their births were both mistakes and how difficult they were as infants. She cared for them well enough, though. The house was clean, the kids well fed and they seemed a relatively normal pair, perhaps a little highly-strung and attention-seeking but certainly not abused or neglected in any way.'

Mr Platt discussed the case with his senior and they both agreed that Lisa and Adam should be received into care and that a short-term foster placement should be found for both of them. Accordingly, in the two weeks that elapsed between referral and reception, Mr Platt began to explore the availability of short-term foster homes for the children.

In an interview shortly after the children's reception, he remembered this fortnight vividly:

'It was dreadful, I spent days and days trying to get one of our short-term foster parents to take the two kids for four weeks. I did not want them split up and I did not want them miles away from their home, schools and the hospital but could I find anyone? – could I hell! First of all, our division only had one or two foster parents available and none of these would take two children. The other divisions came up with a few other potentials but in the end, these were no good for a variety of reasons; one family had two children of the same ages and the other was only interested in babies so I drew a blank.'

Time was running out and it had taken 18 days to get nowhere as far as a suitable fostering placement was concerned. Doreen was to go into hospital in a few days' time and no location had been secured for her children. The planned entry into care was rapidly becoming a crisis.

Mr Platt's experience was not untypical in the area, for local short-term foster parents have always been a rare breed. Mr Platt's senior summed up the situation in the following way:

'Way back in the days of the old children's department, we never boarded out much in the city itself. Kids were placed miles away up country – this applied to residential care just as much as fostering. Some of it was policy, the old children's officers, to say the least, weren't very pro-family, but many of the problems were due to the special nature of our area. It's an almost totally working-class population for a start and for years, both before and after the war, accommodation in the inner city was poor. There just weren't enough suitable places for successful fostering to have a chance. So, there's no tradition of fostering and, of course, consequently there's no tradition of good fostering practice. Quality control and supervision have, in the past, been very poor.'

On drawing a blank, Mr Platt approached the local social services placement panel who have the responsibility for vetting and allocating residential places in the area. Room was found for Lisa and Adam in a small children's home in the city just two days before Doreen was to go into hospital. Thus, good practice and wise contingency planning for children leaving home had to be abandoned. Neither could there be any gradual introduction of children to the placement, nor could Doreen meet the staff who were to care for her children before she went into hospital. Indeed, for Doreen, the fortnight before going into hospital was particularly stressful.

'Well, I didn't really know what was going on, did I? He said he was going to find me a nice foster home for the two of them and then, at the last minute, he tells me that they're going into a home. No, I wasn't happy about that. I said, I don't want my two going into no home. But what could I do? I had no choice. I was worried sick. I didn't want the operation, I tell you. I didn't want no knife-cutting . . .'

Doreen's feelings of panic as the day of her operation drew nearer increased, as did her sense of inadequacy and powerlessness. The two giants of health and social security seemed to be closing in on her.

'What with the doctor not telling me what he was going to do and Mr Platt messing me about, I was at my wits' end. I mean, the specialist said he was going to have a look-see! I mean, what the hell does he mean by that? I kept thinking, what if they find anything else – what if they find cancers all over me? No one would tell me, though. I just felt it was the end, that I would never see my children again. I didn't even know where they were going.'

The evening before she went into hospital, Doreen, Lisa and Adam, accompanied by Mr Platt, went to St Christopher's children's home. The two children nervously clutched tired and stained teddy bears, and Doreen gazed into the middle distance as a kindly residential social worker steered the quartet down the gleaming corridor towards the sitting-room. Mr Platt remembers the children being very quiet and bemused, and Doreen looking as if she had swallowed a handful of Librium:

'She was upset but, to be honest, I don't think she really understood what was going on. She was in a sort of limbo of anxiety about herself and the kids. I don't think she really took anything in. The two kids were really rather sad. It never fails to hurt me when I'm involved in a separation.'

Lisa and Adam's pockets bulged with sweets, tokens of continuing concern from mum, but they were not happy. Mrs Ames, the residential social worker, remembers them refusing the orange juice and cake offered to them as she went through the numerous strategies she had for helping to alleviate their obvious worries.

For the few hours that Doreen stayed with Lisa and Adam, the residential social worker attempted to discover something about the personal preferences of the children – which television programmes they watched, and what their favourite bedtime stories were. As it happened, Mrs Denbow could not read, so this particular question caused some embarrassment.

Doreen's eventual departure from the children's home was difficult as she burst into tears and smothered the bemused children in kisses, entreated them to be good and promised a swift return. Adam apparently appeared distanced and unaffected by this deluge of emotion, but Lisa screamed and clung to her mother's skirts. At one point, Doreen sobbed that she was calling the whole thing off and was not going to leave them. In retrospect, both the field and residential social workers agreed that much of the distress of Lisa and Adam's separation could have been avoided had they and their mother been able to visit the children's home before and familiarise themselves with the place and the staff.

Although Adam expressed the least anxiety, at the time of his mother's departure, he was the most affected in the longer term by the events of that day. He was listless and quiet for many days after and asked for his mother more than Lisa did. He had also apparently brought the wrong teddy and deeply mourned the loss of his 'Moo'. It took Mrs Ames three days to discover that Adam's 'Moo' was an old rug with which he comforted himself at times of stress. As she said, 'It was obviously an important object in Adam's life, but there was little I could do to get it for him. Had I had the time to get to know him better before his arrival he could have brought it.'

Adam and Lisa Denbow's admission into care, like many others in our cohort, was hurried and badly organised. A planned reception had been envisaged by their social worker but this was thwarted by a shortage of foster home placements. The residential option had been dismissed early on as unsuitable but, as is so often the case, was in the end the only facility available at short notice. For Lisa and Adam, entry into care meant staying with strangers in an environment totally unfamiliar to them. Additionally, the residential social workers knew little about Mrs Denbow and her two children when they arrived at the children's home and, consequently, were limited in their efforts to ease the difficulties of separation. Objects important to the children had been left at home and unnecessary embarrassment caused by ignorance of Doreen's illiteracy.

Doreen's first visit to the children's home that was to care for her children was, therefore, an unhappy experience for her as she had to cope not only with the distress of leaving her children but also, in her case, the unhappy task of meeting strangers in a context that conjured up unpleasant memories of her own residential experiences during childhood. Typically, Doreen remembered the feeling of being a spectator of her own behaviour, of being acutely conscious of the verbal and visual messages she was conveying to the social workers about her feelings for her children, of knowing, as she put it, 'that I really should cry and at the same time worrying about making a fool of myself – making a scene'. We shall return to this situation later in our study.

### The James family

When we spoke to Rose James, her recollections of Andrew, Jane and Frances's entry into care were tinged with a deep sense of guilt. She felt it was her fault for allowing the situation in her home to develop to such grotesque proportions. Also, despite Rose being just as much a victim of her husband as were her children, she could not escape a profound sense of personal responsibility for her separation from her children.

It will be recalled that, on arrival at the hospital, the doctor decided that all three children should stay overnight for observation. Rose fretted about the children having no nightclothes and lingered until late in the evening, comforting her children between tearful interviews with the police and her social worker. She finally left at 10.00 p.m.

Andrew, Jane and Frances remained in hospital for the following two days. Rose spent a good deal of each day with them and found visiting the hospital a relatively easy process as it was near her home and the nursing staff were understanding. However, even at this early stage of the case, Rose was conscious that her visits to her children were closely supervised. As she said,

'They [the nurses] were always around when I was there – you know what I mean. I could tell they were only spending so much time with the kids because

I was there. I suppose it was the police – they were asking all sorts of questions – they thought I was involved. Mind, I suppose I was in a way. I should have said something sooner.'

In addition to attempting to sort out the complex facts of the case and Rose's possible role in the abuse of her children, the social worker was trying to organise a more permanent placement for the three children. The case conference decision was that, on leaving hospital, all three should be placed at the local O and A centre where the whole situation could be monitored and kept under control. Although superficially it seemed clear that Rose was not responsible for Frances's injuries, the police were still investigating the case, and social services needed time to consider the long-term welfare of the children. Also, although Ted James had been remanded in custody, no real decision could be made until his case came up at the Crown Court.

In such dramatic cases as this, which are relatively uncommon, the gradual introduction of children to substitute care situations is impossible. However, the degree of trauma experienced by all those involved does depend greatly on the extent to which the social worker concerned is able to cope with the crisis.

Despite many social service departments having complex administrative arrangements for dealing with high-risk situations, few social workers are actually trained to cope with situations of *extremis* and there are few guidelines on rapid risk-evaluation. In the case of Rose and her three children the right decisions were made, but as the social worker said, 'In situations like that, you really have to pull out all the stops and you're not only having to deal with other people's sense of panic but also your own terror of getting it wrong.'

Although a place of safety order was secured for the three James children, Rose was hardly cognisant of its application. All she knew was that her children were being made safe and her husband was being locked up and, like many of our study group parents, she was swept along in the powerful tide of events.

## The Barton family

Let us now turn to our adolescent whose lifestyle, if unorthodox and hedonistic, certainly need not arouse deep sadness or impotent concern. We have seen that Gloria departed for Sunnylands, the O and A centre, having precipitated a scandal, the ripples of which affected her stepfather, Derek, and disturbed the equanimity of her family and friends.

Yet Brenda, Gloria's mother, was not heartbroken at the departure of her daughter and was deeply incensed that 'She brought the police to my door. I won't forgive her for that.' She made no plans to visit her daughter although encouraged to do so by the social worker the next day; indeed, she assumed an air of deep indifference and viewed the sexual molestation of her daughter as trivial. Derek, on the other hand, was treated lightly and, in spite of his impending court appearance, Brenda decided that the whole thing must be part of Gloria's fantasy life – a conviction that remained unshaken in spite of Dean slyly pointing out, 'Mum, Gloria doesn't need one.'

The pretence that Gloria had gone off to stay with friends after a family row did not last long despite valiant attempts by wider kin and acquaintances to maintain the fiction. Indeed, the charade was sabotaged by Dean, who, the next day, had paid one of his uncommon visits to school. As he said, 'This time I had something to tell them, half of the class was going to get done for screwing under age.' That day the school counsellor hardly had time to drink her tea. Soon everyone knew and either eagerly or uneasily awaited developments. Back at the flat, the onslaught on the milk and teabags was renewed while Derek discreetly withdrew to the pub.

Meanwhile, Gloria was brightening up life at Sunnylands and continuing to enjoy her role as 'little girl lost'. She had her own room, a fresh audience and a number of potential conquests: lads remanded to local authority care whose despair at the local soccer club's persistently poor performance had led to an attack on the floral clock and gnome garden, one of the city's prime attractions. Nevertheless, Gloria did have a twinge of regret: 'Really, I didn't want to land Derek in the shit. I just wanted to get back at Mum – all that fuss.' Indeed, after the first few days, heady liberty turned to loneliness and she began to miss the evening promenade in the city centre. As she volunteered,

'I thought of all those scrubbers down by the taxi rank, waiting for the local boys to arrive and here I am instead, watching Coronation Street and earning the privilege to stay up 'till 10 o'clock.'

Naturally, access was restricted to Gloria, although it seemed a rather academic precaution. She was restricted to the grounds of Sunnylands for the first week and Dean, her brother, conveyed all the gossip, suitably embellished, to his sister, via friends who were either day visitors to the assessment centre or resident there but going out to school.

Gloria enjoyed the impression she had made at the assessment centre and the stir at school on the night of her reception into care. As she pertinently commented, 'It will give them all something to think about', and she cheerfully faced a long time in care. Her social worker accurately summed up the situation:

'The goods weren't really damaged and she's a pretty shop-soiled article already, but the law is the law, so she has got to be kept clear of that family for a while. If she runs true to form, she is going to be a damned nuisance.'

## Conclusion

We can see that each of these families has suffered considerable upheaval. The crises present parents with many problems extraneous to the loss of their children. Addresses and/or living arrangements may change suddenly, husbands or co-habitees depart and/or illness and criminal behaviour erupt. These problems in themselves would be sufficient to cause depression, anger and hopelessness in parents already struggling to keep going. They would be unlikely to display equanimity and stoicism regardless of the loss of their children. Hence, it is difficult to assess how much of the anguish a mother experiences as her children enter care springs from separation, from her loss of other support or from the dramatic upset to daily routine. Her sense of order is thrown into confusion by crises, an order by which we all manage our lives and to which we cling in bereavement, hospitalisation and other moments of stress.[11] Several studies have suggested that the disruption of contexts, order and expectations are as distressful to both children and adults as is the pain of separation.[12]

Nevertheless, 'filial deprivation' plays a part in the distress of parents.[13] Anger, grief and disbelief mix with guilt and relief in the feelings of parents. Aldgate noted that the parents of children who returned home quickly were more likely to display feelings of anger and loss than the parents of children likely to stay in care for a long period.[14] Thoburn also shows that relief and gratitude are often replaced by anger and a sense of violation on the part of parents.[15] In addition, she notes that social workers' perceptions of the distress and upheaval caused to clients by separation does not correspond with the actual pain that they experience. Social workers seem to underestimate the shock of events to parents of which separation is only a part. We shall find these suggestions amply borne out as this study progresses. We shall also note that parents feel they are under examination, that their parenting skills and long-term viability are in the balance, yet they complain that they receive very little guidance on appropriate behaviour. Indeed, parents slowly become aware that they have precipitated a course of action about which they have very little information and over which they have even less control. As Thoburn comments,

This makes this group of clients [parents of children in care] different from most recipients of social services, in that they have little choice in the matter. They were 'captive clients'. They might refuse to accept certain aspects of what was offered, but they could not, without going back to court, terminate their connection with the department. The result, as one might expect, was a resentment which distorted the relationship [with the social worker] and their view of the help offered.[16]

Yet the social worker's role is not an enviable one. While in all the cases just illustrated social services intervention was necessary, social workers frequently found their actions severely circumscribed by the lack of suitable placements. The widely recognised advisability of familiarising children and parents with likely placements presupposes an availability and flexibility of resources which certainly did not exist in the local authorities we studied. While parents frequently complain that they were not kept fully in the picture, in many situations social workers are caught up in crises and their decisions cannot be cool and participatory. Unfortunately, just at the time when honesty and trust between social workers and families are at a premium to ensure the easy and rapid return of children from care, empathy and understanding are less in evidence.

## Summary points

1. On the entry of a child to care the social worker has to decide where the child should be placed, what legal status is most appropriate, the amount of work the case demands and the kinds of access arrangements that can be made for parents and child. These decisions are closely interrelated and much influenced both by the social workers' previous knowledge of the family and by their expectations concerning the duration of children's stay in care.

2. As a result, any consideration of access and the problems of maintaining links between absent child and the family must take a wide and longitudinal perspective.

3. While younger children are initially received into short-term foster care, the reception role of many residential settings remains important, particularly the O and A centres and small community homes. Social workers were dissatisfied with a quarter of children's first placements, hindered by the need to keep siblings together and inadequate resources. Parental links were not given high priority in the selection of placements.

4. A preoccupation with maintaining links between parents and absent child should not allow the wider family or social and neighbourhood networks of children to be forgotten.

5. Little consideration is given to alerting or involving fathers who, although frequently separated from the family, may still be able to offer children emotional support and a sense of belonging.

6. Nearly three-quarters of the children entering care rapidly experienced barriers to maintaining contact with their parents and wider family. A third of children had restrictions imposed on specific individuals or aspects of their meeting, while two-thirds experienced barriers to contact which were inherent in their placements.

7. Our case studies suggest increasing ambivalence on the part of parents to social work interventions. They are not involved in the care task nor viewed as a resource. They feel unwanted and their requests for access are often interpreted as demands for the return of their child.

# 7. Are links important?

In this chapter we explore links, the practical, psychological, symbolic and power dimensions which the concept implies. We consider the literature on the significance of parental contact with absent children. We suggest that social work concern over the maintenance or severance of blood-ties is largely irrelevant to the majority of children entering care. Those that stay long in care are usually older children, have well-forged links with family and others on entry, and the provision of stable, substitute parenting is difficult to ensure.

In daily life we give little thought to the complex process by which we maintain contact with family, kin and friends. We reach for the telephone, gossip with our families, remind our children of mother's birthday and annually make out a list of Christmas cards without the guidance of a sociometric test. Like most human games, we have long since learned the rules of maintaining contact with others so that the strategy largely remains unconscious.

Nevertheless, even the shortest separations can add a problematic dimension to maintaining links with our families and inject unfamiliar anxiety. When our needs for contact are frustrated, with ill grace we desperately trudge round vandalised telephone boxes or wait, in agonies of frustration, for the arrival of the Automobile Association, momentarily obsessed by distance and isolation. To cope with longer separations we have developed a wide range of reassurances and rituals which protect us and others from the yawning abyss of feeling unwanted. Thus, we undertake or receive wearisome and regular hospital visits, clutching symbolic fruits and eau de cologne. We write daily letters to absent sailors and, on return from long separations, mime passionate and inappropriate Hollywood embraces. Indeed, it takes much effort to maintain links with the separated, in which time and money, energy and inclination, are prerequisites. Unfortunately, some of these attributes are sparse among the families scrutinised in this study and many of their children in local authority care are still learning the rules of keeping in contact with parents and the wider world. Many of the rules they will learn may preclude the possibility of forming adequate and consistent links in the future. Thus, we shall find as this study develops, that maintaining links between parents and child presents many problems.

There are many ways in which we can link with those from whom we are separated. First of all, we can visit or be visited with a frequency that reflects the depth of our attachment, feelings of obligation and which meets the expectations of others. We have already noted that with children in care many of these visits will be carefully regulated and under scrutiny. Naturally, visiting patterns will vary considerably, affected by culture, by class and by age, although they will have some common features. Interestingly, an event as familiar as a visit has received more attention from novelists and anthropologists than from sociologists and psychologists. Visiting rules have been little explored. Yet managing a visit, either as a guest or a host, is a complex interaction.

Apart from instrumental visits such as to the dentist or the supermarket which are relatively straightforward, visits with an expressive dimension, such as those to family or friends, are more difficult. Rules closely govern our behaviour, there are norms on when to arrive, when to leave, what role to adopt during the visit, what topics of conversation to avoid, and what currency to use in the interaction. The rules that govern our visiting behaviour may be unwritten but they are clear, and gross violations are long remembered. For example, few of even one's closest family would brim with welcome at an unexpected dawn visit, and you usually spare great-aunts the company of transvestite friends. Care must always be taken when managing a visit.

Unlike participants to a local authority care situation, some visitors are very carefully schooled in their behaviour. For example, in the preparation of élites such as commissioned officers, diplomats and senior business executives, correct visiting behaviour is still carefully taught. Polite society in the eighteenth and nineteenth centuries had elaborate codes of visiting behaviour which were frequently observed even among close members of the family. On his honeymoon, the young and punctilious Lord Crewe left his calling card on his wife's dressing table each evening. While today we are more relaxed, one frequently regrets the absence of such forewarnings.

Visiting requires much social skill and the experience can be stressful. There are many uncontrolled variables operating on the interaction. For example, one's infant son may drop icecream on the sofa or, amidst scandalous revelations, the chip-pan can catch fire. Even within close families, some visits are more normatively controlled than others, especially those that may excite an outside audience. One doesn't arrive drunk for a family funeral or christening. Nevertheless, it is permissible conduct at a wedding – and probably the only way to survive Christmas. However, visiting one's wider family or being visited by them takes place in familiar contexts, the rules have long since been learned and occasional violations of expected conduct are forgiven.

In marked contrast, the arrival of a stranger to a family produces tremors of unease in even the best of families, for rules are likely to be broken and skeletons to fall out of cupboards. Thus, the nervous, advancing chatter of brother's new girlfriend or last year's conference amour quickly directs our steps to the bathroom for a shave or hairnet and thrusts our prayers heavenwards that Gran will not mistake the unfamiliar arrival for a brother home from the Somme. Indeed, new visiting procedures are very difficult to establish and we hesitate when to call on the newly-married or bereaved, even on those who have recently moved house, been made redundant or got divorced.

Visiting those we know intimately in strange contexts and before unfamiliar audiences is a particularly fraught experience. We only reluctantly pay visits to hospital although the cool, neutral ethos of the ward and the specific role of the visitor make arrival easier. We take soap and clean pyjamas and desperately try to look pastoral. Visiting our offspring at school or summer camp is particularly difficult. We feel superfluous, uneasily aware that our loved ones are different and cannot incorporate us into these alien settings. Thus wives rarely visit husbands at work, or vice versa, neither do parents, however anxious, brave the disco, looking for their liberated adolescent offspring. The more separate the contexts and specific our role within them, the less easy it becomes to move from one situation to another. For example, it makes the transition from working colleague to bosom companion lengthy and difficult.

By now it should be obvious that a lone parent whose child lingers in the care of strangers in unknown territory, to whom the care intervention is a violation, a parent who is bereft of a meaningful role and is unversed in the rules of this unfamiliar game, will find visiting difficult. These barriers to contact are compounded by the complex feelings of guilt, powerlessness, anger and mourning that most parents experience on the removal of their children to care. No wonder that to ease the interactions of a visit and win indulgence for their unwitting violations, like the Wise Men parents usually take their children inappropriate gifts.

Writing of visiting fathers in a similarly fraught situation, those separated from their children by divorce, Wallerstein and Kelly write:

The visiting relationship which successfully outlived the marriage reflected not the relationship of the pre-divorce family primarily, but the father's motivation, the child's motivation and the psychological capacity of fathers, mothers and children to adapt flexibly to the new conditions of the visiting relationship. Men who could bend the complex logistics of the visiting; who could deal with the anger of the women and capriciousness of children without withdrawing; who could overcome their own depression, jealousy and guilt; who could involve the children in their planning; who could walk on middle ground between totally re-arranging their routine and not changing their routine at all; and who felt less stressed and freer to parent, were predominantly among those who continued to visit regularly and frequently.[1]

We shall return shortly to this valuable study of the relationships between children and parents in situations of separation, but it does emphasise how difficult such visits are and that the early patterns of contact established between parent and absent child tend to persist.

Yet, for us all, seeing is only part of belonging. Apart from the fact that those who do not visit us, those whom we dislike, can be among the keenest reminders of home, we need the reassurance of familiar territories; to see our house, flat, garden and neighbourhood. So we tour our homes on return from a long holiday, checking that everything is in place, like a family of bears fearing the violation of Goldilocks. Frequently, those long separated from home ache for such reassurances quite as much as for familiar faces – a need to belong enshrined in Rupert Brooke's memorably bad lines:

> Just now the lilac is in bloom
> All before my little room
> And in my flower beds, I think
> Smile the carnations and the pink ...
> Stands the church clock at ten to three?
> And is there honey still for tea?

Equally, children find contact with their immediate neighbourhood very important; it provides a sense of belonging, whether they experience the delights of Kensington Gardens or the welcoming chippy and warm launderette. Unfortunately, these aspects of belonging rarely impinge on our planning for separated children. We rarely, if ever, consider returning them on a brief visit to the reassurances of their neighbourhoods. Indeed, to a child, family members removed from familiar contexts take on an almost unreal, surrealist quality and a parental visit can lose much of its impact. Children have very limited perceptions of time, space and appropriate behaviour and adults seen out of context generate great surprise. More wonder and excitement is created among children by the unexpected glimpse of a teacher at a funfair or of the vicar viewed furtively munching in the Kentucky Fried Chicken than anything on home video. Several children illustrated this disorientation in the intensive study: 'It didn't seem like my mum somehow, she had a new coat on, sitting in a room at social services, she could have been anyone's mum' (boy, 12, foster home). And, more ambitiously, a 15-year-old girl in an assessment centre mused, 'I wish we all lived in a bus, then my mum could drive up with the dog and the budgie and everything else, we could row over who does the washing-up, it would be nice, just like it was before'. Both these children illustrate the need for parents to be seen in familiar contexts, and incidentally remind us of the importance of pets, the absence of which is keenly felt.

In addition, the neighbourhood in which we live provides endless reassurance and reinforcement of our family links. When we go out or shop there are chance meetings with wider kin, with brothers and sisters, with friends, one's whole social network and we endlessly channel, sift and embroider family information. To the child, the familiar warning, 'Watch out or I'll tell your mum' is not only a sanction but also a reminder of a powerful presence.

For many children in care it is likely that a return to the sagging tents of the Saturday market or an hour spent amongst the débris of a familiar, disused railway siding would be as therapeutic as an hour spent in pastoral care. One of the problems of maintaining links between children absent in care and their families is that linking is a part of an elaborate package of belonging, each aspect of which reinforces the others. Preoccupation with access, particularly parental access to their children, should not blunt our realisation that belonging for the absent child is a much wider and more complex experience.

Again, failure to be on the scene regularly can make return very difficult for children. Not only have they little in common to talk about to visitors but writing of reconstituting families, Burgoyne and Clarke comment: 'New partners systematically work through past events, they reconstruct personal biographies which they feel are internally consistent and, above all, form a manageable basis from which to develop new relationships.'[2] Such a strategy on the part of parents involves lies and half-truths, thus reconstituting families move home, abandoning familiar neighbourhoods which undermine their new image. Not only are absent children a threat to these fresh parental constructs but, on return, children often have to face unfamiliar localities.

Links are also maintained with home in other ways. On departure, we take things with us – photographs for our locker doors, slippers for anonymous hotel bedrooms; we pack children's toys for a trip as much to give them a sense of continuity as to bring comfort and amuse. On return we bring back odd T-shirts and inappropriate camel stools or *assegai* for the living room – trophies which, by their very incongruity, reinforce homeliness. We have in other studies explored this personalisation of space by children and adolescents and the way it gives them a sense of belonging.[3] Indeed, in times of greatest stress, adults, as well as children, literally hang on to home like sailors clutching mementoes as they jumped from the sinking *Repulse*. It will be interesting to see how these aspects of belonging are managed while children are in care, to what extent and in what ways they personalise space and link with absent parents and distant homes.

Links also have another aspect: a power dimension. Children need not regularly be in contact, be visited, receive letters or phone calls to feel in touch with parents and wider family. Security and a feeling of belonging can come from the knowledge that someone at a distance is watching over you with power to intervene. Just as an anchorite in the desert belongs to the deity, so awareness of parental power can link an absent child with his family. We have seen in other studies that boarding school children rarely express anxiety about maintaining links with their parents, indeed they feel more isolation from their siblings and pets than they do from significant adults.[4]

Hall and Stacey, in their study of hospitalised children, show how important socialisation for absence and awareness of parental competence can be in ameliorating for children the stress of separation.[5] Links between parents and absent child can be quite strong when maintained by reversed-charge phone calls, when there is a 'hot-line' to the security of father's office. Naturally, the power of parents to intervene will depend on their resources and the young person's situation, but whether on a kibbutz or a cadet ship, children value a return ticket, and letters from home are particularly welcome when they contain a cheque. Sadly, almost by definition, this power dimension is little enjoyed by parents of children in care, even in situations where children have entered care voluntarily and can be unilaterally removed. Indeed, the sense of isolation that must be experienced both by parents and children who are largely powerless to change a situation must be severe.

We can see that there are many aspects to the problems of maintaining links between parents and child absent in local authority care. Parents' successful accomplishment of regular visiting is only a small part of maintaining links with children. Contacts by telephone, letters and through others such as the wider family, siblings or friends are also very important. We have noted that return to the neighbourhood also reinforces the child's sense of belonging. In addition, links between parents and absent child have a power dimension, an anchor provided by parents who can do something about their child's situation how and when they see fit.

As we follow our 450 children through their care careers, we can explore the ways in which these different aspects of contact and belonging affect their experience. However, it should already be apparent from our opening chapters that some aspects of links, such as parental power, will be less significant than others. Nevertheless, the ways in which families maintain contact with absent members are varied and it would be wrong to assume that links between parents and children in care should be nurtured in every case. We have seen that some parents are uncaring and indifferent, that some are dangerous, and some by their actions will have forfeited the rights they might once have had over their children. In contrast, some injured children or older adolescents may not be anxious for frequent contact with their parents, they will have seen quite enough of them already. We have seen how complex many care situations are and that the arrangements concerning access and other aspects of contact between parents and child will be very much an individual social work decision. Guidance can only be at a very general level.

## The significance of parental contact

Some of these issues were very much in mind during the framing of the research design. We were discouraged from exploring whether strong links were beneficial to absent children or from examining such controversial issues as blood-ties or psychological parenting. Such a mammoth task, for which we are ill-fitted, would have diverted our efforts. Nevertheless, some brief review of these issues and the light cast on them by this study is appropriate, although it should be re-emphasised that our investigation is not about the consequences of separation for children or the psychological impact of long careers in local authority care.

Through the 1960s and early 1970s the DHSS received conflicting messages from a variety of child-care authorities and from research on the importance of maintaining links between children in care and their parents.[6] Though few studies had actually explored the issue of contact between absent children and their parents, disturbing evidence on the effects of separation was accumulating, much of which seemed relevant to children in care. In addition, a number of scandals had revealed that social workers, mindful of the trauma of separation and its long-term consequences, were often reluctant to remove children from high-risk homes.[7] Some clarification of the role of parents in children's care experience was clearly needed.

The Curtis Report (1946) which gave some unity to child welfare was both influenced by and implemented in an intellectual climate that stressed the child's need for stable, continuous parenting. No doubt mindful of the turbulence and disruption experienced by children during the war, the emphasis in much writing at that time was on stability in parenting, on the importance of the mother's early inter-action with the child and on the traumatic effects of separation. These aspects of childrearing were stressed in the work of Bowlby, Winnicott, Burlingham and Freud, Isaacs and many others.[8] Some authorities, such as Rutter and Kellmer Pringle, pointed out that it was as much the quality of substitute care as its stability that was crucial in child development.[9] While authorities differed both then and now on the extent to which they view the psychological consequences of a disrupted childhood as irredeemable, there is a general consensus of what should be avoided, particularly separation in early childhood and a rapid succession of caring figures.

The consensus was succinctly summed up by Kellmer Pringle and Pilling in their comprehensive review of the literature, *Controversial Issues in Child Development* (1976).[10] They state:

A child is most likely to develop to a maximum level if he has an enduring relationship with at least one person who is sensitive to his individual needs and stage of development. This does not necessarily have to be his mother nor mean that more than one person cannot satisfactorily share this role. An insufficiency of stimulation and responsiveness to the child does not necessarily have effects on later development that are irreversible but they make the attainment of optimum development much more difficult.

While these authors stress that such perspectives on childrearing are general, they also point out that children in local authority care poignantly highlight the issues of continuity of parenting and the effects of separation. Indeed, over three decades a mass of evidence and even more theorising accumulated on separation while the equally fraught problem of return was and remains little explored.

Many influential studies over the years have concerned children in hospital. For example, the work of the Robertsons, Schaffer and Callender, Douglas and others, while disputing some aspects of attachment theory, highlighted the stress caused to children by separation from parents.[11] Subsequently, Hall, Stacey and others followed Yarrow in linking disturbance in children on their entry to hospital as much to the disruption of their social world as to the experience of separation itself.[12] Incidentally, their evidence is supported by earlier studies of the Dartington Social Research Unit into boarding education which stressed the importance of the preparation of a child for separation, research which highlighted the different levels of distress caused to children by leaving for a boarding school.[13] We noted particularly the contrast between working-class and middle-class boarders in levels of anxiety, homesickness and running away.

Yet the situation of children in local authority care was of particular concern, because evidence was accumulating that some children stayed long in local authority care and many of these were in residential institutions. For example, Rowe and Lambert had highlighted that the rapid turnover of children in care concealed the problem of those who 'lingered long' and for whom coherent plans were either thwarted or failed to materialise.[14] Walton and Hayward also drew attention to the numbers of children in long-term care, an issue emphasised by both Boss and Parker who suggested that short-term admissions to care received greater social work attention than those who remained long.[15] In 1974, Kellmer Pringle stressed the damaging effects of instability and change on children in care.[16] She writes,

He has no single person who shares his own, most basic and important memories, no one to confirm whether these memories are in fact correct or figments of his imagination, no one to polish up the fading memory before it was too late. Such deprivation is so damaging, I am not at all sure that we can make up for it artificially.

Nevertheless, the difficulties of providing substitute care, which were reiterated by Trasler and Parker in their studies of fostering, did not discourage local authorities from seeking to provide family placements for children and quasi-family experiences in residential care.[17] This emphasis continues to be very much in evidence in the five local authorities we have studied and in our recent studies of residential settings.

The vision of the nuclear family and the need to keep it together was reiterated in numerous reports, as was the need to substitute a family experience for those children deprived of normal home life. It was stressed in the report of the Ingleby Committee (1960) which led to the Children and Young Persons Act 1963 where preventative work with the family was enjoined on local authorities.[18] It states, 'It becomes the duty of the state to discover such families [those at risk] and help them in every possible way.' Through the decade following the Second World War this stress on the importance of the family and the child's need for parenting emerges as a familiar theme in the reports of the Home Office children's department and those of the Department of Education on the schools for the maladjusted. Indeed, the approved school system which sought to reorientate delinquents through strict, no-nonsense, training school regimes rapidly found themselves out of fashion.[19]

Nevertheless, this emphasis on the importance of the nuclear family and the role of stable, warm parenting within it has led to certain unintended consequences. It means that the failure of preventative work with families and the consequent separation of children on entry to care are viewed as signal defeats by social workers. We have seen that this affects the way in which they subsequently view children, dividing them into short- and long-term care cases. Consequently, the family is seldom viewed as a resource. In addition it has meant that substitute care settings have sought to reproduce the small nuclear family and, failing this, have become preoccupied with small-group living situations.[20] Foster homes are believed to be preferable to residential care although, in many ways, smaller community homes are indistinguishable from larger foster homes in their daily running and can have more stable child populations. Yet few of these developments have been based on hard evidence. Indeed, Parker succinctly questions this drift: 'The love of one's children is unconditional and partisan, try as we will, we cannot produce it to order.'[21] Eric Miller in the same way highlights children's need for unconditional love and the considerable difficulties authorities face in providing stable substitute parenting.[22] Roy Parker also makes the point that this preoccupation with the quasi-family on the part of the care authorities has prevented them from looking creatively at the care experience and from developing new residential and day-care services.[23] Indeed, one of the conflicts that will emerge in the following study is that the comparatively recent family orientation of social work, its generic focus, runs counter to the child rescue, control obligations and strong belief in family and neighbourhood contamination which have much longer and healthier pedigrees in child welfare.

The Rapoports, looking at the changing perspectives on the family over three decades, from 1945 to 1975, provide us with a succinct summary of these developments.

An authoritative set of formulations in the period following the Second World War idealised a conception of the nuclear, conjugal family, with relatively standardised composition, division of labour and life-cycle timetable. This conception that 'normal' mature men would be economic providers while 'normal' mature women will be housewives and mothers has been bolstered by clinical psychiatry (as in the works of Bowlby and Winnicott), by medicine (as in the work of Spock), by sociology (as in the work of Parsons) and by professionals in law, education and social work. But research has increasingly questioned this model, both the data and the conclusions drawn. It has also become clear in recent years that not only is this nuclear family no longer the most typical but that it has problems of its own.[24]

Refreshingly, the evangelical zeal and missionary style which characterised Victorian reformers in child care had not entirely disappeared. Goldstein, Freud and Solnit exerted a great influence in their study, *Beyond the Best Interests of the Child* (1973).[25] Beautifully written, unequivocal and without much evidence, the study stresses the child's rights to parenting and summarily dismisses the accumulating evidence that the effects of separation on children and the achievement of substitute parenting were very complex issues. They write that the child's interest should be paramount once the child's placement becomes the subject of official interest. The authors stress the need to seek the 'least detrimental alternative' to the care of inadequate parents. They emphasise that the neglected child needs

[a] placement which maximises, in accordance with the child's sense of time and on the basis of short-term prediction, his or her opportunity of being wanted and for maintaining on a continuous basis a relationship with one adult who is or will become his psychological parent. . . .

The rights which are normally secured over time by biological parents may be lost by their failure to provide continuous care for their child and earned by those who do so.

This study, and the work of Rowe and Lambert on children who lingered long in unresolved care, were influential in providing extra safeguards for foster parents and children long boarded out by local authorities through the Children Act 1975. In addition, Barbara Tizard examined the development of a group of 30 children adopted from institutions after the age of two and concludes that both long-term fostering and residential care must be considered inferior to adoption. Although these studies are very careful not to draw wider implications for child care from selected groups of children in care, others have been less scrupulous. Yet, it will be seen that very few children in our study of 450 children entering care met the criteria of Tizard in that they remained long in residential care while infants and only 9 of the 88 children corresponding to Rowe and Lambert's criteria were 'waiting' after two years in care.[26]

Yet, research would suggest that the consequences of separation from parents on children is a more complex issue than the protagonists of particular viewpoints will allow. Indeed, Rutter, in his exhaustive and balanced reassessment of literature on maternal deprivation, suggests that the concept has outlived its value: 'It is evident that the experiences included under the term maternal deprivation are too heterogeneous and the effects too varied for it to continue to have any usefulness.'[27]

Inevitably, this review of the situation was dismissed by Goldstein, Freud and Solnit as 'simplistic'. However, since that time several studies of particular relevance to the problems of maintaining links between children in local authority care and their parents have supported the views of Rutter, the Rapoports, Parker and others. These studies come to very different conclusions from those which advocate psychological parenting and the severance of links between child and family.

### The importance of family links in social work literature
Much social work literature differs considerably from many government reports, legislation and research studies in that it also stresses the needs of parents, social workers, foster parents and residential staff as well as those of the children. Many authorities stress that the benefits of contact between parents and absent child affect the family as a whole.

We have seen that the majority of children who are accepted into care have at least one parent alive and ongoing contact with their wider family. Many social workers have expressed concern for the separated child's emotional health if contact with the natural parent is not maintained. Indeed, social work literature implies that the interaction between child and parent allows for a more realistic awareness by the child of their relationship. Victor George writes of the need for parental contact: 'Even if reunion is unlikely, parental visiting is considered conducive to the child's emotional health and he tends otherwise to feel rejected, disloyal or to view his parents unrealistically.'[28] Peter Righton also stresses that even where there is little or no expectation of a return home, the children's parents continue to matter emotionally.[29]

There are a number of studies in foster care which emphasise the importance of a link between parent and separated child. Robert Holman in several articles has suggested that self-knowledge is not a guarantee of success in a foster home but that it greatly helps the foster child.[30] By self-knowledge, Holman is referring to the foster child's awareness of his or her family background and the reasons why he or she no longer lives with his parents. While his study is based on a scrutiny of only 20 children, he suggests that the rates of success in fostering were highest for those children with most self-knowledge.

Exploring the self-image of the foster child, Eugene Weinstein shows that the well-being of the child in the foster home is closely related to the awareness of his or her origins and position as a foster child.[31] Rosamund Thorpe in her study of 160 foster children also found that there was a relationship between an awareness of background and the foster child's happiness.[32] She also points out that contact with the natural parents enabled the foster children to create a more satisfactory picture of their family background and the reasons for their entry into care. Indeed, Thorpe's findings support the suggestion of Weinstein and Holman that foster children with parental contact were significantly better adjusted than those who did not have contact with their natural parents. However, in a very recent study of children in long-stay foster care, Rowe failed to find an association between continued contact with parents and the well-being of the child.[33] But she does emphasise that any firm conclusions are precluded by the fact that so few of her children had really regular parental contact at any time during their stay in care.

Social work literature is also concerned for the natural parent who relinquishes a child. Olive Stevenson, writing about reception into care and its implications for the natural family, emphasises that a continuing relationship with natural parents is necessary for parents, however inadequate, because of the feelings of gratification that parenthood gives.[34] Both the Rapoports and Wallerstein and Kelly reiterate this viewpoint, that the child and parent have a reciprocal relationship and that the development of each is interrelated. Juliet

Berry also emphasises the importance of parents being encouraged to contact their children and the dangers of misinterpreting parental behaviour.

It is only too easy for parents to adopt an all-or-nothing attitude, to opt out completely, to clamour possessively, to interfere obstructively, to appear like a bad fairy at the most awkward moment, to disappear when wanted (e.g. to sign some consent form) and generally to show themselves incapable of carrying through consistent plans.[35]

Berry suggests that social workers, by underestimating parents' distress, tend to encourage their passivity and subsequently use this as evidence of parental indifference to the child. Nevertheless, Berry joins Holtom, Righton, Mason and Thorpe in pointing out that foster parents and social workers find the stress of linking children with their natural parents very difficult.[36]

It is important to highlight five recent studies which are particularly relevant to this issue of maintaining links between parents and child in state care. Three of these studies come from the United States while two others concern separated children in the United Kingdom.

While there have been few longitudinal studies in the United Kingdom of the relationship between children in local authority care and their parents, the USA has provided several major contributions to knowledge. Naturally, as with the deployment of many transatlantic imports, there are dangers in relying too heavily on findings which spring from very different child-care contexts. Nevertheless, the findings of several investigations are of particular relevance to our task.

In the late 1950s, Maas and Engler in the USA studied children in the care of nine communities and showed the virtual isolation from family contact of those who stayed long in care.[37] They also highlighted that repeated movements between placements were common while in state care and that these had a deleterious effect upon children's development and their contacts with their natural families. Stimulated by this study and the work on separation of Bowlby, Freud, Solnit and others, David Fanshel and Eugene Shinn, again in the USA, began in 1966 a longitudinal scrutiny over ten years of both children in care and their parents, looking at 624 children in all.[38]

The children's adaptation to their care experience was assessed through aspects of educational functioning, through careful psychological testing and these were related to children's contact with their natural parents. Their study, *Children in Foster Care* (1978), has been more recently supplemented by Fanshel's study, *On the Road to Permanency* (1982), which looks specifically at the parental visiting of children in state care. The studies also explore those factors which influence a child's length of stay in care.

Fanshel's studies differ significantly in emphasis from our investigation for the following reasons. Although foster care in the United States is a generic term, including in its compass residential care, it excludes delinquents and those with mental or physical handicaps. Whereas many of these children in the United Kingdom are the responsibility of social services departments, most of the placements (90 per cent) in Fanshel's study were provided by independent agencies and they varied greatly in quality. Fanshel's investigation did not address itself to children who stayed in care a short time (less than 90 days) nor to those children who had been in care before or who had siblings in care. The study also excluded adolescents entering care over the age of 12. Naturally, all these factors affect significantly the sample of children that Fanshel studied and contrasts with our investigation which looks at all children who enter care whatever their age and however brief the experience. As we shall note elsewhere, while only 57 of our 450 children meet Fanshel's criteria, his findings echo ours for younger, long-stay children.

Nevertheless, Fanshel's painstaking and illuminating studies highlight certain important features of a child's career in care. He notes the increasing isolation of children who stay long in care: 57 per cent of his group were unvisited by parents and virtually abandoned after five years. He emphasises the child's need for continuity of care and the poor level of social work planning and support. He clearly demonstrates that the children's well-being on a wide range of criteria is influenced by parental visiting and that frequent contact with parents is the best available predictor of the child's eventual rehabilitation with the natural family. Many of these findings will be repeated in the study which follows; indeed, the correlation between parental contact and exit from care is even stronger in our study than in Fanshel's investigation.

Fanshel suggests that much of the responsibility for the withering links between the natural family and the child lies with the caring agencies who fail to appreciate the significance of parental links or to encourage contact. He also highlights the pejorative perspectives on natural parents entertained by care-givers and social workers. The study emphasises that although children might be distressed by contact with parents in the short term, on all enduring criteria of adjustment association with a natural parent is beneficial. In subsequent studies Fanshel has highlighted aspects of contact and visiting which cause problems between care-givers and visiting parents. He concludes:

In the main we strongly support the notion that continued contact with parents, even when the functioning of the latter is marginal, is good for most foster children. Our data suggest that total abandonment by parents is associated with evidence of emotional turmoil in the children. We can think of no more profound insult to a child's personality than evidence that the parent thinks so little of the relationship with him that there is no motivation to visit and see how he is faring. Good care in the hands of loving parents or institutional child care staff can mitigate the insult but cannot fully compensate for it. It is our view that the parents continue to have significance for the child even when they are no longer visible to him.

At the same time, we are saying that continued visiting by parents of children who are long-term wards of the foster care system, while beneficial, is not without stress. It is not easy for the child to juggle two sets of relationships and the case workers report that some children show signs of strain in the process. We maintain, however, that this is a healthier state of affairs than that faced by the child who must reconcile questions about his own worth as a human being with the fact of parental abandonment. In the main, children are more able to accept additional, concerned and loving parental figures in their lives, with all the confusions inherent in such a situation, than to accept the loss of meaningful figures.

Stein, Gambril and Wiltse develop Fanshel's suggestions of the need for a data base for children in state care and explore predictive indices for early return of children to their parents. Their study, *Children in Foster Homes*, provides a recent and comprehensive review of the literature related to parental participation in child care in the USA and offers a code of good practice in many areas of social service delivery.[39] This study of the Almeda project in California demonstrates that where intensive services are offered to parents and efforts are made to rehabilitate children, rapid exit from care is greatly facilitated. An important aspect of intensive work with families and children was the nurturing of contacts between the two, the seeking-out of significant kin and friends, and the encouraging of the participation of both care-givers and parents in the child-care task. However, the writers stress that rehabilitative work with families does not have high priority with social workers, that care plans are infrequently made, and that parental links are insufficiently valued or nurtured by care-givers and social workers. They also stress that shared care and rehabilitative work takes a great deal of social workers' time.

Also in the United States, Wallerstein and Kelly made a study of 60 families experiencing divorce.[40] Although their study group were self-referrals to a counselling centre, many of their findings have wider implications. They highlight the stress placed on family members by divorce and the ways parents and children manage the separation experience. They traced the long-term consequences for members of these families in their book, *Surviving the Break-up*. It is particularly encouraging that the authors take a process perspective, looking at various stages in the divorce and post-divorce careers of children and their parents. They show how enduring natural family relationships are in spite of disruption. In their conclusions, they write:

Within the post-divorce family, the relationship between the child and both original parents did not diminish in emotional importance to the child over the five years. Although the mother's caretaking and psychological role became increasingly central in these families, the father's psychological significance did not correspondingly decline. Even within remarriages, although the step-father often very quickly became a prominent figure to the children, the biological father's emotional significance did not greatly diminish. It has been, in fact, strikingly apparent through the years that whether or not the child retained frequent or infrequent contact with the non-custodial parent the children would have considered the term 'one-parent family' a misnomer. Their self-images were firmly tied to their relationships with both parents and they thought of themselves as children with two parents who had elected to go their separate ways.

Certainly one characteristic of so many of these children was their acute, conscious, sometimes hyper-alert monitoring of their parents and their parents' attitudes over the years. The cool, erratic, openly rejecting behaviour – or even abandonment – by a parent did not seem to dim the child's awareness of that parent and often did not diminish the child's compassion or longing.

Regardless of the legal allocation of responsibility and custody, the emotional significance of the relationship with each of two parents did not diminish during the five-year period that we have studied.

Naturally, such findings would encourage a perspective on separation radically different from those experts who advocate the severance of contact with natural parents and the importance of psychological parenting to children facing long separation. Wallerstein and Kelly conclude:

In taking a position in favour of flexibility and encouragement of joint legal custody where feasible, as a symbol of society's recognition of the child's continuing need for both parents, we offer a view diametrically opposed to that of our esteemed colleagues, Goldstein, Freud and Solnit in their book, *Beyond the Best Interests of the Child.* Although we share a common, psycho-dynamic framework with these colleagues, we have in the course of our research, arrived at findings and recommendations which are greatly at variance with their views. Our findings regarding the centrality of both parents to the psychological health of children and adolescents alike lead us to hold that, where possible, divorcing parents should be encouraged and helped to shape close divorce arrangements which permit and foster continuity in the child's relationship with both parents.

Closer to home, Ivis Lasson concerned herself with a group of 72 children in care in Birmingham who had lived in residential care for at least three years.[41] Her study explores those care-givers who become important to these children over time and whether the links they enjoy with their family influenced other relationships and experiences. It identifies those children who have retained links with their natural families and examines the differences between children who are visited and those who are not. Lasson shows that acceptance by and continued contact with a parent does have a positive effect on children while they are away in care. Her study, in a more modest way, echoes the findings of David Fanshel in New York. She shows that parental contact had a beneficial effect on children's behaviour within the residential home. She concludes,

This study, as with studies of foster children, confirms that visited children are more settled in their placements than unvisited children. This confirms Thorpe and Weinstein who were able to show a greater degree of settledness in the foster home when visiting was frequent.

The sample children who have never known their natural parents are shown to express less trust in caring adults, to know fewer families in the community and have less involvement with other families outside than all the remaining sample children.

Analysis of the data does, however, suggest that if the sample children are to be helped towards making a wide range of social relationships and to enjoy a wide range of social experiences, contact with natural parents, particularly with mother, will facilitate this.

Lasson stresses particularly the importance of contact with relatives and friends and the need to encourage the participation of the wider family.

These findings would indicate that children who have no contact with a parent or relative tend not to go out of the home and make substitute relationships to the family. The reverse position takes place – those children with contact with their natural families go out and make additional relationships to the natural family. Yet, children without contact with their natural family, appear to be inhibited in their contacts with other family groups and individuals. It does seem to be a situation where the children who already have something go out and receive while those without turn inwards and receive less.

Finally, another significant contribution to understanding the needs of children in care for parental contact lies in Hall and Stacey's *Beyond Separation*.[42] Although this study relates the distress of children in hospital to the discontinuities which attend the experience, it has considerable implications for children in local authority care. They found that children differed considerably in the degree of suffering they experienced in hospital, although they were undergoing the same illnesses and treatments. The authors illustrate that these differences were related to the social background of the children, their position in the family, the style of parenting they had experienced and the ways in which they had learned to behave at home.

Hall and Stacey also emphasise that the suffering of children experiencing separation was closely associated with the meaning to them of the hospital experience. They emphasised the discontinuity of experience provided by the hospital ward and addressed themselves to the organisation of the hospital and its unnecessarily alien environment. They also highlight the important negotiating, arbitrating role of the visiting parent. Their study is also particularly valuable in that it explores the impact of the hospital, not only on young children but upon adolescents. They conclude, 'We should be aware of the distress arising from separation, not just in the pre-school child, but in children of all ages, indeed, probably also in adults.' It would be possible to explore further the implications of these studies to our research but space has not permitted more than a cursory glance. Indeed, when we began our investigation three years ago we erred in believing that the controversy between the child's rights to stable substitute parenting and a contrasting viewpoint which emphasised the value of parental links, would pose us with considerable problems. As this study develops, it will be apparent that the dispute neither helps nor reflects the realities of the child's care career. Indeed, the problems as they emerge for the majority of children in care lie not in fraught decisions on the severance of family links but in the difficulties of nurturing parental contact in unpropitious circumstances.

## This study and the 'links' controversy

Can this study throw any light on the dispute between the blood-tie and substitute parenting which has been outlined in the previous pages? We can see that in recent years, research evidence would suggest that maintaining contact between the majority of children in care and their parents is desirable. This study, as it develops, will support such a viewpoint for reasons which lie outside issues of psychological and social well-being for the child. It will be useful to keep the following points in mind as they are more fully explored in the succeeding chapters. The following findings do offer some answers to the blood-tie controversy.

We have seen that Fanshel, Lasson and others have demonstrated that children absent in state care are happier and function better when contact is maintained with their parents or with the wider family. Fanshel also highlights that those children who have contacts with home are likely to leave care more quickly than those who do not. The pages which follow amply support such conclusions. For example, we have analysed carefully those factors which influence the length of stay of children in care and, even after controlling for other variables, find that a weakening of parental links is strongly associated with declining chances of the child returning home. Indeed, a carefully controlled correlation exercise which, because of its complexity, is to be published separately, illustrates that contact with a parent most clearly correlates with an early exit from care.[43]

Naturally, parental links are not a sufficient condition to ensure exit from care, because love and the ability to care may not go hand in hand. Nevertheless, links with the family are a necessary condition for exit because without parental links, apart from the few for whom adoption is a likelihood, children without family contacts will stay in care, however much they improve in health, behaviour and functioning.

Most writers assume that a long stay in care is harmful to the child, forgetting that relying on fitful parental support may not be a less detrimental alternative to separation. Thankfully, it is not our task to arbitrate on this issue. But if early exit from care is an acceptable goal, then the maintenance of strong parental links is a very good way of facilitating departure. Unlike so many variables in the family and care situation of these children, all of which defy social work interventions, keeping links going is well within social workers' capabilities.

Secondly, it will become clear as this study develops that transfer and breakdown of children in placements selected by social workers are common. We shall devote considerable attention to this instability in a child's care career in the following pages. This propensity to disruption is only slightly less common among young children than adolescents and is as likely to occur in foster as in residential care. Residential settings also face the additional problems of considerable turnover in care staff although there is evidence that this movement has declined recently. Consequently, it is very difficult to ensure that some children deprived of normal home life receive a stable, caring, substitute home. In these circumstances parental and wider family links, however unsuitable they may seem on other grounds, may be the only enduring relationship the child enjoys. Indeed, in advocating the denial of access to the children of uncaring and ineffectual parents, Goldstein, Freud and Solnit nevertheless emphasise that

Even if grounds for modification or termination [of parents' access] could be established, there would be no justification for initiating an action if the state knew beforehand that it could not offer a less detrimental alternative. If the state cannot, or will not, provide something better, even if it did not know this at the time the action was initiated, the least detrimental alternative would be to let the *status quo* persist, however unsatisfactory that might be.[44]

It will clearly emerge from our study, how difficult it is to ensure that some children experience a less detrimental alternative to the inadequacies of their own families' care.

Thirdly, the majority who enter and stay in care will be older children and adolescents. They enter care with well-forged links between themselves, their parents, their wider family, their friends, schools and neighbourhoods. These young people wish to maintain many of these relationships and, as we have suggested, such bonds are mutually reinforcing, providing a sense of belonging.

This and many other studies indicate that children resent their parents' roles being usurped in care situations and the inevitable decline that separation brings to many other relationships. We have already noted that fathers in particular get scant consideration, especially from social services and in the child-care legislation. It will also be seen that while many children enter care with siblings and considerable efforts can be made to keep them together, sometimes this is unsuccessful and separation occurs. Yet little thought is given to the nurturing of compensatory relationships with the wider family. Many children do not seek a replacement family experience, nor is the diminution of the role of natural parents and wider kin advisable for it is to the family and/or immediate neighbourhood that the majority of children return on leaving care.

Fourthly, the number of young children who enter and stay long in care is small and those children who through neglect or risk of injury need to be isolated for long periods from their parents are even fewer. It is not disputed that these children need to be in stable alternative family situations and that adoption or long-term fostering seems most appropriate. It was not our task to explore this issue. But, we have already seen that poverty, exacerbated by isolation and ill-health, puts intolerable pressure on some families and that the juxtaposition of many pressures precipitates their children into care. It would be unwarranted to limit the access of such parents without very cogent reasons, punishing them for poverty. One could hardly think of an action more likely to add to the periodic depression of many lone mothers. Indeed, some mothers fail to seek medical care for both physical and mental problems, haunted by the prospect of losing their children and the unequal fight to get them back. In such cases, severance of parental contact to facilitate replacement parenting is not the answer. For such children, foster homes with elements of shared care, however difficult this is to manage, would seem most appropriate.

In addition, we have already noted that wider family networks do exist and need to be tapped. On those rare occasions when parents are absent or dead, the wider family needs to be involved as children in long-stay care have a right to know their family and care circumstances. Many authorities have suggested that for psychological well-being and a sense of belonging we all need to have unbroken personal histories and a map of our lives.

Fifthly, it will become increasingly evident as this study progresses that parents feel frozen out by the care process. The decline in contact between children who stay in local authority care and their parents may in part reflect the indifference of some parents but it also reflects their powerlessness to intervene, their lack of role and their feelings of guilt and inadequacy. We know from research, particularly that of Jenkins and Norman (1972), Thorpe (1974), Aldgate (1980) and Rowe (1983), that these feelings on the parts of parents hinder contact with absentee children.[45] It is also likely that social workers misinterpret natural parents' behaviour at the time of admission, as our own case studies have suggested. They seem unaware that in grieving and mourning for their lost children, parents will oscillate between aggression, anger and rejection and passivity and indifference. Indeed, the widespread comments made by social workers on parental indifference, ambivalence and rejection may reflect parents' outward stance rather than their inner feelings. Rowe comments:

We were frequently dismayed and sometimes angered by the ways in which social workers so often failed to provide the necessary support and encouragement to maintain visiting, sometimes they set up a 'no win' situation for the natural parents, first discouraging visits to let the child settle and later saying that, after such a long gap, renewed visiting would be upsetting.[46]

Finally, there is an assumption that, regardless of whether children seek such contacts or not, the child-care scene is literally overflowing with adults aching to provide unconditional love; many longing to sit up at nights worrying about hedonistic and graceless adolescents or anxious to find deep fulfilment in chasing absconders and bailing out the delinquent. While social work probably has more than its fair share of saints, evidence would suggest that it is far easier to write of substitute parenting and the severance of parental links than it is to provide constant adult support and unconditional love. Indeed, Parker, in reviewing ten years of Seebohm, noted the ways in which the professionalisation of social workers has diminished the status of tending skills.[47]

As this study develops, we shall illustrate that children who stay long in care receive only a perfunctory scrutiny from social workers as time progresses. After some initial activity in the months immediately after reception, social work activity declines. Several studies, such as those by Lasson, Berridge, Rowe and Fanshel, have suggested that caregivers do not perceive themselves as replacement parents.[48] Indeed, Rowe's recent study of long-term fostering shows that, in spite of facilitating legislation, many foster parents do not wish to shoulder the responsibilities of adoption and guardianship.[49] Our study will also demonstrate that many children experience long stays in residential care which, whatever its considerable and usually unrecognised strengths, finds it difficult to replicate family life.

Consequently, substitute parenting and an enduring relationship, are not easily constructed for a child. As a result, the advisability of maintaining parental and wider family contact should be self-evident, particularly as it prevents the child being 'forgotten' while in care. The loneliness and homelessness of many young people who have been in care spring from the low priorities given to parental links by social workers and their failure to appreciate the barriers that parents and children face in maintaining contact. The isolation of adolescents who have long been in local authority care reflects not only their lack of social skills but also our short-term perspectives, a devotion to child care as opposed to adolescent or young adult care. Had these children been lucky enough to be born in other social classes, they would still, as young adults, be making considerable demands on parental love, time and purse.

For these reasons which will be developed as this study unfolds, the maintenance of links between family and child in local authority care should have priority. They amply justify the focus adopted at the outset of our investigations which was to explore the barriers to contact that parents, children and others face.

## Conclusions

We have seen in this chapter that maintaining a link between parent and child has many dimensions. For the child, contact with home is part of a wider package of belonging. We have also explored the ways in which experts differ in the significance they accord to parental links with absent children. We have suggested that aspects of the care situation, particularly the difficulty of providing stable, substitute parenting, makes home and contact very important to the child. This is reinforced by the fact that a child's withering relationships with the family makes an early exit from care highly unlikely.

We can now turn to scrutinise the problems parents and families face in maintaining links with their children as our 450 children move through care. We can explore what sort of links are enjoyed by those children who stay in care. Who visited them, and did they visit their parents? We shall see which children have been cherished by parents and which are ignored. We can also see which children leave care rapidly and the extent to which parental visiting affects the duration of their separation, and which groups of children over time present the greatest 'links' problems.

The value of a prospective longitudinal study will emerge, indicating how many children remain the responsibility of social services at each time-interval, highlighting their characteristics. At each stage of the care process, we shall focus on those aspects of the social worker's decisions which will have an impact on the child's relationships while in care and the links he or she maintains with the family.

Four key social work dimensions will be examined at each stage. First, we shall explore the nature of social work support offered to children, parents and care-givers. For example, do social workers change frequently and how much effort do they actually make with families, children and care-givers? Obviously, these factors will affect the links experienced by children in care and their parents.

Next, we shall look at changes in legislation and the legal categories under which children stay in care. One would expect, for example, that the links enjoyed between parents and child will be different for voluntary receptions to care than for those children admitted on place of safety orders or on care orders for delinquency. It will also be interesting to see whether children in some legal categories find contact easier than others.

Thirdly, placements will obviously be important. We have already suggested that because of the reproach implicit in the situation, the visiting of foster homes can be difficult for parents. Some placements, such as residential care, may by their routine, their geographic separation and totality exclude parents from much contact with their children, or vice versa. It is also important to look at transfers and breakdowns in children's placements. These changes not only affect links between parent and child but, if frequent, they will cogently justify any efforts to maximise parental contact. To have lost contact with parents in efforts to forge a bond with substitute care-givers and then to find that this security is not gilt-edged and is severed by transfer or breakdown, must be very damaging to children.

Finally, we can explore at each stage of the child's career in care how the 'implicit' and 'explicit' restrictions on access which have been outlined in an earlier chapter affect levels of parental contact.

As a result, at each stage of the child's care career, we can see which aspects of the situation such as social work input, legislation, placement and access arrangements most closely affect the links parents have with their children. We shall also note how these aspects change their significance over time. Let us begin by looking at the characteristics, care experience and family contacts of that large number of children who enter care and leave rapidly.

## Summary points

1. Maintaining links between separated family members is complex and difficult. Visits to their children in care require much social skill and can be stressful to parents. Often they go alone to see their children, unfamiliar with neighbourhoods, routes or transport and feel guilty and resentful at their humiliating situation. Bereft of a role and discouraged by the indifferent, sometimes rejecting stance of their children, parents feel unwanted. Care-givers and children also find the parental visit embarrassing and artificial.

2. Links have symbolic and power dimensions which are little considered in social work planning for separated children. Contacts with parents and wider family are only part of belonging for the child, the importance of their friends and neighbourhood should be recognised.

3. The maintenance of links between separated child, parents and wider family is important: (a) because research evidence suggests that the absent child is happier and functions better when parents remain in contact; (b) because frequent contact with home is the clearest indicator that the child will leave care quickly; (c) the majority of very young children who enter care do not stay long, thus long-term substitute parenting is not a dominating issue; (d) stable, alternative care placements for children are very difficult to ensure, thus the parents and family, while unsuitable on many criteria, may prove to be the only enduring relationships the child has; (e) increasingly, older children and adolescents tend to enter and stay in care, and they have well-forged family and friendship links which they wish to maintain. They often resent the conflict of loyalties that the care situation can bring, particularly in foster homes. Nevertheless, fostering is preferred by social workers and is believed to encourage family links; (f) we can see that parents are beginning to feel frozen out by the care process and feel they are expected to be passive bystanders with little to contribute to the well-being of their children.

# 8. Children who left care early*

Here we look at the characteristics, care experience and destinations of those 228 children who left care early, that is before six months had elapsed. We look at the social workers' involvement in cases, the legislation they employ, the variety of care placements the children receive, and the barriers to contact, both specific and non-specific that families experience. The chapter highlights the importance of early social work decisions in influencing children's length of stay in care, the instability of many children's care placements, the considerable barriers to contact experienced by many families and the mercurial quality of children's households which can complicate return and make social work decisions extremely difficult.

Half of the 450 children in our study group were able to leave care quickly and by the time six months had elapsed 228 had left, all but four of them returning home. We have already described the variety of tasks which face social workers when a child enters care and these leaving patterns indicate that some situations require longer interventions than others. Several writers have suggested that children in care seem to fall into short- and long-stay groups, but close scrutiny of early leavers reveals other important divisions and demonstrates the significance of the first weeks of the child's care experience.

Of the 228 children who left, there is a contrast between those who stay for a very short period and the remainder. For example, 53 (12 per cent) of the children stayed in care for less than a week and a further 142 (32 per cent) were able to leave within nine weeks. After this time, there is a marked reduction in the number of children leaving care. This can be clearly seen in Table 8.1.

These patterns are important for several reasons. Initially, they suggest that the events of the first six weeks are a crucial influence on the child's future care career. A child still remaining in care after six weeks has elapsed has a 78 per cent chance of remaining there for over six months and, as we shall see in a later chapter, a 63 per cent chance of still being in care after two years. Yet the monitoring of children in care in all five areas participating in this study is based around case reviews which are usually held quarterly. This evidence indicates that during the first few weeks of entry to care, very close attention to

*In the following longitudinal study, 'leaving care' means that the child is no longer in the care of the local authority. As we shall see, some children return home but remain legally in care. For the purpose of this study, such children are defined as still 'in care'.

Table 8.1 **Length of stay of leavers before six months**

| Duration of child's stay | Number leaving | Cumulative % of early leavers | Cumulative % of whole study group |
|---|---|---|---|
| Less than 1 week | 53 | 23 | 12 |
| 1–2 weeks (i.e. 7–13 days) | 21 | 32 | 16 |
| 2–5 weeks (i.e. 14–35 days) | 89 | 71 | 36 |
| 6–9 weeks | 32 | 86 | 43 |
| 10–19 weeks | 28 | 98 | 50 |
| 20–26 weeks | 5 | 100 | 51 |
| | (N = 228 | 228 | 450) |

children's contacts with parents, wider family, friends, school and neighbourhood would be beneficial and assist more children to return home quickly.

Although we can already see that initial care decisions are likely to colour much of what subsequently happens, in the first few weeks many children remain the responsibility of intake social work teams who are often preoccupied with other problems. Thus, temporary placements of children can persist longer than intended and *ad hoc* decisions concerning their welfare are often made.

Secondly, the pattern by which children leave care either very quickly or after a longer period, does not seem to be a logical reflection of the presenting problems of children and families which, as we have seen, are extremely complex and varied. While certain of the problems which precipitate children into care can be resolved more quickly than others, the wide range of children's and families' circumstances would suggest that the leaving patterns of children should be more evenly spread over time. Why is it, for example, that only 14 per cent of our study group left in the period between 4 and 12 months after reception? As we have seen, social workers define the task in a way that categorises cases into those that can be dealt with swiftly and those that require much longer intervention, perhaps lasting several years, and few situations fall in between these extremes.[1] We shall explore later the possible explanations for these patterns but the value of adopting a process perspective on children's care experience in this study and following them over time begins to be appreciated.

It might be expected that children who are able to leave care quickly would be the more straightforward cases where temporary breakdowns in family care, perhaps due to illness or lack of accommodation, can be swiftly resolved. It also seems likely that such cases will not be complicated by legislative difficulties or decisions about the access that a family and child should have. For example, Aldgate who, in the early 1970s, studied the length of stay of over 200 children in voluntary care in Scotland found that this was closely associated with the reasons for admission.[2]

Several major factors emerged as significant in influencing the return of children from care. Children seemed to have most chance of return when they were received into care from two-parent families who were living in stable accommodation or from one-parent families headed by their mother following marital breakdown. Most at risk of long-term care were young single parent families and one-parent families headed by father following the desertion of the mother. The reason for care itself influenced the outcome. There was widespread poverty among the study families, so it was hardly surprising that eviction accounted for one-third of the receptions into care. Children that had been received into care because of their mother's death, desertion or long-term psychiatric illness were far more vulnerable to lengthy separation.

She also notes the importance of contact with home and, particularly relevant to this study, social workers' involvement during the child's stay in care. Aldgate adds,

Parents' involvement with their children during the placement was a very significant factor in influencing return. This contact is itself dependent on several other factors like the attitude of care takers, distance between parental and substitute home, reactions of children and encouragement given to parents by social workers early in the placement. Social work activity, whether in the form of general encouragement, practical support or more intensive problem-solving help with emotional difficulties had a significant effect on return from care.

Aldgate's findings have been confirmed in a later study of children in care in Scotland.[3]

In our five areas, the procedures for going out of care quickly were straightforward and the moves for return were usually initiated by social workers (36 per cent of cases) or parents who requested their child's return home (54 per cent). It is noticeable for these short-stay cases that neither the children themselves nor extraneous bodies such as courts and health services play much part in decisions about leaving care.

### Reasons for leaving care

The reasons which enable a child to leave care quickly stem largely from improvements in the family situation rather than any changes in the behaviour of the young person or parents. In 131 cases (57 per cent) there has been a beneficial change in the parents' environmental and home circumstances compared with only 61 cases (22 per cent) where parental behaviour was said to have changed for the better. For example, a third of all children left care because of an improvement in mother's health and/or exit from hospital. In a further 28 cases (12 per cent), the child left care early not so much because of an improved situation but simply because new information had revealed that the presenting problems were not as serious as at first feared. Once again, this highlights the variety of functions served by admitting a child to care.

While the prospect of the child leaving care was generally welcomed, in 40 cases some unease was expressed. Social workers felt anxiety over 26 cases while parents and children resisted seven decisions taken to end the stay in care. Sometimes, social workers feared the abrupt recurrence of illness or renewed neglect or abuse in home situations where improvements were more cosmetic than a reality. We shall find later in this study that these fears were frequently justified as placements at home with families broke down and children had to be readmitted to care.[4]

Indeed, for most children, leaving care was by no means the end of contact with social services. Social workers expected to continue their support and estimated that no fewer than 45 per cent of these early leavers would be readmitted to care in the near future, while for a further 25 per cent the prognosis was, at best, uncertain. Less than a third of these early leavers were viewed as unlikely to return to care and this was usually because the child was either too old or because the original problem, such as school non-attendance, had diminished. Hence, social workers were only able to express complete satisfaction with the progress and outcome of the care experience of two-thirds of 228 short-stay cases. Indeed, social workers had considerable reservations about many children who left care and would have preferred more than a third to stay longer.

As nearly all short-stay children were either voluntary admissions to care (188) or place of safety orders (22), close contact between parents and social workers was generally maintained throughout the care episode, disputes were minimal and agreements about leaving care were easily negotiated. Hence, it is not surprising that nearly all of these children returned to the care of one or both parents (94 per cent) and the use of other situations such as adoptive homes or residential institutions was uncommon. Children rarely initiated their own departures and, in half of the cases, were not involved in decisions about leaving care, usually because they were infants or the situation was straightforward. The returning patterns of children who leave care early are laid out in Table 8.2.

Nevertheless, the family circumstances facing children as they return home continue to be complicated. This is highlighted by the fact that the proportion of those children returning to the care of both natural parents (36 per cent) is exceeded by those returning to single parents or step-parenting (59 per cent).

**Table 8.2  Living circumstances of children immediately after leaving care**

|  | N | % |
|---|---|---|
| *Natural family* |  |  |
| mother and father | 82 | 36 |
| mother alone | 99 | 43 |
| father alone | 8 | 4 |
| mother and step-father/co-habitee | 24 | 11 |
| father and step-mother/co-habitee | 2 | 1 |
| other relatives | 6 | 3 |
| *Other households* |  |  |
| other non-relatives | 1 | 0 |
| adoptive parents | 2 | 1 |
| *Residential care* | 3 | 0 |
| *Died* | 1 | 0 |
|  | (N = 228) | |

Other problems faced by these families also persist. There is usually a history of disruption and separation among families. Thus, for the child, entry into care is only one episode in a recurring and turbulent cycle. For example, 116 of the 228 children (51 per cent) who left care early are known to have experienced in their first years of life a separation from their mothers of more than one week's duration. Health and economic problems also abound with no fewer than 43 per cent of the children coming from families where a member suffers a serious or chronic illness. Similarly, two-thirds of these families had no income other than supplementary benefit and a further quarter face difficulties of either housing, prolonged unemployment or criminality. Neither do all aspects of these family situations improve while the child is away. Children leaving care early usually return to better situations with regard to shelter and the capacity of parents to care for them but more deep-seated problems in the family seem to have been scarcely touched during the child's absence.

Many of these family situations underwent radical changes during the child's absence, even though the stay in care was short. Ten per cent of the children left care to join a completely different household from the one where they had been living before admission. In addition, a further 15 per cent returned to families where there had been significant changes in structure. For example, in 14 cases mother had a new baby, whereas for half of the returning children there was a new adult in the home. In a fifth of cases, similar movements affected siblings.

These changes make return difficult for children. Not only have they to cope with separation but they have to adapt to changed circumstances when they go back home. It is not surprising, therefore, that even though the stay in care of children is short, absence can create serious problems of readjustment on return.

**The care careers**
It is useful to look at the care experience of these short-stay cases, seeing what changes occur in their social work supervision, the legislation under which they stayed in care and their placement experiences. All these have implications for the links they will have experienced with their families while in care. We shall see that because of their short stay, the care careers of these 228 children will be more straightforward than for other groups of children whose stay in care is longer and that contacts with home have been less disturbed.

*Field social work supervision*
The oft-made criticism that social workers change rapidly and that clients are denied continuity of care is not substantiated for the short-stay group. Only 16, for example, of the 228 short-stay cases had a change of social worker while they were in care although some of those originally taken into care by intake teams had no specific social worker responsible for them. Nevertheless, there were frequent changes in care situations and as many as 43 moved between placements. This, rather than lack of continuity of field social workers, caused disruption for these children.

Social workers stress that, although these children leave care quickly, such cases are onerous and in the early weeks organising return can be very time-consuming.[5] Much of the professional involvement with children and their families was described by social workers as 'routine case work' with a need for additional 'crisis' interventions in 10 per cent of cases.

During their stay in care, half of these children were visited at least once a week by their social workers and a further 54 (24 per cent) were seen fortnightly. Similarly, social workers usually visited the child's family and placement regularly. Half the mothers were seen weekly and a further 23 per cent every two weeks. Most placements were visited with similar frequency. Hence, three-quarters of children and families saw a social worker at least once a fortnight. However, many of these visits lasted only a very short time and intensive case work with families seems rare. Yet, social workers failed to visit 29 of the children and 32 of the natural mothers, usually in cases where the child's stay in care was very short. Other family members fared even less well so that, for example, 54 per cent of natural fathers had no contact with social workers at all, and the majority of those absent were unaware of their child's entry to care.

While there is very little indication from this evidence of administrative laxity or inadequate professional oversight, there is a potential danger arising in the insufficient scrutiny of some very short-stay cases. Also, there seems to be considerable variation in the quality and quantity of social work input and, although these children returned home quickly, the conditions which facilitated their return were largely extraneous to social work manipulation.

*Legislation*
The care status of children changes little in short-term care cases. Only 12 of the 228 children experienced a change of legal status and all but one of these was consequent on the expiry of place of safety orders. Hence, legislative changes occurred soon after admission and all but one of the changes were uncontested. Issues such as the assumption of parental rights by the local authority rarely arose. Consequently, only a matrimonial care order, which was taken following a deterioration in the child's home situation, required adjudication.

*Placements*
But the untroubled picture surrounding social work supervision and unchallenged legal status is not matched by the range of placements experienced by the 228 children who left care early. While in care, 44 of them rapidly changed their living situation and for six children this happened twice. Some of these changes were planned, such as leaving hospital or assessment centre, but 18 of these 44 changes were not anticipated, resulting from breakdowns in existing arrangements. The situation of a further 13 children was sufficiently fraught to bring forward transfer plans.

Many of these transfers occurred early but even those children who stayed for a very short time (under six weeks) were just as likely to experience change as those who remained longer (18 per cent as compared with 22 per cent). As we have already noted, although social workers usually gained the sort of placement they wanted, they were less successful in obtaining specific choices of foster parents or residential homes. Placements were chosen for control, for assessment needs or (in only a third of cases) to facilitate access between child and parent. However, most of the children were fairly near home – in fact three-quarters of them were placed within 10 miles of home – but there is no indication that subsequent changes of placement improved parental contact. It is also interesting to note that the proportion of children placed first in residential care (39 per cent) is maintained over time as an equal number of children moved into residential establishments as left for foster homes or returned to parents.

Half of the children over the age of 12 moved compared with one-fifth of those under the age of two. Girls were just as likely to move as boys and, as might be expected, children in certain placements such as O and A centres or with legal categories, such as place of safety orders, were more prone to movement than others.

*Placement breakdowns*

However, a closer scrutiny of the 31 placements that broke down reveals a somewhat different pattern from that of transfers.* Although foster children are less liable than others to shift, they are more likely to experience a placement breakdown: 11 of the 132 initial fosterings broke down under crisis conditions compared with only one of the 88 residential placements. There was a clear crisis in 18 of the 31 breakdowns in that the removal of the child was unexpected and urgent. For the remaining 13 children, a clear placement breakdown occurred but this merely precipitated an intended placement change, such as a return home or a move to a long-term foster home.

All the breakdowns led to a new living situation for the child with many moving into residential care. Interestingly, the placement crisis led five of the 31 children to leave care, so that the child actually returned home following one in six of the crisis breakdowns despite the fraught circumstances of many home situations. Indeed, by precipitating placement crises, it seems that short-stay children can generate a fair chance of leaving care.

This placement instability affecting a minority of short-stay cases should cause some concern. While most children seem to settle well and remain in one placement during their separation from home, a fifth of the children change their living situation soon after coming into care, many for administrative convenience but some because of breakdowns and crises. Many of those children who move are very young and social workers express concern at the distress experienced by them as a result of these changes. Neither is there much indication that their new location is deemed by social workers to be particularly beneficial. We shall see, as the study progresses, that breakdowns and transfers experienced by some children in care are numerous. For some children, the goal of a stable caring alternative to home seems very difficult to achieve and no placement seems immune to crises, transfer and breakdown.

*A placement breakdown is defined as any placement termination that was not indicated in a social work plan at the time of selection, either in the termination itself or in the timing of the breakdown. It does not include, therefore, the ending of 'contract' arrangements or the failure of planned placements to materialise.[6]

*Relations with home*
The majority of short-stay children experience some limitation on their contacts with home while they are away in care. We have already suggested that these limitations can be of two kinds: restrictions which are specific to particular individuals either as a result of social work decisions or through family demands; and non-specific limitations on contact imposed by aspects of the placement.

*Specific restrictions on access*
Specific restrictions on parental access arose from social work decisions for 48 of the 54 short-stay children affected. In many cases, the limitations followed a place of safety order whereas others resulted from requests by care providers in placements (29 per cent of the 54 cases), the child's family (9 per cent) or the children themselves (4 per cent). The main reasons for these limitations were to protect the child from abuse, discourage parental disruption of placements, or to moderate friction between parents and child.

These specific restrictions were often severe, perhaps banning all contact between a particular individual and the child. This condition was imposed at some time on the contacts of 38 children (17 per cent) in the short-stay group. Outside contact was often discouraged by deliberately selecting distant and inaccessible placements. Few of these restrictions, however, endured throughout the care period. Nevertheless, it was still the case that one in ten of early leavers were forbidden to see a close relative, or vice versa, at the time they left care. However, this figure is inflated by the fact that half of these limitations were applied to the very short-stay cases who remained in care for less than two weeks.

*Non-specific restrictions*
Non-specific restrictions which arise from the context of separation and substitute care hinder the frequency, duration and style of contacts between children and their families. These restrictions applied to the majority (70 per cent) of short-stay children throughout their care period and difficulties in maintaining contact still pressed heavily as they left care. The impact of these barriers varies depending on the social competence of the families and children involved. Rules about visits, problems of distance and transport combine with the deprivations and insecurities of many families to make the maintenance of links difficult. These restrictions press most heavily on children admitted to care voluntarily – the majority of short-stay care cases – a problem echoed in Packman's recent study of children entering care.[7] Examples of barriers to contact greatly affecting our study group are as shown in Table 8.3.

**Table 8.3** **Percentage of 228 children affected by particular non-specific restrictions and family problems**

| Non-specific restrictions arising from* | % | Family problems affecting links* | % |
|---|---|---|---|
| Rules re. visits | 50 | Health | 29 |
| Distance of placement | 28 | Turbulent relationships | 25 |
| Transport problems | 18 | Economic and employment | |
| Attitude of placement | 11 | difficulties | 18 |
| | | Behaviour difficulties | 11 |
| | | Offending | 9 |
| | | Housing | 4 |

* Categories not mutually exclusive.

Local authority resources available to parents to help their visiting varied greatly and parental awareness of the assistance on offer was even more uneven. Clearly family links are far more easily maintained if a car, telephone or public transport are available. Telephones are especially important as 37 per cent of the children used this to keep in touch with their families, especially if the mother was in hospital. Indeed, one in five of the short-stay children telephoned their parents every day. Although these restrictions on contact were negotiated by families and children in different ways, the majority of these children maintained links with their families, hence their rapid exit from care.

*The maintenance of family links*
The family contacts of the 228 short-stay children in this study are very varied. For 86 (38 per cent) of them, social workers felt that the placements had helped families to continue contact, whereas in 100 cases (44 per cent), placements were viewed as detrimental to maintaining links with home. The attitudes of foster parents and residential staff to family contact were important, far more significant than problems of distance and transport. We found that social workers viewed residential care less favourably than fostering in maintaining links because foster care could be local, offered more flexible visiting arrangements and could work with parents in a way alien to some residential provision. Nevertheless, there are considerable barriers to contact in foster homes as well as in residential care, but these impediments are *different*.

The style of various residential and foster placements is seen as highly influential by social workers in either facilitating or discouraging family contact. However, our evidence would suggest that the significance accorded to stylistic differences between and within each of these sectors, can be overemphasised at the expense of barriers to contact which are intrinsic to separation. While it is obviously easier for a parent to visit an 'inclusive' rather than an 'exclusive' foster home or a local children's home rather than a distant CHE, the non-specific restrictions in all situations are much more severe than most social workers appreciate.

In the case of residential care, parents will usually have previously experienced visits to various institutions and, therefore, will be pre-pared for the routines and rules that they are likely to meet. Further, while the rules of institutions may restrict contact between parent and absent child, such rules may help to put the visitor at ease. Institu-tions, for all their strange totems and taboos give security, an asset during any visit to a child absent in care when the usual order of the visitors' lives will be upset. Thus, parental powerlessness in the resi-dential setting might be compensated for by a feeling of safety, while the foster home may hide reproach and threat.

Parental unease is also affected by the expectations held by those who provide substitute care. Residential social workers will be famil-iar with their role in visiting situations but foster parents' expectations can be quite different; indeed, they may even perceive themselves as taking the role of the natural parents, an expectation which is much reinforced by phrases in the boarding-out agreement that foster parents are required to sign. Foster parents may even be disappointed applicants for an opportunity for adoption. Not surprisingly, this can generate severe barriers to visits or visiting. Parents pressing for access may be perceived by both care-givers and social workers as wanting the swift return of their child although frequently it is contact that families seek, not immediate reunion. We shall see as we follow the careers of children in care that short-term living arrangements often drift into long-term placements without the visiting arrangements being scrutinised.

Stylistic differences among placements are especially significant for the family contacts of children of junior school age who, as we shall see later in this report, present special problems with regard to the maintenance of links. For these children, substitute parenting is difficult to arrange and, unlike adolescents, they are not old enough to fashion their own links with the family.

In spite of these difficulties, of all the 228 short-stay children who left care, three-quarters were in regular contact with their mother and relations with other family members were satisfactory. Yet other chil-dren were less fortunate and it is surprising that 50 of the 228 children who left care early had no contact with their mother during their time away from home. Again, this is partly explained by the very brief stays of some of these cases (21 of the 50 children were in care for less than one week) but among the remaining 29 who had little home contact were five who stayed in care for over one month.

Links between children in care and their families, as we have suggested, involve more than visits and we shall explore throughout this study these other aspects of belonging. For example, children kept in contact with their families by seeing other relatives or friends who acted as go-betweens, by telephone and, very occasionally, by letter. Nevertheless, it is disturbing that three-fifths of the children did not enjoy these sorts of contact and, for them, there were no telephone calls and letters to compensate for a lack of regular parental visiting. In fact, only 60 per cent of those children who failed to see their mothers during their sojourn in care were able to make contact by other means. This was also true of half of the children who were denied any visits from a specific adult. For many children not only do specific restrictions hinder contact with home but their isolation is compounded by wider non-specific restrictions. As in any hospital ward, barrack room or reformatory, those that are cherished are inundated with letters and visits while the rest of the residents look on bleakly.

Although these children go home quickly, the problems of maintaining links between them and their families while in care are very evident. We shall see that for those children whose stay in care is longer, the withering of family contacts becomes an increasing problem. It is not true that by closing one route to contact others take on greater significance for the child; links with home are a package and the smaller the package, the less there is in it.

While short-stay children are fortunate in being able to return home quickly, it is also apparent that for many of them links could have withered at any stage, disrupted by additional family crises, thus extending the separation. Many of the barriers to contact, such as attitudes of care-givers, the distance of placement from home and access to the telephone can be overcome, but other, less tangible, hindrances are more resistant to change, such as the inertia and disintegration of poor families and the cultural barriers to visiting that they experience. It is also clear from the intensive study of 30 families experiencing a care intervention that parents find visiting very difficult for reasons laid out in the previous chapter.

While social workers seem satisfied with the patterns of links enjoyed by the majority of children whose stays in care are short, their answers are now beginning to reveal increasing and deep concern over the problems of maintaining links between children in care and their families. Indeed, an issue that received scant attention at the outset of a child's care career now begins to assume prominence in social work concerns. These anxieties increase as we study those many children who remain in care. Even at this early stage the concerns of social workers about insufficient contact between parents and children outweighs by five to one their anxieties over the detrimental effects of maintaining links.

## Summary
We can see that half of the children entering local authority care only stay a short time, that is, for less than six months. Two-thirds of the early leavers in our study group left care within five weeks. The early leavers are usually young children received voluntarily into care, or those for whom place of safety orders have expired. However, we shall find that a child still in care at the end of six weeks has a 78 per cent chance of remaining for over six months and a 63 per cent chance of still being in care, often away from home, two years later. Thus, the first weeks in care are crucial for the child's rapid rehabilitation with the family.

We shall notice in later chapters that, as time passes, there is increasing stability in the child's care situation – changes in placement, in legal status and in access arrangements all diminish. Once six months had elapsed there was only a slow trickle of departures from care so that 27 of the 222 children in care at six months had left by the 12–month stage and a further 25 by the end of two years. This re-emphasises the significance of the early weeks of the child's care career and the need for maximum social work effort at this time if a child's long stay in care is to be prevented. But as these subsequent exits from care do not raise issues of parental links which are substantially different from those of other children, they will be dealt with later. In addition, 38 children out of all leavers from care during the two years returned to care and doubtless more will do so in the future. These are also dealt with separately.

Short-stay children usually enter care because of a crisis in the parents' ability to provide, such as the hospitalisation of mother or family eviction, and, as these children rarely raise severe problems of neglect, non-accidental injury or control, the majority return home when the precipitating crisis eases. But return is still fraught with difficulties; at home, fresh faces abound, new roles have been assumed and the prodigal's cherished territories expropriated. Indeed, a third of the children returned to households which had experienced a major change in the interim. Thus, short-stay children exhibit family characteristics very reminiscent of all children entering care, of poor, chaotic, rapidly changing households in which they have only a precarious foothold. However, short-stay children differ significantly from long-stay cases mainly in social workers' expectations of their length of stay.

Nevertheless, this chapter makes it clear that the wider problems that precipitated these children's brief stay in care have not been resolved. Children's deprivation and fraught histories are maintained. They have been long known to social services and while the crises that propelled them into care may have been eased – for example, new accommodation has been found or mother's depression lifted – the family's structural position remains unaltered. Poverty, persistent ill-health, wider instabilities and lack of extended family support persist. The crisis symptom that necessitated the child's entry to care implies major structural problems in the families which are beyond the reach of social workers. Thus, they expect 44 per cent of the children who leave care early to return and another 24 per cent are viewed as likely to be readmitted. Indeed, we shall see these anxieties are quite justified, for one-third of those children who left care early came back during the following two years, many to embark on long stays in care.

The experiences of these short-stay children do not substantiate oft-voiced criticisms of child care. For example, there are few changes of social workers and the legislation employed seems suitable and is rarely in dispute. However, we can see that certain serious problems are beginning to emerge even at this early stage.

We know these children enter care for situational reasons, they experience an emergency service and many are already well known to social services. Three-quarters of them will continue subsequently to hover on the margins of social services, vulnerable to return to care and longer separations from their families. Yet the level of family case work or contingency planning seems low and the difficulties children face oscillating between care situations are largely unappreciated.

The insecurity and instability children endure within their families does not necessarily disappear on their entry to care. While the majority of them enjoy stable and supportive situations, some do not. About one-fifth of those children who left care early experienced a breakdown in their placements or were precipitately transferred by bringing forward intended changes. We shall find that transfer between placements and breakdowns within them are a salient feature of children's care careers over the whole two-year period. Fostering is just as prone to breakdown as are placements in residential care and young children are affected as well as adolescents.

These traumas result as much from factors external to the child as from their difficult or unresponsive conduct within placements. Indeed, we shall see that 37 per cent of those children who entered care under the age of two and stayed in care for two years had breakdowns in their placements. Breakdown and transfer are even familiar among early leavers and changes of placement do not necessarily improve a deteriorating situation. As a result, some of the children become more inextricably enmeshed in the care process. The distress and upheaval of transfer can easily lead to a deterioration in child behaviour and what was initially intended primarily as short-term child rescue can easily become long-term child control.

It is also clear that links between short-stay children and their families begin to cause social work concern even though these children's duration in care is expected to be brief. A withering of links with home reduces the child's chances of leaving care and there are many barriers to maintaining contact. Over two-thirds (69 per cent) of short-stay cases were seriously frustrated in their efforts at keeping in touch with their homes by restrictions inherent in their placements or by families' incapacity to visit. For a quarter of short-stay cases, these difficulties were aggravated by specific restrictions on access which applied to key family members. Contact with other siblings who were in care but placed elsewhere was often particularly difficult. In addition, there seems to have been little attempt to involve the wider family or friends, although these may have been significant to the child prior to the entry to care.

While most specific restrictions on access were lifted before the child left care, other barriers to contact remained constant. Indeed, those children who changed placements often found increasing problems in maintaining contact with their families. Frequently, situational barriers to keeping in touch were insufficiently appreciated by social workers. It is also clear that the care intervention itself has a dynamic effect upon families, fathers sometimes reappear to take more interest in the child and either feuds are buried in the child's interest or simmering conflicts can erupt.

Unfortunately, a withering of contact due to placement and distance and to specific restrictions imposed on seeing key individuals in the family does not lead the child to compensate by intensive communications using other means. The isolated child in care is not always using the telephone, visiting siblings, scribbling yet another letter. It is those who have good links in care who are the good communicators. We shall see in the following pages that, among those who stay in care, in many relationships the temperature is already beginning to drop between parent and child. Embraces that were often tepid at the outset of a child's care career get fewer as the weeks progress.

## Case study

However, if we remind ourselves of our case studies, the embraces of Sally March might have been indiscriminate, nevertheless they were heartfelt. Fanned by the guilty indignation of her mother at her grandson's unceremonious removal to the children's home, Sally's sense of defeat and helplessness quickly turned to anger and a sense of violation. Unlike many mothers facing the loss of their children, she did not deny the hurt or sink into passive, grudging acceptance. Together, she and her mother plotted the return of David, only to find that many barriers were ranged against them.

The first barrier was a simple lack of information – where the child was, how long he was to be there, what rights they had to visit – anxieties which were greatly exacerbated by the place of safety order being taken over the weekend and during a work-to-rule by social workers. Sally's mother volunteered,

'We just didn't know what was going on. If you found a telephone box that worked, there was either no reply from the social or everyone was in a meeting. The police didn't help very much, they said it wasn't their responsibility.'

These anxieties were rapidly overcome by mother and daughter arriving at the social services office early on the Monday morning to demand information and access to David. Sally's social worker explained the reasons why the police had taken David from the flat. He also told her that he felt the child should remain in care for a few days until Sally had sorted herself out. Like many parents in our study, Sally was distressed and difficult to communicate with at this first meeting. Her social worker said,

'Her emotions were mixed up. She was expressing both guilt and anger. Her sense of violation was acute and she saw the whole episode as a plot to deprive her of her baby. On the other hand, she knew the basic problem lay within herself and that she had not looked after David properly. Her mother rather aggravated the situation but her reappearance on the scene was a good sign. Of course, one didn't know how long the reunion would last.'

Sally's sense of injustice rested on her feelings that 'they', the authorities, had cheated and used her. She maintained that the possibility of removal of David to care had never been raised by the social worker and, sadly, her previous trust in the social worker evaporated overnight. However, Sally did not immediately demand the return of David, although she was determined that his sojourn in care was to be as short as possible. She accepted that she had many concerns to sort out, mainly rent and other arrears problems. As Sally commented, 'Well, I mean, what could I do? They've got all the cards, haven't they? So we decided to sweat it out.' Social services did, in fact, have all the cards, although some of the pack, such as the possible role of Sally's mother or the help of her elder sisters as temporary caretakers for David, seemed to have been overlooked.

Sally's first visit to the children's home where David was staying was in the company of her social worker who sat with her during the whole of her visit. Her mother was encouraged to stay at home on this occasion. Sally remembered the event as particularly difficult. As a mother, she felt both stigmatised and robbed of her maternal role, a reproach which endured during most of David's absence. Her feelings of anger and guilt were particularly acute during visiting. As she said,

'The point is you don't really know what to do. All the sort of things I normally did with David didn't seem normal any more. Like talking, I used to say daft things to him and have silly names for him and get on the floor and roll about with him. You couldn't do that in front of people you don't know, he felt I was different and I didn't feel he was mine.'

Although the staff of the children's home were sympathetic to Sally's situation, she was self-conscious and hesitant.

'You're just a sort of helper. I mean, I gave birth to him but that didn't count somehow. I used to go there [the nursery] and feed him but you had to do what they wanted. I took some clothes in for him one day. It was a little suit I bought from the catalogue but you know they never once used it. They said it wasn't right.'

The incident over the suit symbolised for Sally her powerlessness and frustration and she often referred to it during our interviews with her. However, there were other problems associated with seeing David. Buses were few and far between, and Sally was convinced that her lack of punctuality was viewed by the residential staff as a sign of her fecklessness and lack of concern for the baby.

'You know – I used to explain about the buses and things, but I don't think they ever believed me. I reckon it was all going down in some little book somewhere and that I was no good and couldn't look after David and couldn't even make the effort to get there.'

Sally was, indeed, under scrutiny which increased her unease, especially as appropriate behaviour was not made explicit. Everything was being recorded in the visiting records and she was watched very carefully, partly because previous unsubstantiated suspicions of injury were still prominent in David's file. However, few of these estimates on her parenting were passed on to Sally who needed considerable reassurance about her capabilities as a mother.

'I just felt lonely and useless and no one would tell me anything. Each visit made things worse because David looked bonny and happy, I felt I wasn't wanted. I used to cry on the bus going home.'

In our first interview with Sally's social worker after the place of safety order had been taken, he recalled that he was not surprised by the events that preceded the order or the police action and that he had half-expected it. However, he had made no contingency plans for dealing with the situation and was forced, as he put it, 'to play it by ear'. After a number of phone calls to the police, the children's home and the health visitor and a brief talk with his senior, Sally's social worker decided that, although the events did not suggest a good prognosis, the chances of gaining either an interim care order or a full care order were remote. Despite Sally's chaotic lifestyle, there was little evidence of serious neglect and none of abuse. As Sally's social worker said,

'We decided to keep David at the home for the week and monitor the situation. Basically, I think I would have liked to have tried for a care order. Probably I could have secured one but my senior wasn't too keen. He wanted the child returned home and some special home help arranged. Just the thing I was planning for originally. My own feeling was that Sally was in a mess and needed a number of things sorted out before she could care effectively for David.'

Sorting out Sally March's problems, in fact, proved difficult because she would no longer confide in her social worker. She felt violated by the loss of David and her mother fanned the flames of resentment. The meetings between Sally and the social worker, although frequent during David's first week of care, were fruitless monologues on the part of the social worker. Sally's antagonism towards him, although mute, was absolute.

But the breakdown in communication meant that Sally never fully appreciated her rights as a parent or had much understanding of what the place of safety order meant in legal terms. Even when David's legal status changed to that of being in voluntary care, as occurred after seven days, to Sally this meant very little. She did not listen as this was explained to her and there was no written alternative that the social worker could use to clarify her position. Indeed, Sally was unaware that she could remove David at will once the place of safety order had expired.

On the following Monday David was transferred to a short-term foster home which his social worker had hastily arranged. He explained why during an interview:

'I wasn't sure what Sally would do so I arranged for David to be fostered with Mrs Rathbone. It was pure luck finding her at such short notice. Although it was all rather precipitate, I thought it best to place him with her as the whole situation seemed very fluid to me. Mind you, getting together the necessary people for the case conference took quite a bit of doing. I thought if he's going to have to spend some weeks in care, I want him fostered. Although the children's home is of a very high quality, it is still a bit institutionalised.'

The social worker was, in fact, still inclined to believe that David should not return home and was now making contingency plans for a longer stay in care. Sally's mother's reappearance on the scene had not impressed him as he felt she was an unsavoury character: 'From what I can gather, she runs something of an "open house" and I'm not convinced of the viability of her offer to give Sally and David a room. Their relationship is up and down like a yo-yo.'

However, both grandmother and Sally visited David regularly in his foster home. Like Sally, grandmother March was convinced that David's transfer was part of a 'plot', as she put it, to remove David from Sally permanently. Her resolve to subvert what was indeed a distinct contingency plan of the social worker was persistent and considerable. She made her views known in no uncertain terms both to the foster parents and Sally's social worker. The perceived threat to David also galvanised Sally's two sisters who visited her and promised future support.

As a result, David's three-week stay with the Rathbones was, from their point of view, by no means tranquil. However, their considerable experience in short-term emergency fostering and coping with the mercurial, aggressive responses of parents in this case proved extremely valuable. Both Sally and her mother exercised their rights to see David to the full. Grandmother also telephoned regularly demanding all manner of information about what they were feeding him and when he was going to bed. On two occasions her visits ended in abrasive exchanges with the Rathbones with grandma sternly reminding them that they were only 'temporary minders' of David and not to get any ideas about keeping him. Thankfully, unlike some very young children newly separated from home, David was not upset by the visits of mother or gran. This made parental visits less fraught for the foster parents.

At the end of David's four weeks in care, the child was returned to Sally as she had moved into her mother's house. Arrangements were made for Sally to pay her debts over time and, as her accommodation was suitable, there was no ostensible reason for the child to remain in care. Sally had missed the child considerably and viewed his return to her not only in terms of personal joy but also as a victory over social services. The fact that David's last three weeks in care was something of a deception in that social services had no legal power to keep the child meant little to her as the memories of the place of safety order still burned bright.

Although David was not in care for long, Sally found visiting a difficult and stressful experience. She received little advice from the social worker on visiting and felt that some children's home staff were particularly unsympathetic to her transport problems. Little was done to provide Sally with a role during her visits to her son and this thrust her into a passive, patient relationship with the staff. The kindly, consistent concern expressed by the staff about David's welfare, although not alien to Sally, was disconcerting as it reflected constantly on her fitful parenting. Sally felt a mixture of incomprehension, guilt and inadequacy at the home when she watched staff effortlessly and enthusiastically perform tasks, like changing nappies, that she found boring and demanding. Consequently, Sally's praise of the care that David received was always tinged with a sense of inadequacy and resentment.

Sally found visiting the foster home easier than her calls at the children's home because the foster parents repeatedly stressed their temporary role and she felt in greater control of the situation. This seemed to be entirely due to her mother's reappearance and her vigorous involvement in maintaining contact with David. In the absence of a trusting relationship with her social worker, Sally's mother assumed control.

An interesting dimension to this case which illustrates the complexity of the issues involved in child care is that the social work intervention had partly been used by Sally to re-establish her relationship with her mother. In a very frank and perceptive interview after David's return, Sally admitted that much of her behaviour prior to the place of safety order and, in particular, leaving David alone that Saturday night was to draw the attention of her mother to her unhappy situation. As Sally said, 'All along, all I wanted was my mum to sort me out. I knew she wouldn't leave me to stew. She loved David and is ready to take on anyone.' Sally's social worker, on reflection, also sensed that David March's entry into care was not simply a question of a child being rescued from danger. He had suspected that some of Sally's health problems were part of the same complex strategy to activate her mother's sympathy. His major concern remained the fragile and possessive aspects of the mother and daughter relationship.

While David's entry and exit from care have some peculiar characteristics in that his mother was healthy and viable, access restrictions were not imposed and there were few barriers inherent in the location and style of placement. Yet we can see that his family situation was typical of the majority of households facing a care intervention. The baby's home situation was precarious and even the shift of Sally back to her mother might only prove temporary. As with most short-term care cases, improvement stemmed largely from changes in the family situation, its location, membership or finance rather than from major shifts in parental or child behaviour or from the benefit of intensive social work intervention. Here, the extended family has rallied round, although it is noticeable that neither the father nor his family were encouraged to participate. Indeed they were not even informed.

The intervention of social services has acted as a catalyst in a simmering situation and in this case, Sally's hostility and sense of violation were important factors in getting the child out of care. While the social worker was uneasy about David's long-term prospects, a case for the child's continued sojourn in care did not exist. Above all, the frequent, sometimes abrasive visits and telephone calls of both Sally and her mother demonstrated clearly to all that the child was much loved. In this situation, David merited an early exit from care, indeed but for fortuitous circumstances, the visibility of the case and lack of contingency planning, he need not have entered care at all.

The case also suggests that the use of place of safety orders for short-term removals of children can have unintended, unfortunate consequences for the trust and cooperation that should exist between social worker and client. Although the use of the order was quite justified in this situation, its wide powers, adversarial status, pejorative antecedents and wording make it a somewhat blunt instrument for a delicate task.

**Summary points**
1.  Half of the 450 children in our study group left care by the time six months had elapsed; indeed, two-thirds of them left within the first six weeks.
2.  However, a child that remains in care for more than six weeks has a 78 per cent chance of spending six months in care and a 63 per cent chance of still being in care after two years have elapsed. This highlights the significance of early decisions and the need for vigorous social work activity on the child's entry to care. Yet case reviews and social work oversight do not always accord with this short timescale.
3.  This pattern of children's exit from care does not reflect the complexity of children's problems on entry but more the expectations of social workers on children's length of stay in care.
4.  The majority of children leave care early because mothers recover from mental or physical illness or because the threat of injury or neglect either diminishes or has been overestimated. Most of these early leavers were in voluntary care and their legal status remained unchanged while they were the responsibility of social services.
5.  The families of early leavers continue to show disruption and dislocation, thus a third of the children returned to households where there has been a major change in membership and/or location. This makes maintaining contact and return very difficult for some children.
6.  As a result, nearly half of the children who left care early were viewed by social workers as likely to return to care in the future and for one-third of the leavers, social workers had strong reservations about the wisdom of children's departure.

7. The oft-made criticism that social workers change rapidly and consequently children are denied continuity of care, is not substantiated for this short-stay group. It is the changes and breakdowns in placements that disrupt the care experience of these children, not the mobility of social workers. While these breakdowns are uncommon among early leavers they increase the longer the children stay in care.

8. Those children whom social workers believe will leave care early are visited more frequently than those who are expected to remain long (see Chapter 9).

9. The majority (77 per cent) of even short-stay children experience some limitations on their contact with home; 25 per cent of the children who left care early experience a specific restriction, usually on a parent, while 61 per cent of children endured non-specific restrictions, that is, barriers inherent in placements.

10. Nevertheless, three-quarters of children who left care early had regular contact with a parent, usually mother. This enabled them to go home, but it is surprising that a quarter of the leavers had little contact with home usually because they were in care for such a short time. Generally, the wider family was less involved in contact and children's exit from care was largely related to changes in their home situation.

# 9. Children who remain in care at six months

In this chapter we look at the characteristics and care experience of the 222 children who have stayed in care for six months. We find that, although these cases received less social work support than early leavers, continuity in social work care has been encouraging, nearly three-quarters of the children have had the same social worker throughout the care experience. Changes of legal status have affected half of the children during the six-month period, usually in the direction of greater social work control. Changes and breakdowns of care placements continue to rise and the characteristics of these vulnerable children are explored. By this stage, the family links can be seen as being increasingly difficult and serious limitations on contact were affecting four-fifths of the children.

We have seen that just over half of the original 450 children who entered care left before six months elapsed. As a result 222 children were still in care at the six-months stage. Of these, 124 were boys and 98 were girls, the same ratio as that for all children at the time of their entry to care.

Those children who stay in care display certain distinct characteristics, notably, they tend to be the older children. On admission, 60 per cent of the 222 were over the age of 10 and 45 per cent over the age of 13, compared with 36 per cent over the age of 10 and 19 per cent over the age of 13 amongst those who had left care by this time. Likewise, only 12 per cent of the long-stay group were less than two years old, in contrast to 27 per cent of the early leavers. There were also differences in the crises that precipitated these children into care. The young people who stayed in care were more likely to display child- rather than family-focused problems. Thus, behaviour difficulties, moral danger, or neglect and abuse were more common presenting problems than situational factors such as parental illness or inability to care. However, we shall see that family attitudes and viability become important reasons for the child's remaining in care.

In retrospect, the family circumstances of these long-stay children at the time of admission into care exhibited severe dislocation. Compared with those children able to to leave care quickly, the parents of long-stay children were more likely to be absent from home and a greater proportion of long-stay youngsters were living with grandparents or with step-parents before entering care. Indeed, some children seemed almost rootless and abandoned and although this long-stay group had many siblings already in care, they were more likely than those who left early to have been admitted on their own. This suggests that the impetus towards their family disintegration has continued over time.

We can see issues highlighted in our previous chapter silhouetted even more clearly as time passes. After six months in care, some children's problems had been resolved or ameliorated, enabling them to return home, while the hopes of others for return to their families were rapidly fading. Indeed, we shall see that for the majority that remained, the last bus home had already left. Hence, while 28 of the 222 children were actually living at home although still legally in care and a further 14 were fostered with close relatives, the remaining 180 were away from home, stranded by a complex set of interacting problems (difficulties of family, health and behaviour) although no single issue seems to dominate. Table 9.1 indicates the reasons for the child's continuing separation.

Table 9.1  **Reasons for the child's continuing separation from the family**

|  | *No. of cases* | % |
|---|---|---|
| Parents unwilling/unable to care | 55 | 31 |
| Behaviour of child | 46 | 26 |
| Risk of neglect or abuse | 45 | 25 |
| Mental illness of parent | 11 | 6 |
| Abandoned/deserted | 10 | 6 |
| Serious family problems | 8 | 4 |
| Death of parent(s) | 4 | 2 |
| Physical illness of parent(s) | 1 | 1 |
|  | (N = 180) |  |

It is interesting to contrast the reasons for the children's entry to care with those constraints that kept them there. The difficult behaviour of the child becomes a less pressing concern as time passes while parental incapacity or indifference greatly increases. The biggest changes are for those originally admitted because of behaviour problems, neglect or parental inability to cope. These children tend to stay in care because of wider deterioration in home circumstances. Neglect is an issue for 12 of the 27 under the age of two, whereas behaviour problems are much more marked among children over six years of age and keep 42 of the 113 young people over the age of 12 in care.

Each of these reasons is supported by other cogent factors. For example, we shall see that parental inability to care for their children may spring from a lack of community or extended family support, may be due to the increasing isolation of lone mothers, to hostile relations between parents and children and in a few cases to the imprisonment or agreed separation of parents. Similarly, the child's behaviour problems may have a family focus, such as being beyond control, or a community focus, such as delinquency or school non-attendance. Even fears of abuse and neglect are varied in detail and include cases where the risk is of sexual exploitation rather than physical assault.

While it is clear that the reasons for children remaining in care are varied and complex, at six months a polarisation of cases becomes clear. A small number of children appear to be on the verge of going out of care so that, for example, social workers plan for ten of the children to leave during the next three months and a further 37 are expected to be discharged within the coming year. Most of these are young children under the age of six. For the majority, however, a longer stay is anticipated, and 74 of the 222 (33 per cent) are seen as likely to be still in care two years hence, that is, some 2½ years after their original admission.

Let us now look at those four aspects of children's care situations that we found useful in scrutinising those children who left care early. Let us look at the oversight they received from social workers, their changes in legislation, placement experience, access arrangements and family links.

## Social work oversight

Of the 222 children still in care at six months 67 had experienced a change of social worker since their reception, and most transfers occurred after the child had initially settled in care, two-thirds taking place ten weeks or more after reception.

The reasons for these changes in social work responsibility were almost all administrative, such as the movement of the child from an intake to a long-term social work team (42 per cent) or replacing a social worker who had left (33 per cent of changes). While the move to an area-based team was important for supervising the children who stay in care, it is noteworthy that administrative reasons initiate changes of social worker, not the needs of the child. Moves to an individual social worker with specialised skills were extremely rare during the first six months, occurring on only two occasions. However, there is a tendency for certain types of cases to be allocated to those staff members who are seen as unlikely to move. Hence, children on care orders for neglect and those for whom parental rights have been assumed are much less likely to have experienced a change of social worker than others. In contrast, children with school difficulties, other behaviour problems or offences will experience more frequent changes in their social workers during the first six months: 55 per cent of these children experienced a change in social worker.

Naturally, children in those local authorities that had intake teams experience more changes of social worker. Intake teams act as a filter to protect social workers from the daily avalanche of requests for help received by social services.[1] While our research would confirm that the intake team approach can successfully filter out many minor problems, we shall find that this does not always follow in practice. The efficacy of an intake team seems to depend on the workload, calibre and experience of staff and their relationship with area teams. However, whatever its other benefits, the intake system does increase a child's chance of changing social workers. We shall also note that, as time passes, some children, even after 12 or 24 months in care, were still the responsibility of intake teams and had not been allocated an area social worker.

Settling a child into care is a demanding task. More than half (57 per cent) of children still in care at six months were visited more than once a fortnight by social workers, and 83 per cent of them were seen at least monthly. The children's families were visited less often with only a quarter of mothers being seen at least once every two weeks. If the child's father was living at home he also was unlikely to have regular meetings with the child's social worker. Indeed, in the six-months period, social workers made no contact with 34 per cent of fathers who were known to be alive (compared with less than 10 per cent for mothers) and only one in seven of fathers saw a social worker more than once a fortnight. While these visits to families might be regular, social workers did not exude a sense of urgency in seeking the child's rehabilitation at home. Rather, they displayed a sense of wait-and-see, in contrast to the early leavers described in Chapter 8. Considerable social work effort was made to facilitate their return home, with 74 per cent of mothers and 31 per cent of fathers being seen at least once a fortnight. The lower level of social work contact for children who remain in care may be a reason for their continued stay, a feature which will be noted later in Chapter 11.[2]

It was also clear that social work oversight varied considerably across the five areas involved in our study. Despite a few cases of maladministration, such as some children who had no current social worker or the families who have remained with intake teams because plans for transfer have been thwarted, social workers do offer some stability in relationships. Some 70 per cent of children had the same worker during their first six months in care as they had on reception. It is also clear that children, mothers and placements are visited regularly, although foster situations received scanter scrutiny than did residential care, a finding which parallels other studies.[3]

## Legislation

Half of the 222 children still in care at six months had changed their legal status since reception. All the legislative moves increased social work control. The original 44 care orders remained in force without modification and by six months a further 82 care orders had been made. When twelve interim care orders and four matrimonial orders are included, we see that no fewer than 142 (64 per cent) of the children remain in care under the legislation which gives complete control to local authorities' social services.

There is a shift away from voluntary care where responsibilities are shared between the local authority and the child's parents. Of the original 97 children voluntarily received into care, a third now experience care legislation which restricts parental rights, leaving only 66 (30 per cent) in care voluntarily. As might have been expected, the 75 place of safety orders have changed, all but one being followed by care orders, 11 of which are still interim.

It seems that those families whose children stay in care for more than six months experience increasing social services control. The moves to assume greater power over children and, indirectly, their families, are consistent and undeviating. Care orders for neglect and abuse increase from two to 50, and there is a rapid rise in numbers of children in care for moral danger and for being beyond control, which helps justify increasing and varied constraint. Interestingly, care orders for delinquency or for educational problems rise less over the six-month period although they were relatively common initially. It will be noted shortly that moves towards greater control by social workers of the child's care situation which could facilitate links between children in care and their parents seem, in fact, to increase parental passivity and indifference.

After six months, the number of care orders in force contrasts

Table 9.2   **Percentage of full care orders in various categories**

| *Children and Young Persons Act 1969* | *Admission* | *6 months* |
|---|---|---|
| | % | % |
| s.1.2(a)(b) neglect/ill treatment | 4 | 38 |
| s.1.2(c) moral danger | 4 | 8 |
| s.1.2(d) beyond control | 2 | 12 |
| s.1.2(e) FT education | 29 | 11 |
| s.1.2(f), 7(7) offending | 51 | 24 |
| Other | 7 | 4 |
| Matrimonial causes | 2 | 3 |
| | (N = 45 | 130) |

sharply with the situation at the time of the child's reception into care. Issues of neglect, abuse and control come to dominate the care orders, while the significance of full-time education and offending diminish. These differences become even more marked when the twelve cases that are still covered by interim care orders are fully resolved. Table 9.2 shows the proportions of children in care under various categories:

**Children's changes of placement during the first six months in care**
The changes and breakdowns in placement which we have noted characterised some short-stay children continue to cause concern with those children who stay in care, since 136 of the 222 children still in care at six months had changed their placements following reception. Some moved to more suitable placements, others left temporary situations. In a number of cases, however, the substitute care arrangements simply broke down. Hence, when we compare the children's situations at six months with their initial placements, we can see that some children shift more frequently than others. For example, few children remain in hospital and some have moved to community homes with education. Overall, there is a drift towards residential care rather than to fostering, with 26 per cent of those initially fostered now finding themselves in residential care at six months, while only 13 per cent of children leave residential homes for fostering. There also appear to be fewer children leaving foster placements for home, much less than for residential establishments. These patterns are indicated in Table 9.3.

**Table 9.3   Changes in type of placement between entry and six months**

| Placement on entry | Placement at six months | | | |
|---|---|---|---|---|
| | Home or fostered with relatives | Foster home | Residential | N |
| | % | % | % | |
| Home or fostered with relatives | 86 | 5 | 9 | 22 |
| Foster home | 4 | 70 | 26 | 57 |
| Residential | 15 | 13 | 73 | 143 |
| | | | | (N = 222) |

During the first six months in care, 117 of the 222 children (53 per cent) experienced some kind of residential placement and 97 (44 per cent) a foster placement. Within the residential sector, some placements were more common than others with O and A centres being used for 86 of the children.

## Placement breakdowns

As we have already indicated, 38 of the 222 children experienced a placement breakdown in the first six months and had to be moved elsewhere. For some children, this happened more than once so that in all 48 placements were involved. Of these, two-thirds (32) broke down under crisis conditions necessitating the hasty and unplanned removal of the child, whereas for the other 16, the breakdown precipitated intended plans. The majority of these crises (60 per cent) occurred in the residential sector and 37 per cent in foster homes.

**Table 9.4   Frequency of breakdowns in different types of placements**

| | *Numbers of breakdowns* | | | |
| *Type of breakdown* | *Residential* | *Foster home* | *Home* | *Fostered with relatives* |
|---|---|---|---|---|
| Crisis | 17 | 9 | 5 | 1 |
| Precipitating intended change | 12 | 4 | 0 | 0 |

When we examine all the living situations experienced by the 222 children, including the one in which they were currently placed, we find that there are 420 placements in all during the first six months; 13 per cent of these placements have broken down, two-thirds of them under crisis conditions. Looked at in this way, the residential context, with a breakdown of 10 per cent fares slightly better than fosterings, where there is a breakdown rate of 13 per cent, and placements at home with the family, where the rate is 14 per cent.

**Table 9.5   Percentage of breakdowns in different types of placements**

| *Type of breakdown* | *Residential* | *Foster home* | *Home* | *Fostered with relatives* |
|---|---|---|---|---|
| Crisis | 6 | 9 | 14 | 7 |
| Precipitating intended change | 4 | 4 | 0 | 0 |
| | (N = 270 | 100 | 35 | 15) |

These figures, of course, are the *minimum* rates of breakdown for various settings as they include ongoing placements which might collapse in the future. Another way of calculating rates could have looked at the proportion of breakdowns among only those placements that are finished, that is, excluding the child's current situation. However, such comparisons are misleading as home and fostering placements are more likely than residential care to be concluded because of a breakdown. Hence, the proportions of breakdowns in both of these would have appeared unduly high.

Breakdowns add a complication to any care plan. One in eight of all placements experienced by children still in care at six months have broken down prematurely, two-thirds of them in crisis conditions. In addition, a quarter of all placements completed by children during the first six months have broken down. While such disruptions only affect a minority of children in care, social workers express considerable anxiety over their frequency because subsequent satisfactory placements are more difficult to achieve.

Naturally, the reasons for placement breakdowns are very varied. For a third of the children, social workers admit the original placement was inappropriate. They suggest that good foster homes are difficult to find and require considerable support. However, in residential situations disruptive behaviour and persistent absconding on the part of the child were the main reasons put forward. In foster situations less responsibility was placed on the child for collapse and frequently moves from fostering were precipitated by problems within the foster home itself. Marital tensions, the need to care for elderly relatives, pregnancy and illness of the foster mother can all precipitate difficulties for the foster child. Interestingly, problems posed by the child's parents were rarely a factor leading to placement breakdown. While this is frequently advanced by social workers and care-givers as a reason for restricting parental access, difficulties with parents led to placement breakdown in only five cases.

The role of residential care is particularly important in providing for children who have experienced disruption. Fourteen children who experienced a crisis either at home or in foster care were transferred into residential placements. In contrast, only four children left residential care for either foster care or home.

It is clear, therefore, that 61 per cent of the children who experienced a placement breakdown moved to residential care, especially to O and A centres or to ordinary community homes, which seem to cater for these crisis admissions. Indeed, a third of the young people living in O and A centres at the six-month stage and 18 per cent of those in children's homes have changed their type of placement as a result of crisis, compared with only 10 per cent of those in foster homes.

## Characteristics of children at risk of breakdown

All children in care risk a breakdown in and/or transfer between placements. Girls are slightly more vulnerable than boys and those expected by social workers to remain long in care display equally unsettled care careers as do those whose return home is imminent.

Adolescents, however, are more prone to placement crises than are the younger children and a quarter of children in care over the age of 12 at six months will have experienced a placement breakdown. In addition, children taken into care for neglect or behaviour problems are more prone to placement crises than are those whose families can no longer care for them. Hence, children removed from home under place of safety or care orders experience more unintended changes than do voluntary receptions. While, in general, limitations on parental contact imposed by distance, location or access arrangements did not appear to affect the transfer and placement breakdown of children, regular contact with natural mother greatly moderates the crisis nature of many breakdowns and transfers as will be further explored in Chapter 11.

Placement breakdowns are an important feature of the child-care process. They are frequent, having already affected one in eight of the children still in care at six months and account for a quarter of all changes experienced in children's living situations by this time. Breakdowns also severely limit future placement possibilities and frequently propel children into residential care. It is also clear from our evidence that all children in care are vulnerable to breakdown and no one group can readily be identified as presenting a disproportionately high risk. While adolescents seem more prone to sudden moves, these often merely bring forward anticipated changes, whereas for younger children and for those expected to remain with substitute families, breakdowns usually arise from serious crises. This has clear implications for children's future careers, the options open to social workers and the decisions about the role of the child's natural family in the care process. As was apparent from our scrutiny of early leavers, for some children stable care is difficult to achieve.

### The family and their links with the separated child

We saw in Chapter 8 that social workers became increasingly concerned about the family links of children as they stay in care. Yet in the selection of placements, contact with home is only one of several influential factors. As we have seen, the placement choices are primarily concerned with matching the child's individual needs with the provision available, and access to the natural family is usually a secondary consideration. Indeed, it only seems to have been discussed as an issue for two-fifths of those still in care at six months. This pattern is especially clear when we examine social work reviews which should be undertaken on the child at regular intervals.

By the time six months had elapsed, 169 of the 222 children had been reviewed, and case conferences were imminent for many of the remainder. The reviews of children's care situations carefully evaluated current placement experiences and just over half in their conclusions recommended a continuation of the arrangements. Residential placements in particular received close attention and much closer scrutiny than did foster homes.

The discussions sought confirmation of existing care plans rather than consideration of fresh initiatives. For example, the reason for the child's original admission to care, the suitability of the current placement and conditions at home at the time of review received much greater consideration than expectations about the child's future or why the child had to remain in care, a feature also noted by Fruin and Vernon.[4] Consequently, while attention focused on situations at home, the child's access arrangements to the natural family or the contact he or she was enjoying featured less frequently in discussion. Indeed, in 39 per cent of cases, access between the child and natural mother was not even raised as an issue, and contact with father or the wider family received less consideration still.

There was even less concern over children's social networks outside the family. School, youth club and neighbourhood friendships were seldom raised, except to express concern over some undesirable peer-group relationships. Yet, we know that, particularly in adolescence, friendships outside the family, usually centred on school, have great significance for children.[5] This may partly explain why adolescents in residential care often maintain contact with other children in the care system rather than develop friendships outside; it may also account for Lasson's finding that good links between absent children and their families facilitated the maintenance of other wider social networks.[6]

Overall, when considering children's family and wider social networks, there is an intrinsic assumption in discussion that everyone, including the child himself, is familiar with the reasons for access arrangements. As a result, and quite unintentionally, a wait-and-see policy often becomes an acceptable course of action, especially for adolescents, and little additional social work effort into the maintenance of links between child and family is recommended. This was often at odds with social workers' expressed intentions.

In situations where family links were an issue at case reviews, half (51 per cent) of the recommendations were to change existing policies. For 30 per cent of the 222 children, these decisions were to try to increase contact as opposed to 21 per cent to reduce it. Although social workers express satisfaction with these arrangements and family contacts do not loom large as an issue in case reviews, social worker anxiety over access arrangements and family links is considerable. It is the one issue on which the uneasy consensus put up at case reviews can disintegrate and call into question all other decisions.

The families of children in care as we have already noted, are by no means simple in structure or unchanging. The crises, when they occur, frequently affect all children in the family. Thus, many children in care are placed with siblings. This situation applies to 85 of the 222 children still in care at six months, that is, 40 per cent of those children who have brothers and sisters. Clearly, the requirements to keep siblings together will affect placement decisions or raise the issue of maintaining sibling contact. This was mentioned by many social workers as a serious limitation to the care plans that they could adopt. While siblings were often placed together, occasionally different placements were deliberately selected for each child. Half of these arose because children were seen to have different needs but for the remainder there was simply the problem of too many children for one placement. Sometimes this was solved by using residential care. Naturally, when siblings are separated this greatly complicates the parents' ability to stay in contact or for siblings to enjoy a continuing relationship. In addition, 20 children were actually separated from their siblings during the first six months in care because of difficulties within the placements.

The turbulence which characterised the families of children who left care early is an even more marked feature in the homes of children who stay in care. As time progresses these instabilities greatly affect the maintenance of links with parents. For example, 85 of the 222 children in care at six months came from single-parent households and in only one-third of cases are the natural parents still married to each other. In addition, half the households have a fluctuating and unstable membership. For example, the families of 95 (43 per cent) underwent a major structural change during the six-months period. In addition, 115 of the children who remain in care have natural, half- or step-siblings living outside these households all of whom could raise additional problems in the maintenance of contact. The families present a wearying kaleidoscope of arrivals and departures, of moves and returns.

Indeed, from Table 9.6 we can see that many of the households from which these long-term children come into care will change radically even in the space of six months; if anything, they are likely to lose rather than gain members. The child's situation is not simply one of indifferent relatives or parents ignorant of their child's whereabouts (in only 10 per cent of cases did parents actually not know their child's address) but contact is hindered by constant upheaval in the households and diminishing prospects of ever being able to care for the child.

Younger children (under the age of 5) are far more likely than adolescents to come from families undergoing major changes and this is reflected in their placements and care histories. For example, 50 of

**Table 9.6  Changes in children's family structures in first six months of care**

| Leaving the pre-care household | | Moving into the pre-care household | |
| --- | --- | --- | --- |
| | N | | N |
| Mother | 16 | Mother | 1 |
| Father | 27 | Father | 5 |
| Siblings | 10 | Step-parent/co-habitee | 21 |
| Grandparents | 2 | New baby | 3 |
| Step-parent/co-habitee | 10 | | |

(Total study group N = 222)

the 95 children experiencing family changes are in foster homes, 13 are living with their natural families or relatives, leaving 32 in residential care. Yet the quality of family relationships is not necessarily related to the extent of these changes. Many children whose families have reconstructed or dissolved are expected to leave care in the foreseeable future while others begin to loom as long-term care problems. In 42 per cent of cases, social workers indicated that even in the short time since the child's reception to care, there had, in their opinion, been a significant change in the feelings of the child towards mother – 27 per cent for the better and 15 per cent for the worse. This is reciprocated by shifts in the mother's relationship with her child – 27 per cent improving and only 10 per cent deteriorating. Similar patterns obtain for other members of the family who may be significant to the child: fathers, step-parents, grandparents and siblings.

These changes in relationships have serious implications for policy and practice because the relationship between the mother and her child is closely related to the contact she chooses to make. These feelings can change even within six months. However, there is often a time-lag and specific restrictions on contact are slow to change and remain in force long after improvements in relationships have taken place. In addition, non-specific barriers to contact, that is, those inherent in the placements, can endure for much longer. Similarly, the children's feelings for their close relatives frequently improve as the care experience continues, and here again improved relationships do not necessarily lead to greater contact and often access arrangements remain unaltered for long periods. Children find it difficult to influence patterns of contact in any way, and many with irregular contact with their parents fail to agitate social workers for increased links, although some resourceful adolescents fitfully evade access restrictions.

In any discussion of the problem of maintaining links between child and parents, we can see that the child's family situation is not constant even for a short period. While family members can be preoccupied with adapting to new structures, similarly children have to forge new understandings and cope with changes in the qualities and patterns of relationships amongst their closest relatives. Clearly, this is no easy task for them to manage or for the social workers who befriend and counsel them. There is scope for much professional development here and a need to incorporate more effectively into reviews, planning and practice the changes that occur in the child's family and in the attitudes of parents, care-givers and in the children themselves.[7]

### The maintenance of family links

The polarisations noted earlier are clear when we examine the contacts between children and their natural families. Many children in care are able to enjoy frequent contact with their relatives and have homes which are stable if still unable to care. But for other children their families have not only changed in structure but also have lost touch and the child's chances of returning home seem slight.

By six months, as a result of turbulent homes, changes and break-downs of placements, the restrictions on contact both imposed and inherent in placements, links with home are increasingly difficult to sustain for many children. Indeed, by six months a serious limitation on contact with the natural family was affecting 182 of the children, that is, 82 per cent of the children who remained. It will be remembered that in the previous chapter we distinguished between those barriers to contact which were specific to individuals such as a step-father or siblings and those barriers which are inherent in the place-ment (non-specific restrictions). After six months has elapsed, it is interesting to see the extent of these limitations on the relationship between parents and those children who were still in care.

### Specific restrictions

At six months 109 children (49 per cent) out of the 222 still in care were experiencing a specific restriction, that is access to a child of a significant adult, usually parent or step-parent, was restricted. For the majority of cases (94) the specific restriction was part of the social work plan for the child, while for the other 15 the restrictions were imposed by relatives or by the children themselves. Naturally, such restrictions will affect ongoing relationships. In 30 per cent of the cases it was the child's mother who was restricted, compared with 28 per cent for fathers and 15 per cent for step-parents. While some of these restrictions were imposed to protect the child from abuse or distress, social workers believed that many specific restrictions helped to maintain the stability of placements. The varied reasons for restricting access of individuals to children are laid out in Table 9.7.

**Table 9.7 Reasons for imposing specific restrictions on links with the child's natural family***

| | % |
|---|---|
| Child alleged to reject or to be indifferent to parents | 54 |
| Parents alleged to reject or to be indifferent to child | 53 |
| Child in danger of abuse or neglect | 53 |
| Parents likely to disrupt placement | 38 |
| Parents have actually disrupted placement | 17 |
| Parents a bad moral influence | 17 |
| Child likely to be delinquent | 7 |
| Child likely to abscond | 7 |
| | (N = 109) |

* Categories not mutually exclusive.

In 49 cases, children were forbidden all contact with parents, while the remainder enjoyed only controlled links with home. Many restrictions were imposed on the frequency of visiting, the place of visit and strict insistence on supervision of the contact, although the functions of such supervision were not always clear to participants.

Specific restrictions enforced by social workers are clearly more easily applied under certain legislation and in particular placements. They are most frequent among children for whom parental rights have been assumed and where care orders have been taken for neglect, moral danger and matrimonial disputes. Although restrictions are much less common for voluntary and other types of care situations, specific restrictions, usually applied by children or relatives, still affect a third of those children in voluntary care. Our evidence also indicates that specific restrictions affect younger children and will be most common in foster placements. Nevertheless, it is surprising how frequently specific restrictions imposed by the child's relatives impinge even on children placed at home or with relatives, indicating that such placements do not necessarily resolve family difficulties and are seen by social workers to require careful supervision.

*Non-specific restrictions*
Non-specific restrictions on contact with home, that is, limitations inherent in separation and placements, were also very widespread amongst children in care at six months, affecting 65 per cent of the 222 children. They generally sprang from rules governing the frequency and places of visiting, particularly in residential care. In addition, the

health, financial and shift-work problems faced by families often presented great difficulties to maintaining contact.

## Changes in restrictions

It is important to note, however, that these restrictions on contact between parents and children, do not remain static during the six-months period. During this time both specific and non-specific restrictions change considerably. For example, of the 109 cases where specific restrictions are in force, 72 have operated continuously since reception while 37 have been applied subsequently. Only 25 of the children who experienced specific restrictions at the time of their admission now find barriers to access removed. Hence, for only half of the cases (46 per cent) affected by specific restrictions has the same pattern persisted throughout the full six-months period. The longer the social workers expect the child to stay in care, especially in foster homes, the more likely the care plan will increase restrictions on parental access. Restrictions of contact do not diminish over time and patterns set early on tend to prevail.

These patterns are reflected in the frequency of visiting and contact with close relatives recorded for our study group. Among the 222 children still in care at six months, there is considerable variety in the amount of contact they have with their natural families. At the six-months stage, 28 per cent of the children were seeing their mothers at least once a week, and 59 per cent more than once a month. Younger children were usually visited by their relatives or, in fraught situations, met their parents on neutral ground. Adolescents, in contrast, were more likely to visit parents from placements, especially if in residential care. However, at six months, no clear arrangements have emerged and all children meet parents in a variety of settings. In contrast, 17 per cent of children have no contact at all with their parents during this period. These are mostly children in care for neglect, abuse or desertion. The patterns of contact are clearly shown in Table 9.8.

Naturally, in individual cases there will be considerable variations from these patterns – some children will experience an increase in contact with parents, others a decline. For half the children, levels of contact have remained constant. Nevertheless, overall these figures should give some cause for concern. Decline in parental contact was affecting one in five of our study group after six months in care had elapsed. The care experience for a minority is one of increasing isolation from home while for others there is continuous contact and hopes of eventual rehabilitation. Our statistical prediction described elsewhere on children's length of stay in care confirms that children iso-

Table 9.8   Frequency of child's contact with close relatives*

|  | Natural mother | Natural father | Step- mother | Step father | Siblings | Grand- parents |
|---|---|---|---|---|---|---|
|  | % | % | % | % | % | % |
| More than once a week | 28 | 12 | 1 | 6 | 35 | 9 |
| Once a week–once a month | 31 | 20 | 3 | 8 | 16 | 14 |
| Less than once a month/irregular | 16 | 19 | 3 | 4 | 11 | 7 |
| No contact | 17 | 43 | 14 | 14 | 8 | 9 |
| Not applicable | 7 | 6 | 79 | 68 | 28 | 33 |
| Not known or cannot be accurately assessed | 1 | 0 | 0 | 1 | 3 | 28 |
|  |  |  | (N = 222) |  |  |  |

* Frequency is based on pattern prevailing for at least 75 per cent of study period.

lated from their natural families by this stage have no hope of leaving care (except if adopted) by the time two years have elapsed.[8]

Nevertheless, it is also important to note that half the children are able to maintain links with relatives in other ways, such as by telephone and, less frequently, by letters and contacts through friends. A quarter of the children in care at six months were contacting their natural families in this way at least once a fortnight, but again for a minority (11 per cent), there were neither visits nor contacts of these other kinds.

For just under two-thirds of the children (61 per cent), their families (64 per cent) and social workers (64 per cent), these patterns were perceived as satisfactory, even where there was little or no visiting. In a few cases, the child's best interest seemed to be served by a lack of contact and for some, relations between the child in care and the family were often fraught with unresolved emotional tensions. It certainly does not follow that the more frequent the contact, the greater the satisfaction. Indeed, our intensive study indicates that more important than the rate of how often contact occurs is the freedom for parents and children to manage visits and interaction on their own terms and unimpeded by the covert barriers we have already described. Hence, it is significant that nearly all (90 per cent) those children and families who were dissatisfied with existing arrangements sought more contact with each other and more freedom in managing the meetings, a *rapprochement* viewed less than enthusiastically by social workers.

At the six-months stage, therefore, we can see several interesting patterns with regard to the care experience of our study cohort. Some have managed to retain regular links with their families while others have lost contact: some are content in their placements while others are unsettled, some seem likely to return home shortly but others are clearly destined for long stays in care. And as we have seen, the care experience itself is not always stable and placements are often difficult to sustain.

While only a minority (17 per cent) of children living away from home appear seriously unsettled in their placements at six months, problems can be aggravated for some by lack of parental contact and the indifference of close relatives. Indeed, our evidence indicates a clear association between a decrease in family contact and unsettled behaviour. We have noted that at six months, in only a third of the placements is the child fully settled. For example, while two-thirds of fosterings appear to be satisfactory for the child, many young children still find this sort of placement insecure. Anxiety is even greater in residential homes which are often holding or temporary shelters, particularly for older children presenting behaviour problems. This becomes clear in the intensive study from the assessments made by foster parents or residential staff of the children's adaptations to their current placements at the six-month stage.

Table 9.9  Child's adaptation to current placement

|  | *Foster homes* | *Residential* |
|---|---|---|
|  | % | % |
| Fully settled and integrated with adults and peers | 68 | 23 |
| Strongly identified with placement but holds back in relationships | 15 | 16 |
| Not really integrated within placement, is not at ease | 7 | 13 |
| Child at ease in placement, but conscious of temporary nature of situation | 8 | 31 |
| Child not integrated in placement, is something of a stranger | 2 | 8 |
| Too early to say/not known | 0 | 8 |
|  | (N = 59 | 121) |

Generally, in residential placements we have found that children with little contact with parents are the most ill-at-ease, confirming Lasson's findings on children in long-stay homes and echoing the work of Hall, Stacey and Oswin on children in hospitals.[9] Increased contact with home also reduces problem behaviour in absentee children.

In foster care the situation is more complex as both the studies of Weinstein and Thorpe have demonstrated.[10] Children who do not have regular contact with their mother show diverse patterns, with over half well settled while the remainder show various signs of stress. Children in foster homes are more upset by changes in existing arrangements, either when long-absent family figures reappear or, more often, when there is a reduction in contact with home. Relations between the child's foster family and the natural parents are also likely to deteriorate.

These relationships are clear for children in care at six months as shown in Tables 9.10 and 9.11. Social workers' and other care-givers' estimates of children's adaptation to placements associate children's difficulties with levels of parental contact and changes in visiting patterns.

**Table 9.10  The effects of frequency of parental contact on children's adaptation to placement**

| | Foster care | | | Residential care | | |
|---|---|---|---|---|---|---|
| % of children | More than monthly | Less than monthly | N* | More than monthly | Less than monthly | N |
| | % | % | | % | % | |
| Well-settled | 57 | 34 | 83 | 63 | 22 | 49 |
| Not settled | 59 | 36 | 22 | 54 | 44 | 50 |
| Other | 25 | 75 | 12 | 67 | 29 | 55 |

*Notes:* Results significant at .05 level on chi-square test, except for frequency of parental contact and placement adaptation in foster care ($p < 0.2$).
* For remaining children, categories do not apply.

These patterns, however, are clouded over time, for at two years there is no clear relationship between parental contact and children's placement adaptation. This is because, by this stage, some children in foster homes are ready for adoption and are settled although they have no links with their natural families and many adolescents in residential care are on the point of leaving. Hence they can display 'gate fever' and be very disruptive yet still have strong family links.

Nevertheless, as time passes the relationship between family contact and child behaviour continues to apply to groups of children in care, such as those who have neither family links nor satisfactory placements. These children, as we shall see, cause social workers concern on many criteria. It will be recalled that Lasson, Wallerstein and Kelly

**Table 9.11  The effects of changes in frequency of parental contact on children's adaptation to placement**

| % of children with behaviour problems | Foster care | | | Residential care | | |
|---|---|---|---|---|---|---|
| | Increase | Decrease | No change | Increase | Decrease | No change |
| | % | % | % | % | % | % |
| Some | 18 | 47 | 46 | 32 | 65 | 47 |
| None | 82 | 53 | 54 | 68 | 35 | 53 |
| | (N* = 34 | 32 | 48 | 53 | 31 | 64) |

Results significant at .05 level on chi-square test.
*For remaining children, categories do not apply.

and Fanshel found a strong correlation in their studies between parental visiting and child functioning, but it is important to stress that they were only considering sub-groups of children in care and the more complex patterns revealed here spring from the scope of the study group – all children entering care.[11]

Interestingly, although 30 of the 195 children in care at six months were unsettled in their placements and 67 were difficult in behaviour, social workers' and foster parents' estimates of disturbance are considerably lower than those obtained in clinical surveys of children in care, such as those discussed by Wolkind.[12] This sanguine attitude to child disturbance is further evidenced by the frequency with which social workers are surprised by placement breakdown.

Frequently, the response by social workers to difficulties posed by children consequent on changes in parental visiting patterns is to reduce contact further. Consequently, social workers are faced with an extremely serious situation as the child's isolation from home is exacerbated by a miserable care experience. The child rapidly becomes a candidate for transfer or breakdown. Ten children can be clearly identified as facing these problems at the six-months stage with a further 20 likely to present such problems in the near future.

## Conclusions

The picture of children still in care at six months is one of transitory light and shade with gathering squalls. Depending on one's perspective of social work interventions, the findings can offer modest satisfaction or cause considerable misgivings. It should be stressed that 40 per cent of the children in care at six months are in stable settings, have experienced continuity of social worker and satisfaction is expressed by parents, care-givers and social workers over their situation. Even the majority of children in their behaviour as reported by social workers or in interviews with us are quiescent. In addition to the majority of children who have already left care, a small number will be expected to leave, during the next six months as situations improve, with most of them returning home. Indeed, there is a widening of the polarity we noticed in Chapter 8, where some children were highly likely to return home while for others the prospective length of stay in care increases. Naturally, as we trace the careers of those children that stay in care over time the less comforting will be the picture presented. Just as those children who enter care can be seen as the failures of preventative efforts with families, so many children who remain in care increasingly appear as the casualties of the system.

Nevertheless, it is this group of prospective long-stay cases that should cause anxiety. We have seen that there is a shift in the reasons why children stay in care compared with the causes for their admission. Secondary problems appear both within the child's family and the placement. As increasing knowledge of families' and children's difficulties accumulate, social workers revise their perspectives and seek wider controls. Thus, there is considerable legislative change involving those who stay longer than six months in care. Voluntary participation of parents in the care process declines, ideals of shared care wither and care orders increase.

The families from which these children come remain poor, disrupted and either unwilling or unable to care. The same radical changes that characterise the families of those children who left care early are even more noticeable among those children who stay. By six months nearly half (43 per cent) of the children will have experienced a major change in their family structure. There is a familiar succession of evictions and resettlement, of dissolution and reconstitution, with the arrival and departure of co-habitees, lodgers, relatives, half- and step-siblings, while the extended family sits censoriously by. Indeed, the rapid change in relationships and settings, reminiscent of an endless and wearying game of Postman's Knock, is a marked characteristic of the families of children in care. These oscillations are most noticeable among the families of younger children, a factor which not only prevents their return home and affects their wider relationships, but also greatly hinders contact between parents and children.

Yet, the instability and insecurity we noted among children whose stay in care was short still characterise a minority of those who stay longer. More than half the children still in care at six months will have moved their placements, although the majority that shift will have experienced planned changes, for example from an O and A centre to a children's or foster home. One in six of those children who are in care at six months will have experienced a breakdown in their placement and will have been transferred. It is regrettable that a minority of children should have had their previous rejections, insecurities and anxieties reinforced by their care experience.

### Summary points
1. 222 children were still in care at six months (124 boys and 98 girls). Sixty per cent of those who stay were over the age of 10 and 45 per cent over 13.
2. Children stay in care increasingly because of parental incapacity or indifference. The households from which they come continue to show turbulence and disruption. Contact between absent child and parent is hindered by such upheavals and by the diminishing prospects of the child ever returning home. Relationships between mother and absent child fluctuate during separation and

these need constant scrutiny by social workers because these changes affect the contacts mother chooses to seek.

3. Declining chances of return are reflected by changes in children's legal status – by now 64 per cent of children remain in care under legislation which gives complete control to social services.

4. While the majority of children in care continue to enjoy stability in their contacts with social workers, changes of social worker have affected one-third of the children at six months. These moves are almost entirely for administrative reasons. The visiting of children remains frequent but social workers show no sense of urgency in seeking the return home of the child, in contrast with the efforts made with those children who left care early. Visits to the child's parents begin to decline.

5. While social workers increasingly express concern over links between absent child and parent, in the selection of placements and reviews of children's situations, access arrangements and levels of contact were not given high priority.

6. By six months 20 per cent of children had experienced a placement breakdown or a precipitate transfer. These occurred because of inappropriate initial placements, because of the difficult behaviour of adolescents in residential situations and because of changes within foster homes. Disruption of placements is very rarely caused by parental visiting. While this may arise because potentially abrasive parents have been denied access, the exclusion of many parents for this reason seems over-zealous.

7. By six months many children in care were able to enjoy frequent contacts with parents and relatives and a small number were on the point of going home. But declining parental contact was affecting 20 per cent of those children who remained in care.

8. 109 (49 per cent) of the 222 children still in care at six months were experiencing restrictions on their access to specific adults; 65 per cent of the children also suffered non-specific restrictions on contact, problems inherent in placement routines, distance and accessibility. Restrictions on contact generally do not diminish. The longer the social worker expects the child to stay in care, especially in foster homes, the more likely it is that the care plan will impose restrictions on parental and family access. Restrictions set early on tend to linger.

9. More distressing to parents than the frequency of contact or access restrictions on specific individuals are the limitations placed on parents and children's freedom to manage visits and interaction in their own way.

10. In residential placements children are happier and function better as the result of parental and family contacts while in foster situations changes in parental visiting seems to cause stress in children and friction with care-givers.

# 10. Children still in care at twelve months [*]

Between six and twelve months, a further 27 children left care, leaving 195 children still the responsibility of social services. This chapter looks at their characteristics and continuing care experience. We shall see that, as time passes, things settle down; social work involvement with children diminishes markedly, there are fewer changes in the child's legal status and fewer planned changes in the care placements. Nevertheless, placement breakdowns and the precipitate transfer of children continue unchecked. By twelve months, the problems of maintaining links between parent and absent child have increased, with as many as two-fifths of the children virtually isolated in care. We explore the reasons for this withering of parental contact with their children and how significant social workers now view the child's situation.

One advantage of adopting a process approach to child-care careers is that it highlights fluctuations in social work practice.[1] At some points, access arrangements are scrutinised, parental contact is carefully examined, appropriate legislation is sought and children rapidly pass through a variety of placements, while at other times the situation is more tranquil. We have seen that the first two months of the child's stay in care, for example, were particularly significant, with 30 per cent of our study group leaving care, while for those who remained the early months involved much change and disruption. During the early days of children's care careers, families were also turbulent, unable or unwilling to cope with their children.

In the period between six and twelve months after reception into care, things seem to settle down and there is a considerable drop in the number of changes experienced by children. Let us look at the careers during the second six months in care of those young people who remain, assessing changes in social work oversight, the legislation employed, the child's placement experience and the links enjoyed with the natural family.

Only a small proportion (27) of the study population were able to leave care in the six months period leaving 195 of our original 450 still in care after one year. The changes experienced by those who stay are not only less frequent but also less radical than in the first six months, and they consolidate rather than reverse the trends noted earlier. The ratio of boys to girls, for example, remains constant at 56:44, while the age distribution of children confirms the tendency for adolescents to remain in care along with a few long-stay younger children. The latter are often the victims of severe neglect. Adolescents, consequently, form a greater proportion of the total as time passes.

Table 10.1   **Ages of children in care at various times**

| Age of child | Admission | 6 months | 12 months |
|---|---|---|---|
| | % | % | % |
| 0–2 years | 18 | 12 | 11 |
| 3–5 | 19 | 13 | 10 |
| 6–11 | 25 | 24 | 25 |
| 12 and over | 38 | 51 | 53 |
| | (N = 450 | 222 | 195) |

The reasons why children stay in care or remain away from home have also altered little from the situation described at six months. There is hardly any change of emphasis in the main reasons given for children remaining in care. Social workers stress that parents are unwilling or unable to care, that the child risks neglect or that behaviour remains problematic. These constraints apply to three-quarters of the children still in care at twelve months.

Other aspects of the care situation change little. The use of residential care is still extensive, with no increase in the use of fostering, but movements between placements are less common than in the earlier period. Changes in legislation decline as time progresses. Access arrangements remain similar to those at six months with the non-specific restrictions inherent in many placements continuing to discourage parental links. Indeed, the earlier social work strategy of wait and see now emphasises the 'wait' rather than the 'see', for social work activity with this group of long-stay children shows a marked decline. Indeed, during this time there is almost no change in social work plans with the exception of six children for whom adoption is now a serious consideration.

Let us now look in greater detail at the careers of the 195 children still in care at twelve months. As the findings reiterate much that is familiar from earlier chapters, we have chosen to highlight changes in children's situations rather than repeat previous details. Let us first consider the provision of social work oversight.

**Social work oversight**
Forty-one of the 195 children (21 per cent) changed social worker in the second six-months period, a slight reduction on earlier patterns.

As before, the reasons for change were largely administrative, and were not the result of new social work plans or allocations to specialist workers. Generally, the arrival of a new social worker which occurred in nine cases did not seriously affect social work plans for the child. Although there are a few examples in the cohort where major decisions, such as a child's placement or patterns of family links, have been radically changed by a new social worker, these changes are uncharacteristic of the care careers of the majority of children. In any case, during their first year in care, as many as 57 per cent of the 195 children who remain in care have had the same social worker throughout: a further 37 per cent of children have experienced only one transfer.

Although there are few changes in social worker, they are less involved with children and their families during the second half of the year: levels of social work input decline. Social workers report that, for half their cases, contact with clients and support for families, placements and children is less than before. At twelve months, 39 per cent of the children were being seen once a fortnight compared with 56 per cent at the six-months stage. Social workers also see less of the child's natural parents, with only 17 per cent of mothers and 6 per cent of fathers receiving regular visits. In some cases, contact has been lost altogether, and 15 per cent of mothers and 40 per cent of fathers are no longer in touch with the child's social worker. Indeed, by twelve months care situations have stabilised to a point of acceptance or resignation by all participants. While a sense of urgency over the continuing care careers of children has seldom been a feature of case reviews, by twelve months acquiescence in the present situation is general.

### Changes in legal status
The legal status of children who remain in care at twelve months did not change radically during the latter part of the year: only 16 children (8 per cent) of those remaining in care at the end of the year experienced new legislation compared with half during the first six months in care. These changes increased social work control, usually because of a deterioration in the child's situation, echoing the patterns we have described earlier. By twelve months, the proportion of children in care under voluntary legislation had fallen to 24 per cent whereas 68 per cent of children are on care orders, and for a further 6 per cent full parental rights have been assumed.

It is important to remember, however, that the care order category may only reflect one aspect of the behaviour of children and the category selected may be one of several possibilities. For example, much delinquency is accompanied by problems of school attendance and the general term 'beyond control' implies a wide range of behaviour. Some of the factors justifying the initial care order may also decline as time passes and the major social work problem at twelve months may not be the same as that implied in the legal category, as Table 10.2 indicates.

Table 10.2   **Factors present as a reason for continuing care**

|  | Reasons for staying in care at 12 months | Reasons for being away from home |
|---|---|---|
|  | % | % |
| Non-accidental injury, neglect, abuse | 59 | 49 |
| Educational needs | 27* | 21* |
| Offending | 13 | 9 |
|  | (N = 195) |  |

* When only those children of school age (5–16) are considered the figures rise to 34 and 27 per cent, respectively.

From this table, it can be seen that the danger of neglect and abuse is a major reason why half of the children have to stay in care or be away from home. Educational needs, especially the requirement to receive full-time education, are also strong, affecting a quarter of all children in care and as many as 34 per cent of those of school age. A high proportion of these have to live away from home. Offending, in contrast, seems to decline as a problem over time so that although many young people come into care because of delinquency, this only continues to be a major issue at the twelve-months stage for 13 per cent of those in care and for 9 per cent of those both in care and placed away from home.

Finally, it is interesting to consider the group of children who have remained in voluntary care throughout the year, as by this time they form nearly a quarter of our study population. It is clear that these children remain in care for a wide range of reasons, principally a refusal to live at home, desertion by parents or homelessness of the family; but even these constraints only apply to a third of all cases and almost every other possible reason for being in care is represented. Yet it is significant that over half (55 per cent) of all these voluntary cases are expected to stay in care for at least another two years, and for a further 13 per cent of children the outlook is said to be unclear. What is more, 55 per cent are in residential care, mostly in children's homes. Only 40 per cent are fostered, a ratio that is no more favourable for voluntary receptions than it is for all young people committed to care. It is also important to note that while the majority of this group (47 per cent) are over 13 years, there is still a core of young children in care voluntarily with 17 per cent under the age of 7 and 11 per cent under 3. We shall return to this group later, but it already seems clear that the consumers' experience of social work intervention does not always reflect the subtleties and nuances of legislative categories, neither does their legal status necessarily reflect their current problems.[2]

## Changes of placement during the first year in care

Although only 44 (23 per cent) of the 195 children still in care at twelve months have been in the same placement throughout their stay in care, changes are less frequent during the second six-months period. Changes of placement affect one-third of the children during the second six months as compared with 60 per cent during the first six months. Slightly more children than before are now living at home or with relatives, and fewer are in residential care. There is little change, however, in the patterns of fostering. Changes of placement do not appear to be associated with major changes of social work plan, particularly as 31 of the 67 children who moved did so because of breakdowns in the original placement.

These patterns become clear when we compare the type of placements of the 195 children at entry and 12 months later, which shows that 69 per cent of those first placed in foster homes and 60 per cent of those in residential care are still in this type of provision twelve months later. Compared with the earlier period, it seems that fewer children have remained at home throughout and there is a slight increase in those moving from residential care into foster homes as time progresses.

As might be expected, during the second half of the year the use of O and A centres declines, and is experienced by only 12 per cent of the children, but CHEs become increasingly important and now shelter as many as 15 per cent of the children still in care. Only 39 per cent of the children have been fostered during this latter period, the same number as have had a residential experience other than a CHE. Thus, at twelve months, the children's placement is very much as at six months with some children moving towards home and, for a few adolescents, towards independence, while others seem destined for a long stay in care.

As would be expected, placement choices are closely related to children's ages and the legislation under which they remain in care. For children under the age of seven, 27 out of the 42 are living in foster homes compared with only six in residential care. In contrast, 62 per cent of adolescents aged 13 and over are in residential care and only 15 per cent are fostered. Surprisingly, the figures for residential

care are also high for the 7–12 age group. This reflects social workers'
uncertainty about the prognosis and the plans for many such children.

Table 10.3   Ages of children in different types of placement

| Placement at 12 months | Age of child on reception | | | |
| | 0–2 | 3–6 | 7–12 | 13–13+ |
| --- | --- | --- | --- | --- |
| | % | % | % | % |
| Home or with relatives | 18 | 25 | 20 | 23 |
| Foster home | 72 | 55 | 29 | 15 |
| Residential care | 9 | 20 | 51 | 62 |
| (N = | 22 | 20 | 49 | 104) |

The legislation affecting children is also likely to be associated with
some types of placement more than others. Fostering is used for voluntary admissions and children on care orders for neglect or for whom
parental rights have been taken. Residential care and placements at
home, in contrast, are more likely to be employed for adolescents on
care orders because of behaviour problems.

Nevertheless, by the twelve-months stage, each type of placement is
beginning to have different time implications for the child's future in
care. For most of those who live at home, leaving care is imminent,
whereas placement with relatives implies a much longer stay in care.
In the residential sector, special schooling has longer time expectations while placement in a CHE has a shorter prognosis. Children's
homes also shelter those children whose stay will be long or those with
uncertain futures.

In other respects, there is little change from the situation at six
months. Generally, social workers seem more satisfied with both the
category of placement such as residential care or fostering and with the
actual placement enjoyed by children at the end of the year. If unease
is expressed, it is about particular residential placements for children
with educational and control problems. In addition, there is concern
about the living situations of many younger children. One-third of
those under five and 40 per cent of those on care orders for neglect
cause social worker anxiety.

**Breakdown of placements**
While changes of placement diminish as time progresses, the frequency of placement breakdown continues unchecked. Thirty-one of
the children in care at twelve months (15 per cent) had experienced a
breakdown during the second half of the year. It will be recollected

that 38 of the 222 children (17 per cent) had experienced a breakdown in the previous six months. By twelve months, eleven children had experienced breakdowns twice and the total number of children experiencing a breakdown during the whole year reached 58. This represents almost 30 per cent of the 195 children still in care at twelve months. As before, two-thirds of these movers precipitately changed placements as the result of a crisis and usually they entered residential care. The significance of breakdowns as a reason for changing placement also increases as they now account for 42 per cent of all completed placements and the unease expressed by social workers in our previous chapter at the frequency of breakdown gathers as time progresses.

The pattern of movement noted at six months continues so that foster children have moved less than those in residential care. As before, if transfers from foster homes do occur, they are very likely to be the result of a breakdown. However, it is also noticeable that placements at home show a much greater tendency to run into difficulties as time progresses. As noted earlier, hasty transfers tend to propel children into residential care rather than the reverse.

An attempt to identify the vulnerable groups reveals that, after twelve months, young children are just as prone to transfer as adolescents although, of course, the latter are more numerous. Seven of the 15 infants admitted to care before the age of two have suffered a placement breakdown, three of them under crisis conditions. Girls are still more prone to precipitate transfer than are boys. In addition, breakdowns seem closely related to certain features of parental contact. Factors such as distance between the child and family and the frequency of visits seem to be less significant than *changes* in patterns of parental visiting. Indeed, two-thirds of the breakdowns followed either an increase or decrease in parental contact. As we noted at six months, breakdowns are associated with the unsettling effect of a situation and changes in the visiting patterns of parents.

Equally important for our understanding of care careers is the effect of a placement breakdown on social workers' expectations of the child's future. Thirty-one of the 58 children whose placements broke down prematurely are now expected by social workers to remain in care for over two years, compared with only 13 of the 58 at six months. Placement breakdown is viewed, therefore, as a secondary adjustment problem seriously affecting care careers and likely to propel into or maintain children in residential care. Breakdown also lengthens social workers' prognosis of children's duration in care.

### The maintenance of family links

Decisions about links between the child in care and the family continue to be made as time progresses, even though there is little overall change in the second half of the year. Children's situations were reviewed periodically, but the frequency of large case conferences on children declined. Of the 170 children reviewed during the year, access to the natural family was viewed as an important issue in all but 50 cases. Continued oversight of the existing arrangements was the most frequent recommendation, decreased contact was advised for 20 per cent of the children whereas for 30 per cent more access was to be encouraged. As other aspects of the care situation were more tranquil, social workers also appeared to have more influence on the decisions made concerning access in these later reviews and case conferences. As a result, in only five cases were social workers unhappy about the final decision. Two of these concerned children with school attendance problems.

Indeed, the second half of the year would have offered good opportunities to nurture and encourage parental contact with their children. Not only have changes within the care system diminished considerably but the families also seem less disrupted than in earlier months. The fraught kaleidoscope of household dissolution and reconstitution moderates, children's natural families seem more stable with changes in household structures affecting only 67 of the 195 children still in care, that is, a fall of one-third compared with the earlier period. Unfortunately, by this time many parental and family relationships with the child have cooled.

Naturally, some children who stay in care remain more vulnerable to family upheaval and turbulence than others. For example, the families of children admitted voluntarily and children for whom parental rights have been assumed are more quiescent than the families of those in care for neglect, abuse or delinquency. While, in general, family turbulence declines over time, if it continues the prognosis of early return to home for some children rapidly diminishes. This is particularly noticeable for younger children who are expected to remain long in foster homes. This group see their parents less and less and move further away as a result of placement changes. By the twelve-months stage, a third of these younger children are more than 20 miles away from home, all reflecting social work plans to place them with an alternative family.

In general, the declining contact between parents and absentee child noted at six months continues as the year progresses. In a few cases improving relationships and more tranquil home situations were clearly associated with an increase in contacts of all kinds. Hence, for 19 children, weekly visits were now possible as a result of improved family relations and these contacts were carefully nurtured by social workers. But improvement is not the rule and the number of isolated children in care continues to grow. By twelve months, 38 of the 195 children in care had lost all contact with their mother, and 70 per cent of children had no contact with their father. As we have seen, children who have lost contact with their families are a very varied group, comprising cases where social workers have deliberately restricted links, adolescents who refuse to live at home and children whose family contacts have simply withered.

## Specific restrictions
Limitations on access between children and families continue to be severe, so that at the end of the year 152 out of the 195 children in care were experiencing serious limitations to contact with their natural families: 102 young people faced some restrictions on access and 122 children suffered considerable barriers to contact as a result of their placements. Seventy-two children had to cope with both specific and non-specific restrictions on contact. Of the access restrictions in force after one year, 60 children have been continuously restricted since reception while new constraints on contact with specific individuals have been introduced in 42 cases. In contrast, for 27 children specific restrictions have been abandoned. Hence, when policy changes do occur, they seem likely to increase control over contacts with home rather than diminish constraints over access already imposed. As at six months, specific restrictions are often part of the social worker's strategy, but levels of restriction vary and the most extreme situation where the child's address is withheld from the natural family is occasionally employed. For example, of 180 natural mothers alive or whose whereabouts are known by social workers, 18 do not know the child's address at this stage and in 11 of these cases this is a deliberate social work decision, six of these children are infants and all but one are younger than 11 years of age. Interestingly, one of these children is still in voluntary care.

The reasons social workers offer for imposing specific restrictions remain unchanged. They are dominated by fears of abuse, mutual rejection and a desire for continued placement tranquility.

## Non-specific restrictions
During the twelve months the barriers to contact imposed by certain placements, distance, problems and cost of travel continue undiminished. These difficulties were affecting 80 per cent of those children still in care at twelve months. Indeed, the manipulation of these non-specific restrictions to control contact with home, with siblings and others becomes increasingly noticeable as time progresses. In this sense, the distinction that we have made between restrictions that are specific to individuals and those barriers that are non-specific, that is, inherent in the separation experience and placements, begins to blur.

We find that distance and unwelcoming placements are now part of social workers' strategy for discouraging parental contact and facilitating substitute relationships, as we have just noted with some young children in foster homes.

The selection of placements to control access between the child and the family is very marked – such placements affect 45 per cent of the children. A quarter of foster home choices are now being made to restrict links compared with 20 per cent at the six-months stage. Children are also no nearer to their homes than they were previously, and after twelve months in care, 28 per cent are living over 20 miles from their natural mothers and fathers, and only 37 per cent are within 5 miles of home, figures that show little change from the earlier situation. Indeed, for many, distance from home continues to be a very important aspect of the separation experience. Thirty-one per cent of the 195 children in care for one year have never been nearer than 20 miles to their homes and only 46 per cent have been within 5 miles. While distance is not the major barrier for parents in maintaining links, such placements hardly facilitate regular, enriching contact. In addition, such distances isolate children and hinder them from maintaining contact with neighbourhoods and wider social networks at home. We have already suggested that children's links with their family should be seen in the wider context of belonging, in which contacts with the neighbourhood are an important part.

It is also noticeable that restrictions on access and wider, non-specific restrictions now become associated with expectations of long stays in care. While a few children are likely to leave care rapidly, particularly those living with parents or relatives 'on trial', the majority of other children are now expected by social workers to remain long in care. Indeed, by twelve months, many have lost contact with their natural families. This may not be unexpected, for example, if adoption is pending but for the remainder of children the decline in parental contact is particularly serious for their future.

One of the problems in charting the care careers of a large study cohort such as this is the diversity of children's needs, characteristics and care situations. A conclusion drawn for one group can be contradicted by the experiences of another. It is important to stress, therefore, that no one type of case dominates the care population at twelve months, but several small groups of children stand out as continuing to present particular links difficulties. Young children and adolescents can present problems, both those in foster care and in residential homes. For example, after twelve months 28 per cent of the 95 children in residential care are unsettled and experiencing relationship and school problems. Many do not appear to be well integrated either into their natural families or home neighbourhoods or into substitute care. All but one of these children are over 11 and most have been in their placements for about three months. Social workers express particular concern about eight of these 95 children in residential care. They have lost contact with their parents, their isolation is intensified by this and contributes to their unhappiness.

The adjustment of children in foster homes, in contrast, appears to improve over time and is generally better at one year than previously. Only 11 per cent of the 57 children are said to be unsettled and only 7 per cent of these have no family contacts, a pattern which amply demonstrates the value of maintaining links between parents and children in foster care, as has also been found by Weinstein, Thorpe and Holman.[3] We can see that even at twelve months, certain groups of children can be viewed as likely to present links problems in the future. As time passes, while those causing concern are not yet numerous, the inexorable increase in isolated, unhappy, long-stay children should be noted.

## Conclusions

At the end of one year, 195 out of our original entry of 450 children remain in care. The majority of these are adolescents, over 11 years of age. We noted that 228 children left before six months had elapsed from their reception into care, but the exodus from care that characterised the first six months of our study has now ceased. In the latter half of the year, only 27 children followed. As the months pass, the majority of those children who stay in care find things settle down. There are fewer changes of social worker, only one-fifth of the children experience a new relationship in the latter part of the year. Movements between placements are fewer, although breakdowns continue to cause concern, and even children's families seem relatively quiescent.

The turbulence and change in households that characterised the first few months decline and patterns of access and contact between child and family are little disturbed. Now that control has been achieved over the majority of cases, social workers find little need for legislative change; twelve interim care orders have become full care orders and six children are being considered for adoption. The gradual decline of voluntary care continues. Indeed, in comparison with the earlier months, the care situation at one year is remarkably static.

Such tranquility should be given a guarded welcome because it reflects a general acquiescence in the care situation on the part of most participants. Parents display a fatalistic, passive acceptance, social workers' satisfactions increase, care-givers are involved even less in decision-making and most children settle down. Nevertheless, breakdowns in placements, fostering as well as residential care, continue to accumulate. By this time, nearly one-third of children still in care at one year will have experienced a breakdown in their placement and three-quarters will have moved placements during the year. Indeed, for some children, it seems very difficult to find a supportive and stable alternative to their chaotic and disadvantaged families.

The heterogeneity of children in care continues with the emergence of the 8–12 year olds as a particularly problematic group. Their care plans lack certainty and many are causing concern to social workers within placements. Adolescents continue to display school and control problems and these are beginning to displace the reasons for which they were admitted to care.

The problems of maintaining links between parent and child continue; barriers inherent in placements remain unaffected as time passes, while restrictions on the access of key family figures to their children marginally increase. While many separated siblings remain in contact, members of the extended family or the wider social networks of the child are out of touch and half of the children will have spent the year in placements which are distant from home. At the end of a year, two-thirds of the children were experiencing difficulties in links with their parents and were virtually isolated. Prolonged separation was causing considerable distress to some children and affecting their response to placements.

The most disturbing aspect of the care picture after one year is the decline in social work activity. Vigorous rehabilitative efforts with the family, which have seldom characterised the children's experience, seem virtually to have disappeared. At the end of one year only 17 per cent of mothers and 6 per cent of fathers were receiving regular social work visits. Just over a third of the children and placements were being seen once a fortnight while the remainder were scrutinised less frequently. On social workers' own admissions, the content of such visits seems largely perfunctory. Indeed, in our intensive study group, four of the 22 parents of children still in care remained unvisited for three months and the social worker was largely inaccessible by telephone or visits. There seems to be a tension in social services departments between managing entry into care and work which is concentrated on rehabilitation once the child is in care. When resources are scarce it is clear that one of these activities takes precedence over the other.

With the exception of a few children living at home or with close relatives and the older adolescents, the majority of children who have spent a year in care are destined to stay there. Indeed, at crises or at case reviews, social workers' expectations of children's sojourn in care seem to be extended. It will be interesting to see how many of the 195 children still in care at twelve months out of our original 450 who entered care remain for yet another year.

**Summary points**

1. Between six and twelve months 27 children left care leaving 195 out of our original 450 entries remaining in care after one year had elapsed. Slightly more boys than girls linger, and the majority of children are adolescents (more than half are over 11 years of age).

2. By the time a year has elapsed things are beginning to settle down; there are few changes in the child's legal status, their reasons for staying in care remain largely unchanged, and even the households from which these children come seem more tranquil.

3. While planned changes of children's placements diminish over time, the frequency of placement breakdown continues. By twelve months 30 per cent of the 195 still in care had experienced a placement breakdown and eleven children had suffered this disruption twice. Girls are more prone to breakdown than boys and, while more adolescents break down than younger children, those under 11 are proportionately as prone to disruption as older children.

4. Failure in placements still reflects inappropriate or unsatisfactory earlier locations of the child, many of which were recognised as deficient by social workers at the time of placement. Fluctuation in parental visiting also seems significant, particularly in foster homes. Breakdowns in placement and precipitate transfer markedly increase the length of time social workers expect children to stay in care.

5. Social work activity with families, children and care-givers shows a decline. At the end of one year only 17 per cent of mothers and 6 per cent of fathers were receiving regular social work visits. However, one-third of the children were being seen once a fortnight. These visits seem rather perfunctory and do little to emphasise the significance of parental and family contacts for the child's happiness and stability. Children's situations were periodically reviewed but, by this time, large case conferences on children are rare. Generally, case reviews largely confirmed existing situations.

6. By 12 months, 38 of the 195 children in care had lost contact with their mothers and 70 per cent of these children had no contact with their fathers. These children are a varied group; for some access has been denied, for others links with home have withered and some children are reluctant to reciprocate parental and family interest.

7. Of the 195 children still in care at one year, 152 were facing considerable barriers to contact: 102 children now experience specific restrictions on access, while 122 children suffered non-specific barriers to contact with 72 children experiencing both specific and non-specific barriers to contact with home. Parents seem

increasingly disinclined to visit, they feel deskilled, diminished and stigmatised.

8. While heterogeneity still characterises the children who remain in care at twelve months those aged between 8 and 12 years are beginning to cause concern. Their care plans lack certainty, some are causing problems in their placements, breakdowns occur and they are highly likely to spend their adolescence in care.

# 11. Children still in care at two years

This chapter looks at the characteristics, care experience and prognosis of those 170 children who have stayed in care for two years. We shall see that adolescents are an increasing proportion of those in care and that those children who remain have increasingly complex reasons for staying which differ noticeably from the reasons that necessitated the child's entry to care. We shall also see that social workers' prognoses are increasingly pessimistic about some children's chances of leaving care. Once again, we shall look at changes in the children's legal status, their placements and what social work oversight they have received in the preceding months. We shall note that the majority of children still in care at this time are having difficulty in remaining in contact with their parents and that the proportion of those isolated has increased.

We saw in our previous chapter how changes in children's care careers diminished over time. Looked at one year later, movement is even slower. Only 25 children left care during the second year with the result that 170 (38 per cent) of the original 450 children are still in care after two years; 92 are boys and 78 girls, a proportion which has been constant throughout the whole period.

In this second year, the contrasts already noted between children's care careers become even more marked. Some young people are on the point of leaving care or are ready to return home while for others the chances of rehabilitation remain small. Social work activity continues to decline in most cases but the children's care experiences do not necessarily become more stable. While the need for changes in legal status seems to have disappeared, movements between placements, breakdowns and restrictions over access to the natural family are still widespread among the children in care at two years.

Children remain in care for complex reasons. These reasons often differ from those that necessitated reception to care, especially where family structure has changed, and each cause has different time implications for the child's continuance in care. Thus, the majority of children admitted to care because of parental illness, unexpected absence, or their inability to provide have left care compared with only half of those cases where there are behaviour problems or children suffered neglect or abuse. Nevertheless, for those who do remain, certain situations imply a long stay in care. Over time, features such as imprisonment, isolation and physical illness of parents are less cogent factors in lengthening children's care careers than the absence of the natural family, its inability to cope or when plans for children's adoption are advanced.[1] All these magnify the chances of children's staying in care. While behaviour problems posed by the children and unsatisfactory family relationships dominate throughout the two years, these generally characterise adolescents in care and their situation has short-term implications. But long stays are likely when neglect or the inability of the family to care endure over time, factors which are more likely to affect younger children adversely.

These features will affect the age distribution of those remaining in care after two years and it is no surprise to find that only 14 per cent of the 170 children who stay in care are aged under five and that the majority are adolescents and young adults. Indeed, as Table 11.1 shows, 68 per cent are aged 11 or over and a quarter of these are aged 17 and over.

Table 11.1   Ages of children on entry and after 24 months

| Ages of children | % of study group on admission | % of those still in care at 24 months | % of original still in care at 24 months |
|---|---|---|---|
| 0–4 | 33 | 14 | 21 |
| 5–10 | 24 | 19 | 36 |
| 11–16 | 43 | 51 | 51 |
| 17 and over | 0 | 17 | — |
| | (N = 450) | (N = 170) | |

This tendency can, of course, be partly explained by the fact that our study group is now two years older than at reception. Yet it is also clear that adolescents have a greater chance of remaining long in care even when they are received voluntarily into care. Only 21 per cent of those admitted to care before the age of four are still there after two years compared with half of the adolescent group.

This pattern greatly influences social workers' expectations of children's length of stay in care. For example, the expected stay of young children who are 'at risk' and still in care after two years will be very long while many adolescents may be ready to return home or live independently. Social workers expect 30 of the 170 children who still remain in care at two years to return home when they reach school leaving age and others will soon be leaving care as they attain the age of 18. This statutory cut-off point in children's care careers leads to an apparent drop in the numbers expected to remain in care for a further two years. But it does not detract from our conclusions that social workers' expectation of children's length of stay in care generally increases the longer the child remains.

At reception, 140 children were expected still to be in care after two years; in fact, 170 remained. Similarly, at 12 months, 22 per cent were expected to go out of care within a year whereas only 13 per cent did. These differences are not great but the accumulation of a small number of cases at each stage of the care career means that after two years there is a growth in the 'longer than expected' group of children who remain in care. These have little prospect of leaving in the near future.

Let us look at those aspects of the child's care career which we have noted affect the links they have with their family. Let us begin with the efforts of social workers, see what legislative changes have occurred, and look once again at children's placements and breakdowns. Finally, we shall see what significance these situations have for the links that children enjoy with home.

## Social work oversight

A quarter of the 170 children experienced a change of social worker in their second year of care. As before, all but three of these changes arise from administrative requirements rather than any change in social work plans. For example, three-quarters of changes of social worker arose simply because staff moved to other employment. This means that 79 (46 per cent) of the children still in care had one social worker throughout the two years. A further 54 (32 per cent) had experienced only one change in social worker. There is, therefore, little general evidence to support the widely held view of a lack of continuity in the field social work oversight which children experience. However, there are some examples among our long-stay children of inconsistent management. For example, three of the 170 children had four social workers during the two-year period.

Change of social worker, however, is not consistent across all groups. Certain categories of children in care are more likely to experience change than others. Slightly more susceptible are adolescents on care orders imposed to ensure full-time education. Similarly, children on care orders for neglect and those in voluntary care are more likely to change social workers. Delinquents and those beyond control receive more stable oversight although a few of the more recalcitrant individuals do get passed on. Those faring best are children for whom parental rights have been assumed and children on care orders because of moral danger, three-quarters of whom have been under the same social worker throughout the two-year period. It seems that where the need for control is dominant, the greater is the stability.

We were concerned in the preceding chapter that the social workers' contact with families, children and care-givers noticeably diminished as time passed. If many parents continued to visit their children and remain in contact in other ways, it was without the active encouragement of social workers. Generally, we find that social workers' level of involvement with clients continues to diminish during the second year. As a result, contacts with many families had withered and there was virtually no communication with a third of mothers. Fathers fared even worse, with 80 per cent of them uninvolved with social workers. Social workers also made little contact with the wider extended family or children's close friends. Neither did the children in care or their placements receive regular visits from social workers, for at two years, nearly half the children (45 per cent) were receiving visits from social workers at less than monthly intervals. Unfortunately, the sanction given in the Boarding Out Regulations (1955) to diminishing social work activity over time not only affects scrutiny of foster situations but also comes to affect those in residential care. This study has demonstrated that any decline in social work activity over time is much to be regretted.

Table 11.2    Frequency of contact between social workers, children and families

| Frequency of contact | Child | | Mother | | Father | |
|---|---|---|---|---|---|---|
| | at 6 months | at 24 months | at 6 months | at 24 months | at 6 months | at 24 months |
| | % | % | % | % | % | % |
| At least once per month | 83 | 55 | 47 | 30 | 22 | 14 |
| Less than once per month | 16 | 42 | 32 | 42 | 33 | 38 |
| No contact | 0 | 3 | 9 | 20 | 32 | 39 |
| Not applicable | 0 | 0 | 13 | 8 | 12 | 9 |
| (N = | 222 | 170 | 222 | 170 | 222 | 170) |

Indeed, at two years, social workers were stressing the difficulties of offering long-term oversight to such families or their children. In a quarter of these cases, social workers were clearly concerned at the inadequacies of the care they had to offer. In addition, they were surprisingly pessimistic about the effects of their involvements. While they stressed that many children had been helped and displayed some satisfaction with the outcomes in four-fifths of the cases, they generally had deep reservations about their impact on the wider problems faced by children and their families.

**Legal status**
In the first six months of care, we noted that changes in children's legal position were frequent, indeed, half of the children experienced a

change of legal status during their early months in care. Nevertheless, as social workers' control over the cases increases, legal changes decline so that in the second year of care legal issues cease to be of much concern. In fact, only five of the 170 children changed their care status during their second year.

When compared with legal status at reception, the legal position of the 170 children still in care confirms the clear shift towards greater social work control we have described in earlier chapters. Only 15 per cent of the children remained in voluntary care throughout the two years, whereas the proportion under care orders has risen sharply. Of the original 97 place of safety orders 67 children are still in care after two years and all but three have been followed by some type of full care order. Indeed, it is clear that while the legal status of the child at two years seems to make little difference to his or her immediate care situation and experience, certain early decisions, such as seeking a place of safety order, can have long-term consequences. In addition, these legal statuses at two years seem very firmly established. Only in one case, an interim care order, was the child's legal position still under review.

Table 11.3  **Legal status of children at two years**

| Legal status | Entry | 2 years |
|---|---|---|
| | % | % |
| Voluntary care (s.2, 1980 Children Act) | 34 | 15 |
| Parental rights assumed | | |
| (s.3, 1980 Children Act) | 0 | 8 |
| Care orders 1969 CYP Act: | | |
|     interim/detained | 2 | 1 |
|     neglect, abuse | 1 | 31 |
|     moral danger | 1 | 6 |
|     beyond control | 0 | 8 |
|     full-time education | 6 | 6 |
|     offending | 14 | 18 |
| Matrimonial care order | 1 | 4 |
| Place of safety order | 39 | 0 |
| Other | 2 | 3 |
| | (N = 170) | (N = 170) |

In the majority of cases (85 per cent), social workers expressed satisfaction with the legal situations of children at two years. The legislation was viewed by them as both facilitating control and the most appropriate for their strategies. Legislative matters are resolved quickly after the child's admission to care and they cease to preoccupy social workers as time passes.

Nevertheless, social workers generally take a rather cavalier attitude to the legal situation regarding many children in care. In interviews they were often unable to specify the legal constraints surrounding their charges or which care order was actually in force; in addition, they had only hazy ideas how legislation limited or facilitated their power. In fact, legislation seems hardly to influence social work actions and, for clients, differences which should be important administratively do not appear to affect their care experience. For example, we have already noted the frequency with which non-specific and other restrictions are placed on children in voluntary care.

### Placement histories

Sixty-nine of the 170 children changed their placements in this second year of care. While this is an encouraging decline in the movements of the previous year, transfer still affected over 40 per cent of our study group during the second year. Thus 83 per cent of children had experienced a change of placement at some point during the past two years. As these changes tend to occur early in their career, many children will have stayed in the same situation during the past 18 months. Nevertheless, a small proportion continue to be very unsettled with 18 per cent having had three or more placements in the past twelve months and over the two-year period, 56 per cent of the

Table 11.4   **Placements of children in care at two years**

|  | N | % |
|---|---|---|
| home on trial | 44 | 26 |
| foster with relatives | 14 | 8 |
| foster home | 45 | 26 |
| *Residential:* | | |
| O and A centre | 3 | 2 |
| children's home | 30 | 18 |
| CHE | 13 | 8 |
| hostel | 6 | 4 |
| special boarding school | 2 | 1 |
| residential nursery | 1 | 1 |
| *Other:* | | |
| independent/co-habiting/friends | 7 | 4 |
| penal institution | 3 | 2 |
| whereabouts unknown | 2 | 1 |
| | (N = 170) | |

children will have had three or more placements and 14 per cent of them will have had more than four.

Many of these changes, of course, reflect intended care plans and result from the completion of an adoption or a return home to the natural family. Other transfers are less happy, for it is clear that placement breakdowns continue to be widespread. During the second year of care, the placements that predominate differ from those employed early on, for example, at some time in the previous year fostering was experienced by 41 per cent of the children, while hostels or children's homes were used by a further 41 per cent and placement at home was enjoyed by 31 per cent. The need for control and education is emphasised by the 17 per cent experiencing a CHE. Observation and assessment centres, in contrast, declined in significance and were employed during this period for only one in 20 of the children still in care. After two years, therefore, the 170 children still in care are in the placements shown in Table 11.4.

There is a clear relationship between the age of the children and their placement at two years. All of the very young children in our study group are either at home or fostered, but as Table 11.5 shows, residential options are used extensively for all other groups, especially those aged between 6 and 11 on reception who, of course, by now have reached ages between 8 and 13 years, respectively.

Table 11.5   Placement of children of different ages

| Age on admission | Home or fostered with relatives | Foster home | Residential | Other | (N) |
|---|---|---|---|---|---|
| | % | % | % | % | |
| 0–1 | 32 | 68 | 0 | 0 | 19 |
| 2–5 | 33 | 44 | 22 | 0 | 18 |
| 6–11 | 23 | 34 | 43 | 0 | 44 |
| 12 or over | 40 | 10 | 36 | 13 | 89 |

When categories of placements at entry and after two years are compared, it will be seen that fostering and placement in a children's home seem the least likely to change.

There is, however, still a great deal of movement of children within the same categories of placement, that is within foster homes, children's homes or CHEs. Hence, when we examine the placements themselves, we find much higher rates of movement. Indeed, apart from those fostered with relatives, children are highly likely to move from their first placements as they stay in care, for example 31 of the 43 initial fosterings moved placements.

Four other features of children's placement histories continue to be important. First, 51 per cent of those children who have brothers or sisters in care are in their placements with a sibling. This is an increase on the figure of 42 per cent at the six-months stage. Statistical analysis of children in care tends to emphasise the *individual* features of cases, whereas the reality of the care experience is more likely to involve groups of siblings coping with separation from home.

A second feature that emerges is the continuing distance between placement and home. A greater use of home placements means that the numbers living within two miles of their family increases from 23 per cent at the twelve-month stage to 34 per cent after two years in care. However, it is important to note that 22 per cent of all children continue to be over 20 miles away from home. Indeed, when we exclude those children placed with their families or nearby relatives, over a third of the children away from home are more than 20 miles distant, and 17 per cent are more than 50 miles away. Thus, some children in care remain very far from home and family.

The third factor that remains equally noticeable over time is the enduring contribution of the residential sector. As we have seen, 32 per cent of those in care after two years are still in residential care and 80 per cent have had a residential experience. Indeed, when we examine the 170 children still in care after two years and chart the settings in which they have spent the greatest period of their time in care, the significance of children's homes and CHEs is emphasised. Children who remain in care, however, are not seen by social workers as likely to stay in residential care. When asked which placements were likely to be employed in the next two years, social workers suggest that only 12 per cent of the 170 children had a strong or even moderate chance of being in residential care compared with half likely to be at home or with relatives and 32 per cent in foster homes. However, we have seen that social workers constantly tend to over-estimate the amount of fostering that will take place and to under-estimate the contribution of residential care.

Fourthly, it is also clear that placements continue to cause concern to social workers. For 59 per cent of children they express general satisfaction over the two-year period with the category of placements chosen, such as fostering or residential care, but they often had greater reservations about the actual placements experienced by children. Thus, 63 of the 170 children still in care at two years were viewed by social workers as unsuitably placed. Many of these were adolescents, particularly those in residential care because of moral danger, and a large number were younger children, especially those on care orders for neglect.

**Placement breakdowns**

We have emphasised earlier in this study that placements often break down, a pattern which continues unabated during the second year of care. In the second twelve-months period, for example, 34 children (20 per cent) experienced a placement breakdown. Indeed, the rate of placement breakdown continues unchanged. For 31 of these children, the placement terminations were abrupt, resulting from a crisis which necessitated the immediate removal of the child. This brings the total of children experiencing a placement breakdown over the two-year period to 67 out of the 170 who are still in care; and 55 of them have experienced a crisis breakdown. As some young people undergo a number of hasty transfers, the total number of breakdowns in the whole two-year period is 107, 78 of these in crisis situations and 29 which were unexpected but which brought forward intended changes.

In all, the 170 children have experienced 505 different placements, of which 335 have been completed. These are made up as shown in Table 11.6.

**Table 11.6   Placements experienced by children**

|  | *Number of placements over 2 years* | *Number of placements completed* |
|---|---|---|
| Home | 66 | 22 |
| Foster with relatives | 18 | 4 |
| Foster home | 105 | 60 |
| Residential | 287 | 229 |
| Independent | 29 | 20 |
| Total | 505 | 335 |

When we examine the placements in which the 107 breakdowns occurred, it will be seen that 36 were in foster homes, 47 were in residential settings, and 24 were elsewhere. In order to identify patterns, these figures have to be compared as a proportion of not only all living situations which children have experienced, including those which are ongoing, but also of completed placements. This arises from the fact, noted earlier, that fosterings change less than residential placements but when they do, the cause is more likely to be a complete breakdown in the care of the child. Hence, when completed placements are scrutinised, some very high figures are found. Overall, 32 per cent of all completed placements broke down prematurely, 23 per cent of them under crisis conditions which arose unexpectedly and necessitated the hasty removal of the child. When different types of placements are compared, it is found that 60 per cent of the moves from foster homes followed a breakdown whereas the figures for residential settings are lower, 36 per cent in CHEs, 22 per cent in children's homes and 13 per cent in O and A centres. Equally unstable are placements at home or the independent living situations usually experienced by older adolescents.

**Table 11.7   Placement breakdowns experienced by children**

|  | Types of breakdown | | | Breakdown as: | | | |
|  |  |  |  | % of completed placements | | % of all placements | |
| Placement | crisis | precipitated intended move | total | crisis | all | crisis | all |
|---|---|---|---|---|---|---|---|
| Home | 10 | 5 | 15 | 45 | 68 | 15 | 23 |
| Foster with relatives | 1 | 0 | 1 | 25 | 25 | 6 | 6 |
| Foster home | 31 | 5 | 36 | 52 | 60 | 30 | 34 |
| Residential | 32 | 15 | 47 | 14 | 21 | 11 | 16 |
| Independent | 4 | 4 | 8 | 20 | 40 | 14 | 28 |
| Total | 78 | 29 | 107 | 23 | 32 | 15 | 21 |

When all placements, including those that are ongoing, are examined, it is found that a disquieting level of breakdown still emerges, although differences between types of placements are less distinct. Thirty-four per cent of all fosterings, 28 per cent of all independent living situations, 23 per cent of all placements at home, 17 per cent of placements in smaller community homes and 24 per cent of those in CHEs broke down. Children who stay long in care, therefore, have a considerable chance of experiencing a placement disruption – nearly 40 per cent of those children still in care after two years will have been affected and 21 per cent of all placements selected will have broken down.

We have already commented on the characteristics of children who experience a breakdown and at two years the picture is little different. As before, it seems that girls are more vulnerable than boys to placement difficulties. A surprisingly high percentage of younger children will also have been affected, 37 per cent of those admitted to care under the age of 2 and 50 per cent of those aged between 2 and 5 will have had a precipitate change of placement. Adolescents are also especially vulnerable to premature transfer, although for them breakdowns are more likely to bring forward intended changes rather than to lead to a serious crisis and *ad hoc* placement.

**Table 11.8  Placement breakdown by age of child**

| Age on admission | % experiencing breakdowns (all types) | (N) | % experiencing crisis breakdown |
|---|---|---|---|
| 0–1 | 37 | (19) | 31 |
| 2–5 | 50 | (18) | 44 |
| 6–11 | 18 | (44) | 14 |
| 12+ | 48 | (89) | 39 |

One other important change in this second year is the increasing significance of links between the child and his natural family for placement stability. During the second twelve months there is a marked tendency for placement breakdowns, especially crisis breakdown, to be associated with low levels of parental contact and reductions in family visits. Children who, at the two-year stage, seldom see their natural parents or who have no other forms of contact are more prone to breakdown than those who maintain regular links. This pattern has become more apparent in the second year of care.

In addition, 59 per cent of those whose links with natural mothers over the two years have declined, have experienced a crisis breakdown at some point whereas those who had little contact throughout display much lower rates. Indeed, it seems to be the *changes* in links patterns that unsettle the child. Curiously, however, an increase in family contact is also associated with placement breakdowns but rarely of the crisis kind. This is because some adolescents re-establish their family links over time and difficulties in the placement merely bring forward their return home.

**Table 11.9  Placement breakdown by change in child's contact with mother**

| Change in mother/child contact over two years | % of children experiencing a crisis breakdown | % of children experiencing a breakdown which precipitates intended change | (N) |
|---|---|---|---|
| Increase | 37 | 30 | 30 |
| Same | 26 | 11 | 97 |
| Decrease | 59 | 26 | 22 |
| Not applicable | 29 | 5 | 21 |
|  | ($\chi^2 = 9.3$, p $< .01$) | ($\chi^2 = 8.4$, p $< .02$) | |

One other factor seems relevant to our understanding of placement breakdown. It seems that features of the placement itself rather than the characteristics of the families or child are important. While there is a relationship between unsettled behaviour by the child and transfer elsewhere, half of the crises arose in situations where neither the child nor the parents offered problems to the placement. Indeed, disruptive contributions from the child's family figure in only a quarter of cases. This is an important finding because it indicates the need for social workers to give greater attention to placement dynamics and to examine closely the history and potential of parental interference when making access restrictions. Simple instrumental factors such as distance between the placement and the child's home are less important than the relationships among and the aspirations of care-givers in the placements.

Placement breakdowns are also significant for children's care careers. The patterns noted at six and twelve months by which breakdowns lead children into residential care are maintained throughout the two years. While 57 of the 107 breakdowns were followed by transfer of the child into another placement of the same type, in 36 of the fostering cases there was a subsequent move into residential care compared with only four transfers the other way. Indeed, only a quarter of fostering breakdowns were placed directly with new foster parents.

The shift towards residential care is maintained during the second year with children's homes receiving 27 of the 107 breakdowns, O and A centres 19 and CHEs 14 compared with only 13 children entering foster homes and nine returning to parents. Of the 36 fostering breakdowns, 22 were followed by a residential placement compared with only nine directly fostered again. In contrast, only three of the 47 residential breakdowns and one of the 15 crises at home were followed by fostering.

Placement breakdowns continue to be an important part of the child-care process throughout the two-year period. They are numerous, affecting 40 per cent of all children still in care, and account for a third of the changes in children's living situations. Because of the continuing risk of breakdown, the cumulative effect over the two years has been considerable and has affected all types of children in our cohort. The effects on children's care careers are inevitably serious, closing options and causing children to go into residential care. For some adolescents these changes may bring children closer to home but for the majority the disruption is severe. In addition, the impact on children's education and their wider social networks will be deeply unsettling.[2] It is also worth noting that while 'failed' foster parents usually rapidly compensate for their loss with new arrivals and other boarded-out children, the rejected child cannot easily make up for severed parenting. Foster parents usually terminate their relationship with the child when breakdown occurs, but the displaced child continues to mourn his or her loss and longs for contact. While relationships between child and care-givers are usually less close in residential care, movement from a small community home can be equally distressing for the child.

## Children's relationships with family

At the end of two years' stay in care, 126 of the 170 children still in care were away from home, although 14 of these were fostered with relatives. Their absence was dictated by the need to ensure control, to protect from moral danger or neglect and to meet educational requirements, thus contact with their families was frequently of secondary importance. Indeed, the relationship between care-givers and children's parents was a continuing source of concern to social workers over the whole two-year period, and in a third of all children who remained in care at the end of two years, social workers admitted the placements had done little to help their families' welfare or to maintain and develop family contact and relationships. In addition, social workers expressed deep unease about many placements during the child's care career; they suggested that unsuitable settings and insufficient options accounted for the frequency of transfer between and breakdown in children's placements.

Social workers intimated that parents generally acquiesce both in the living situations of their children and in the access arrangements that are made. Our intensive study of 30 families experiencing care would confirm this. We have noted that access restrictions in themselves arouse little grievance, it was more the difficulties of maintaining contact within the boundaries of the restrictions that caused anger. The problems presented by distance, lack of money, the vagaries of the transport system, elusive social workers and care-givers aroused more parental hostility than the access arrangements themselves.

Nevertheless, access arrangements and contact between parents and children received some scrutiny as time passed. Contact with home was reviewed for 80 per cent of all children during the second year, although consequent changes in arrangements and visiting patterns diminished rapidly.

Yet, the resilience in the relationships between the child and the natural family over two years is remarkable for, as we have seen, the children's family situations and households changed considerably during the period. Indeed, so turbulent is the continuing history of many families that links with their absent children are unlikely to preoccupy parents for long. Major structural changes within the child's natural family persist while the child is away in care. They affected 34 per cent of the 170 young people during their second year of care. In all, 107 of the 170 children (63 per cent) still in care at two years had been affected by a major change in family structures. These changes at home, when linked with the frequent placement changes and break-downs in care experienced by some children, inevitably affect contact with the family.

While changes in the structure of children's families are frequent it is difficult to predict exactly what form these will take or to foresee their effects on the links parents develop and maintain with their children. With the younger children in particular, the consequences seem to be varied, perhaps promoting greater stability in the natural family but in other cases this is not so. This latter point is particularly important because it is clear that younger children are so vulnerable to changes in family structures.

Changes in the structure of the natural family affect certain groups of children more than others and while boys and girls are equally vulnerable, younger children on care orders for neglect and living in foster homes are particularly prone to this experience. The natural families of nearly three-quarters (73 per cent) of those admitted to care before the age of 11 have changed radically during the child's absence as compared with just half (54 per cent) for the older age groups. Children on care orders for neglect or because of moral danger display much higher rates of family change (84 per cent) than do those in other legislative categories, such as those in voluntary care (50 per cent), care orders for being beyond control or in need of full-time education (48 per cent), delinquency (53 per cent) and cases where full parental rights have been assumed (54 per cent). In the neglect cases, changes in family structures seem to be particularly damaging and there is a tendency for a deterioration in the relationship between the child and the family to accompany these structural alterations.

Certainly, these changes do not necessarily lead to greater stability for the child's natural parents. While death is rarely a reason for family breakdown (only four of the 170 children lost a close relative in the second year), other features associated with dislocation remain. For example, at the two-year stage, 32 per cent of the households from which the children were originally admitted to care are still single-parent families, and 35 per cent of the children have natural, half- or step-siblings living away from these households. Only 29 per cent of natural parents are still married to each other. Families also experience major changes in employment, health and housing. Indeed, social workers are understandably pessimistic about their ability to affect these situational problems facing families and in only 17 per cent of cases did they feel that they had wrought any improvement.

The cumulative effects of all this can be very serious for the child.

According to social workers, half the relationships between parents and children at any one time are disrupted by family turbulence. They report deteriorations in relationships as frequently as improvements, and there is a surprisingly high number of cases where the quality of relationships is difficult to assess, especially those involving the child's natural father.

As a result of these and other changes, 27 per cent of the 170 children in care after two years were not in contact with their natural mothers even though their mothers were known to be alive. This represents a considerable increase in isolation as children move through care. Although by this time 51 per cent of children are in regular contact with home, another 39 per cent are rarely seeing their mothers. This is despite the fact that more children than at any time during the two-year period are now living at home while in care and a greater proportion of children than before are maintaining contact by regular visits home (71 per cent of those with regular contact in residential care and 67 per cent for those in foster care).

**Table 11.10   Frequency of child's contact with natural mother**

| *Frequency* | *6 months in care* | *12 months* | *24 months* |
|---|---|---|---|
| | % | % | % |
| More than once per month | 59 | 52 | 52 |
| Less than once per month | 16 | 16 | 12 |
| Seldom/never | 17 | 23 | 27 |
| Not applicable/not known | 8 | 9 | 10 |
| | (N = 222 | 195 | 170) |

With natural fathers, relationships are even more distant. Indeed, the majority of children in care seem to have little or no contact with their fathers. For example, only 31 per cent see their natural fathers regularly (that is, more than once a month) while 58 per cent have seldom or no contact at all. Poor contact also characterises other relationships, so that 55 per cent of children with step-mothers and 59 per cent of those with step-fathers see these relatives just as infrequently. Similar isolation affects other members of the child's extended family, such as grandparents, aunts, uncles and cousins. Frequent contact is, in fact, more likely to be with siblings, and 79 per cent of those children with a brother or sister, either in or out of care, see them more than every four weeks. This is an improvement on patterns of sibling contact noted earlier. However, for some children, contact with family members clearly withers the longer they stay in care.

The reasons why 63 of the 170 children had little or no contact at all with their mothers are varied, as are the explanations for the 98 who rarely see their natural fathers. Generally, children in most frequent contact were likely to be adolescents in care because of behaviour problems whereas those who had lost touch were children and young people whose families had suffered severe dislocation. In this, neglect and abuse were less significant than continuous family turbulence. In this, neglect and abuse were less significant than continuous family turbulence.

Seventy children were able to maintain contact with their families by other means, such as by telephone, letter or through friends or relatives. Of the 46 children not in any contact with their natural mothers, 21 were said to be in touch with a close relative by phone or letter. Yet the patterns noted earlier still persist; those children with parental links enjoyed a wider set of contacts of all sorts than did those children whose parental ties had withered, a situation highlighted by Ivis Lasson in her study of residential child care.[3]

Finally, links are clearly fashioned by social work decisions. At the two-year stage, 66 per cent of the 170 children experience serious barriers to contact with their families. As more children than before are living at home, this figure which suggests an improvement on the four-fifths of children previously experiencing difficulty, is somewhat deceptive.

### Specific restrictions

Specific restriction on contact, that is a limitation which is specific to a child and a particular member of his or her family, continue to affect 46 per cent of the children still in care at the end of two years. This indicates little change over time. Three-quarters of these specific restrictions form part of the social worker's policy for handling the case but by this time the arrangements seem subject to far less scrutiny at case reviews. For 19 of the 78 children affected, the placements enforce specific restrictions and for a further 16 the child or family impose constraints. Yet in only eight cases do these limitations have the backing of a court ruling. Specific restrictions continue to be enforced by various methods ranging from clear rules about contact to deliberate choice of distant placements, especially foster homes, that will discourage family visiting or other contacts.

In 46 of the 78 cases characterised by specific restrictions, the limitations have been in force throughout the care period. They are applied mostly to the natural parents but for 29 children, siblings are also affected. Fourteen of the 25 children with step-fathers are restricted from contact with them as are ten of those with step-mothers. Specific restrictions only affect other relatives in seven cases. For 48 of the 78 children concerned, the limitations on access are severe and there is a complete ban on contact with the relative concerned. This represents a significant increase on earlier figures of 45 per cent and 39 per cent at the six- and twelve-month stages, respectively and indicates that when specific restrictions continue over time they are likely to become more severe. In 19 of the 48 cases, specific restrictions were imposed by some family members over others, such as mothers refusing fathers' participation or mothers' relatives banning fathers' access. In the majority of cases (29 of the 48), however, it was a social worker who imposed access restrictions in order to facilitate the care plan. Indeed, 19 natural mothers were not only restricted from seeing their children but were actually denied knowledge of the child's address by social workers. All but two of these were young children in long-term foster care because of neglect and for whom full parental rights had been assumed.

There were a further seven cases where the mother did not know the child's address either because she was absent or not interested. Social workers also refused to inform 13 natural fathers of their child's whereabouts and seven placements requested that children's locations be withheld from the families. When parents who are not in touch or who are dead are taken into account, the startling conclusion is reached that at the two-year stage 41 of the 170 children in care had a natural mother who did not know their address, a figure which rises to 62 for natural fathers. It is clear that for some children isolation has been exacerbated by the care process itself as well as by family attitudes and presenting problems.

The reasons for imposing specific restrictions continue to be numerous but over time the risk of neglect, abuse and moral danger and the need to protect the stability of placements become increasingly significant. In contrast, behaviour difficulties, such as absconding or offending, decline as a reason, as Table 11.11 shows.

Table 11.11 **Percentage of cases where specific restrictions are applied***

|  | 6 months | 12 months | 24 months |
|---|---|---|---|
|  | % | % | % |
| Risk of neglect/abuse | 53 | 50 | 69 |
| Child rejects parents | 54 | 47 | 46 |
| Parents reject child | 53 | 56 | 56 |
| Parents have disrupted placement | 16 | 16 | 10 |
| Parents might disrupt placement | 37 | 36 | 45 |
| Parents bad moral influence | 16 | 16 | 33 |
| Child may abscond | 7 | 7 | 5 |
| Child may be delinquent | 14 | 14 | 8 |
|  | (N = 109 | 102 | 78) |

* Categories not exclusive.

These risks will apply more to some groups of children than to others and the characteristics of children likely to be affected are much clearer after two years than they were earlier. Children facing specific restrictions tend to be young children under the age of seven, in care on orders for neglect or following matrimonial proceedings, or because full parental rights have been assumed. Most live in foster homes or children's homes. Less affected are adolescents who are in care because of behaviour difficulties. These are likely to live either at home or with relatives or in residential settings. These patterns are very marked. For example, at the two-year stage, 31 of the 37 children under the age of seven faced specific restrictions compared with only 22 of the 86 who were over 13. Similarly, specific restrictions affected only nine of the 34 children who were in care on care orders for delinquency. Likewise, such restrictions were in force for 32 of the 45 fosterings and 19 of the 30 children in children's homes.

Specific restrictions on contact with the natural family, therefore, continue to be a major feature of the care experience for many children. While it is younger, long-stay groups who are most affected, some adolescents are also greatly deprived of family contacts. The disturbing features at two years are the increase in specific restrictions imposed on younger children for whom the social work plans aim at rehabilitation to the natural family, the failure of social workers to scrutinise closely access arrangements and the manifest isolation of some children.

**Non-specific restrictions**
Other limitations arising from the placement of children in substitute care continue to be important. These we have called non-specific restrictions, and half the children still in care at two years were affected by these. The decline over time in the significance of barriers inherent in placements is more apparent than real, mainly due to the increasing numbers of adolescents who are now able to live at home. As before, non-specific restrictions arise from several sources, all inherent in the provision of care for separated children. Rules for visiting, problems of distance and transport continue to be important. Obviously, non-specific restrictions can change radically as children move into new placements so that half of the restrictions still in force at two years have come into being since the child's initial reception into care. Non-specific restrictions also affect nearly all separated children so that young people of all ages are affected, including adolescents in residential care, especially those in children's homes and CHEs.

Some children are more seriously affected by restrictions intrinsic to their placements than others. For example, neglected children found themselves facing severe restrictions and generally, it is the 6–11 year olds who face the most serious limitations of this kind. Such children are likely to be away from home, they are often in residential care, yet they are not old enough to manage or fashion their own contacts with home or, as is frequently the case with adolescents, to evade the restrictions imposed.

## Conclusions

At the end of two years the hints we received early on in this study of the care careers of children have become more manifest. More than a third (38 per cent) of the children who entered care two years earlier are still the responsibility of social services. The contrast noted earlier between long-stay cases, those whose departure is imminent or children who have left care in the interim remains. We can see that those children admitted to care because of parental illness, imprisonment or family disturbance have gone home, while half those admitted for behaviour problems, delinquency, neglect or abuse continue their care careers. While education problems cause diminishing concern to social workers, nevertheless, the need to ensure schooling remains a contributory factor to keeping many adolescents in care. Only one-fifth of young children admitted to care before the age of four remain while half the adolescent group stay. Indeed, by two years, 68 per cent of the children who remained from the 450 who originally entered care are over 13 years of age. Older adolescents are now beginning to leave care as they reach 18 years of age, the majority returning home and a smaller number to independent living situations.

For those who stay in care, disturbance and distress are more frequently engendered by the common experience of placement transfer and breakdown than change of social worker. Nevertheless, the level of social work involvement with families, care-givers and children declines as time passes. By two years contact with many families seems perfunctory and placements can go unvisited for long periods. Social workers adopt an oversight role and the level and quality of interaction with clients varies very considerably. Many social work tasks seem ill-defined, care plans for children are incoherent and, on their own admission, social workers feel that they have little to contribute to the major structural problems that families face. Generally, social workers stress that they have insufficient resources and time to meet clients' needs adequately. They are preoccupied with a succession of crises, still child- rather than family-oriented and focused on child rescue and case control.

The legal concerns which were salient during the early months in care have disappeared. By two years the control of social services over the majority of long-stay children in care is very considerable. Three-quarters (76 per cent) of children are on care orders and for a further 8 per cent parental rights have been assumed. While there is little evidence of shared care (that is, where the parents are encouraged to participate in the care situation) the increase in children, particularly adolescents, living at home yet still in care means that for some children shared care exists in practice. Nevertheless, the disappearance of voluntary care cases over time needs justification. It may be that from a professional viewpoint lack of control hinders social work planning. But many other aspects of the child's care career militate against successful planning and our evidence would suggest that whatever the legal status, children's care careers are much characterised by *ad hoc* crisis management. It should also be noted that legislative categories and procedures receive rather scant attention from social workers. Often their actions, particularly regarding access arrangements, exceed their legal powers. Were parents more cognisant of their rights and less passive and uncritical of care decisions and situations, social workers would be in a vulnerable position. We and others, such as Fruin and Vernon, have seen in a number of ways how early social work decisions continue to exert an influence on the care careers of children.[4] In this case, the social workers' preoccupation with achieving control in the early months of the child's care career, while maximising social workers' freedom of manoeuvre, has the effect of discouraging parental participation.

Many parents adopt a passive stance to their children's continuance in care. This is because their participation in the care of their children is discouraged, they have been found wanting and, bereft of a parent role, they receive little information on what they could contribute. Some parents had sought help with their children and found themselves subject to increasing scrutiny and control while other parents, initially neglectful, become increasingly indifferent to their children as time passes.

Over time the delivery of social services seems smooth, administratively the system works, clarifying and limiting social work responsibility, ensuring that statutory responsibilities are met, particularly on sensitive issues such as non-accidental injury and place of safety. But administrative competence does not necessarily achieve consistent and high-quality care.

Many families continue to add to their histories of dissolution and reconstitution, as well as accommodating other changes in membership, shelter, employment and health. These concerns mean that links between parents and absent children remain difficult. Parents have many other pressing concerns which take their time. Indeed, at any moment, social workers estimate that major changes are affecting families of half the children in care and that these are sufficient to place considerable strain on the links that children enjoy with their parents.

As a result, by the time children have spent two years in care, only half of them are in regular contact with their mothers and the rest have very infrequent contact or none at all. Only 31 per cent of children have any regular link with their father while the wider family suffers even greater isolation from the absent child. This is particularly sad for grandparents who were often important sources of support on the child's entry to care. Some encouragement comes from the continuing importance of siblings, both those in and out of care. Four-fifths of the children still in care at two years enjoy regular contact with at least one of their brothers or sisters.

This withering of contact is not just the result of the inevitable discouragement that comes to any efforts to maintain contact at a distance, but social work decisions also play a part in the dissolution of family links. At two years, nearly half the 170 children still experience restrictions specific to key adults. Many of these restrictions had not been scrutinised at case reviews during the past year. Indeed, for younger children in care, these restrictions on access had increased over time. In addition, the barriers to contact inherent in placements such as geographic isolation, placement routine or the unwelcoming stance of care-givers remain potent for half the children still staying in care. The apparent slight fall in the proportion of children suffering constraints on their family contacts, both specific and non-specific, is due to the increase during the year of adolescents living at home.

As time passes, more adolescents leave or are on the threshold of leaving care and the majority of them return to home or to its immediate neighbourhood. These adolescents, however disrupted their care career and family links, feel that they belong somewhere and have kept links going, often in defiance of regulations. In addition, there are a few young children who have stayed long in care and who by this time will be in stable foster placements and/or preparing for adoption. For these children the withering of links with their natural family is likely to be compensated for by the increasingly important role of their psychological parents.

Several groups, however, emerge at two years as particularly problematic. First are the 6–11 year olds, long away from home, increasingly isolated, still experiencing transfer and breakdown in placements, often lingering in residential care and unable to fashion their own links with parents or wider family. Incidentally, it was just this age group that Wallerstein and Kelly identified as being most stressed by divorce and who found subsequent adaptation to dual loyalties and step-parenting difficult.[5] These children, as they stay in care, will be ill-equipped to deal with the stress and transitions of adolescence which, with depressing accuracy, social workers forecast is likely to be spent in care, often in residential care. It is this group of children who should excite growing concern at two years as they seem to belong nowhere.

A second group that causes concern are those adolescents who have lost contact with their families. Teenagers leaving care remain in a very vulnerable position. Some emerge at 18 for the shelter of lodgings and friends. Usually, they locate themselves in familiar neighbourhoods or, in the case of those who have few social contacts, in the vicinity of their residential or foster home.

While it would be unfair to suggest that the care experience has added social isolation as an additional burden to these children's already diminished life-chances, we can see that social workers should have given family, neighbourhood and peer groups links a higher priority. It is also to be regretted that the legacy of 'less eligibility' still survives; the care experience is not seen by social services as an opportunity to enrich or to enhance the life-chances of those children who stay long in care. Present social work interventions do not seek to offer, as did the great charity schools and foundations of Tudor times, much chance to escape from the cycle of deprivation. These adolescents emerge from care deficient in social skills, educational attainment and with diminished chances of permanent employment.

Neither should one receive with unqualified enthusiasm the finding that a third of these children who are still in care at two years are now living with their families, 44 of this group of 58 are at home and 14 are sheltered by relatives. This study would suggest that those children who go home yet remain in care continue to need considerable social work support; return home is not the end of the story. We have seen that these prodigals are highly likely to face placement break down and return to care, some for a long stay, consequently repeating a process which this study has only partially glimpsed. Indeed, the high level of breakdown among those still in care yet with their families is particularly distressing because these children are viewed as having more viable home circumstances.

Finally, while this scrutiny of children's care situations at the end of two years indicates that the proportion of children who become isolated while in care is not high, about one in seven of all long-stay cases, we shall see shortly that the national implications of this proportion for the total population of children in care is very disturbing.

## Summary points

1. During the second year 25 children left care with the result that 170 children (38 per cent) of the original 450 entry still remain in

care. Of these long-stay children, 92 were boys and 78 girls; adolescents continued to dominate: 68 per cent of the children were aged 11 or over while 17 per cent are aged 17 and over. Generally, social workers' expectations on children's likely future duration in care rises as time passes.

2. Nearly half (46 per cent) had experienced care from the same social worker over the two-year period and a further 54 children (32 per cent) out of the 170 had experienced a change of social worker. Thus, the lack of continuity in field social work support of children has been over-estimated. Nevertheless, social work activity continued to decline during the second year. There was virtually no contact with one-third of mothers, four-fifths of fathers remained uninvolved, and nearly half the children were receiving visits less than once a month.

3. Legal control has increased during two years: only 15 per cent of children remain in voluntary care and care orders predominate. Particularly noticeable is the rise in the proportion of children in care for neglect.

4. There is a welcome decline in the number of planned placement changes of children. An increased number of children are now placed at home on trial (26 per cent) and the remainder are equally divided between residential placements and foster homes. Some of these settings are far from home – over one-third of the children are now more than 20 miles distant from home and 17 per cent of children more than 50 miles away.

5. During the two years, 67 children have experienced a breakdown in placements, 55 of them in crisis situations and 12 have had intended changes brought forward. Many children have had more than one placement breakdown. This means that more than a third of long-stay children will have changed their placements in crisis situations.

6. During the two years, children's difficult behaviour and breakdown in placements are increasingly associated with low levels of parental and family contact.

7. The households of long-stay children in care continue to show disruption during the second year. The natural families of 73 per cent of those admitted to care before the age of 11 have changed radically during the two years, as have those of 54 per cent of those children over the age of 11. The family relationships of over half of the children who have stayed in care have been disrupted by family turbulence.

8. At two years, two-thirds (66 per cent) of the 170 children still in care experience serious barriers to contact with their families. This decline from the higher level shown at 12 months, however, is due

to the fact that a third of the children still in care are now living with their family (44 of them with a parent and 14 with relatives).

9. Of children away in care after two years, 46 per cent experience specific restrictions, and over half of these have been in force during the whole care period. Non-specific restrictions are pressing, affecting almost all children away in care. These press particularly on children of primary school age. Many of these restrictions remain unscrutinised as time passes. At two years, 41 of the 170 children's mothers were unaware of their child's address in care as were 62 of their fathers.

# 12. The case studies at two years

This chapter traces the perspectives and care experiences of three of the families that opened this study, the Denbow and James children and the adolescents, Gloria and Dean. (It will be remembered that David March left care to live with his mother, Sally, at the grandmother's home.) We can now pick up their stories two years on.

Previous chapters have concerned themselves with the passage of children through care. We have seen the numbers and characteristics of children who leave care at various times over two years, we have looked at the reasons which facilitated leaving and highlighted the problems of those that remain. At each stage of the child's journey through care, we have seen the consequences for family links of certain social work decisions. Aspects of social work oversight, legislative decisions, placements and access restrictions have all been examined and their consequences for family contact with the absent child have been suggested. The problems of maintaining links between family and child absent in care have been explored in a wide context because many decisions which may not appear immediately influential in relationships between parent and child have considerable implications for contact.

David March was an early leaver who, somewhat unexpectedly, has subsequently stayed out of care, living with his mother and gran in the 'open house' that filled the social worker at the outset with so much unease. No doubt the sense of violation etched on the family's memory by the taking of a place of safety order has contributed to Sally March's distancing herself from social services. Yet the other families have remained very much the responsibility of social workers and it is useful to see what has happened to them. How did Mrs Denbow fare after her operation and was she early and easily reunited with her children? What happened to the paranoid Mr James? We can also resume our contact with Gloria Barton, that liberated adolescent whose career highlights the impossible contradictions between care and control and the difficulties, barring a long sojourn in maximum security, of protecting someone from moral danger, a particularly difficult task, especially when that rather quaint Victorian perspective is incomprehensible to the client.

## The Denbow family at two years
Two years is a long time in the lives of young children, and in the case of Adam and Lisa Denbow a lot has happened since we described the

events surrounding their reception into care. Although their mother's illness propelled the children into care voluntarily, surprisingly, we find both children still in care after two years. Indeed, by this time, the prospect of their returning home to their mother is very uncertain, and the social worker now forecasts at least another year in care for both of them. The Denbow children illustrate a number of the characteristics and experiences of those children we have traced through their care careers.

Superficially, the Denbow case appeared relatively straightforward at the time of reception. Two young children needed substitute care for a short time during their mother's hospitalisation. From the outset, however, the case was complicated by the social isolation of the family, Mrs Denbow's history of mental illness, and the absence of the children's father. There was also some concern about the mother's ambivalent feelings towards her two children. While the social worker had expected an easy return home, he entertained some reservations about Mrs Denbow's constancy and stability.

We have seen that Adam and Lisa's entry to care was rushed and poorly planned. This was due not to the social worker's negligence, but to the limited availability of suitable short-term foster homes and a reluctance even to consider the potential strengths of residential care. This indecision caused a great deal of distress to the children, their mother and, in all fairness, their social worker, Mr Platt. But, as we have seen, the failure to secure a foster home resulted in both children moving into a children's home the day before their mother's operation. Their social worker envisaged this placement lasting perhaps six weeks in order to allow Mrs Denbow time to convalesce.

Neither child was taken to see the mother while she was in hospital and very little information was exchanged between mother and children. It was here that the absence of the wider family was most keenly felt, as was Mrs Denbow's lack of close friends. Children and mother were virtually isolated from each other for three weeks. Interestingly, neither field nor residential social workers considered this particularly unusual. Plans had not been made to facilitate visiting or the exchange of information between the family. The children were left in limbo waiting to be visited.

Ominously, when Doreen returned home, somewhat low after her operation, the social worker found her reluctant to talk about her children, and particularly resistant to any attempts to arrange an appropriate date for the children to return home. In fact, in discussion, the social worker volunteered that he found the mother 'difficult and obstructive'. Unfortunately, the mother's increasing indifference to the welfare of her children rather alienated Mr Platt. Quite understandably, he was deeply concerned at the uncertainty surrounding their situation and embarrassed by the repeated questions of both residential staff and the children as to when they were going home. Thus his positive role in encouraging and arranging for Mrs Denbow to see her children was somewhat reduced. However, Mrs Denbow was receptive to the idea that the children should visit home from time to time accompanied by the social worker.

During this period, events were further complicated by Mrs Denbow taking in a lodger, a friend of her former husband. The social worker commented that her interest in the children seemed to fade even more with the lodger's arrival. As a result, social work concern about returning the children to their mother increased considerably. Twelve weeks after first entering hospital, Mrs Denbow had seen her children only three times and had failed to keep numerous appointments to visit the children's home. The visits of the social worker had also declined: he had only seen the children three times and had visited Doreen twice. He was somewhat discouraged by his inability to get anywhere. In the end, Doreen was virtually forced to resume the care of her children as the team leader insisted on their return. The children left care but not for long. Two weeks after their return their mother took an overdose of painkillers after a fight with her lodger. He disappeared, somewhat predictably, clutching her social security money.

The social worker took both chilnden back into care, this time using interim care orders as he found that the children had been hit occasionally by the lodger. There was also a suspicion that Mrs Denbow might have been less than protective. Lisa and Adam returned to the now familiar children's home where the staff noted how disturbed both children had become in the short space of three weeks. As one residential social worker remembered,

'They were both bed-wetting when they came back and this certainly wasn't a feature of their behaviour before they went home. Lisa kept having nightmares and Adam threw terrible temper tantrums the like of which I had never seen before.'

Mrs Denbow confessed to the social worker at a subsequent interview that on two nights she and her lodger friend had got drunk and that each occasion had ended in violence. Evidently, both she and her friend had hit the children because they would not go to sleep.

All these events shifted opinion within the social services department further towards the view that the Denbow children were seriously at risk, that their mother was inadequate and that they needed a longer period in local authority care. Therefore, a full care order was successfully applied for and plans were made for the children to be placed with long-term foster parents. The medical and social work consensus was that Doreen Denbow's instability and history of mental illness meant that the prognosis for the children was poor. There was apparently little sympathy for the mother either among the care-givers or the social workers; she had clearly failed the 'parenting test' by her fitful and very infrequent visits to her children when they were in voluntary care. In addition, there was the suspicion of non-accidental injury.

After the care order had been taken, Mrs Denbow was not allowed to see her children for three weeks and she complained that she was kept in ignorance of any care plans that were being made. When we spoke to her, although her views were somewhat confused, she had clearly become very hostile to her social worker whom she now saw as unhelpful and unsympathetic. This was in marked contrast to her dependent stance towards Mr Platt at the time of the children's first referral:

'I know I was wrong, but I just couldn't cope. Everything was getting on top of me, the operation and everything was terrible and I just needed more time. It's not that I don't love my children. They're mine. But I wasn't in a fit state to look after them properly. I thought social workers were supposed to help. I went to the social for help – and what did I get? They took my children away and accused me of neglect and worse.'

It took the social worker three months to find a foster home for Lisa and Adam. During this time, Mrs Denbow was allowed to see her children once a week, but she received little active encouragement from her social worker. The foster parents later considered her 'odd', to say the least; her company unnerved them, particularly when she lost her temper and swore. She was also viewed as having a disturbing effect on the children when she visited. When we talked to the foster parents, what seemed to irk them most was not so much Mrs Denbow's displays of temper but the gifts of sweets and toys she would usually bring her children. As one of the foster parents said,

'It was a bit like Christmas every weekend and we don't think that is any good for anyone – and besides, it was all a bit shallow. She was buying them off, she never talked about having them back. Of course, they were difficult children. Lisa was very disturbed. The children were often upset by her visits and they were difficult enough already.'

This particular foster home placement lasted six months. Lisa's very disturbed behaviour and Adam's continuing temper tantrums gradually exhausted the foster parents' tolerance and they eventually requested the children's removal. By this time, Mrs Denbow's visiting had been reduced to once a fortnight. However she had calmed down a great deal, was less disturbed and was behaving much more rationally. This might have provided a good opportunity for a carefully supervised reunion.

Unfortunately from the children's point of view, Mrs Denbow's lodger friend returned at this critical moment, a reconciliation took place, and he seemed to have taken up permanent residence. So, despite Mrs Denbow's now strongly expressed desire to have her children back, the social services department was very reluctant to sanction their return. Opinion within the social services was, however, by no means unanimous. There were some social workers who felt that the children should return home despite the risk of further abuse while others urged a long-stay foster placement. This led to a great deal of vacillation as to what should be done. In the end, caution ruled the day and, after a short period in another children's home, a new foster home was found. Meanwhile, Mrs Denbow had received a clear message that she was no longer considered a suitable mother for her children.

The children moved into their new placement – the fourth since their reception into care – and the mother's visits and telephone calls to her children rapidly declined. Her hopes of having the children back had been dashed and she began to view the social services with increasing bitterness:

'I mean, what's the point? Once they've got your number, that's it, isn't it? They don't bloody forget! I could give them [Lisa and Adam] a decent home, at least I don't kick them out when they act up, not like them Phillips [the first foster parents]. Well, now the social can bloody stew in their own juice. I'm not going to help, what's the point? I'd always have the social round my neck when I did have the children back.'

Two years later we found that a new social worker has been allocated to the Denbow case who brought some new perspectives on the children's future. Lisa and Adam are still living with their second foster parents but there are indications that even now all is not well. Adam still goes purple with rage and Lisa is difficult to control. As a result, the placement might crumble in the near future. Both children are being seen by an educational psychologist to help resolve their still severe emotional problems. While Doreen's original lodger has long since disappeared she is now living with another man. The new social worker plans to raise at the next review the possibility of placing both children at home for a trial period. The difficulty is that Mrs Denbow has now been separated from her children for two years. She has a job and is enjoying a life without the responsibility of parenthood, which is, in fact, a distant memory for her.

In conclusion, the Denbow case illustrates a number of issues that are common in the care careers of children. In the first instance, despite the fragile relationship Mrs Denbow had with her children, little effort was made to nurture contact while she was away in hospital. In addition, as is not uncommon, the hysterectomy had a disturbing psychological effect and Doreen Denbow became self-obsessed and preoccupied. The social worker, rather than recognising her behaviour as temporary and gently easing her back to caring for her children, came to view Doreen with some hostility and had problems in working with her in the interests of the children. Mrs Denbow was left to organise her own visits and to cope with the complex and conflicting emotions that contact with the children provoked.

The children's short return home after their mother's recovery from illness proved unsatisfactory. The co-habitee was not adequately investigated and the children's return to care was accompanied by greatly increased control being exercised by social services. This time, the children's voluntary care status was changed to a care order. As a result, both children became increasingly isolated while in substitute care. We can see how the insecurity of their position and withering contacts with mother made both Lisa and Adam very difficult to manage. As a result, their first foster placement lasted only six months before they moved to new foster parents via a children's home. Secondary problems are beginning to assume importance, decisions are postponed and Mrs Denbow's timid efforts to maintain contact have received little official encouragement. She feels defeated and, quite understandably, has sought refuge in transitory relationships. Motherhood for Doreen was over for, as she said, 'If they think I am no good for the children, then they had best stay where they are. I'm not likely to get much help, am I?'

What is an even greater cause of concern, and not uncharacteristic, is that Lisa and Adam's new foster home also seems troubled and likely to fail, although it is uncommon to find both mother and children's behaviour proving the main source of stress and leading to placement breakdown. A new social worker, fired with ideals of family casework, hopes to rekindle Doreen Denbow's maternal interest. Nevertheless, even she is uncertain of the children's future length of time in care:

'They could stay quite a while, at least another year. Of course, the older they get, the more easily Mrs Denbow will find it to cope on their return. But I'm not sure she really wants them back.'

### The James family at two years
Andrew, June and Frances James, like the Denbow children, are still in care after two years. However, unlike the latter they are not separated from their family but are living at home with their mother, Rose. They are visited regularly by the social worker, usually every two weeks.

Once the anxieties of living with their paranoid step-father and their dramatic removal from home on a place of safety order were over, life for these children became less fraught. They left the hospital, in which they were initially placed, for an observation and assessment centre where they stayed until a suitable foster placement could be found. The children were deeply distressed by their experiences and the residential staff noted how they each displayed their anxieties in a different way:

'Andrew cried a great deal and would get himself into the most awful states, sometimes he looked as if he would burst. June and Frances, on the other hand, were very subdued and less expressive. June often wouldn't eat and would 'wet' a lot and Frances would withdraw and sit staring into space for long periods of time or pace up and down like some caged animal.'

From the outset, Rose was encouraged by her social worker, Mr Arkwright, to visit her children and was, in fact, taken regularly to the children's home by him. Her visits were, however, closely supervised and a watchful eye was kept on her interaction with the children. Rose was conscious of this scrutiny, just as she had been in the hospital, but she accepted it as an inevitable consequence of her inability to stand up to her husband. Nevertheless, Rose found the watchfulness of the care staff rather difficult. As she explained,

'It's a bit like trying to do some shopping while there's a store detective watching you. You can't enjoy it – it sort of worries you and you feel guilty although you haven't done anything wrong. I mean, who'd've thought I'd run out of talk with my own kids? I did though. I used to sit there and think, what the hell am I going to say next?'

Despite these not uncommon difficulties, Rose continued to visit the children regularly. The unhappiness caused by her separation from them was severe; she mourned their loss. Disbelief, anger, despondency and guilt jostled with each other as she sought to order her sense of loss.

When the place of safety order lapsed, the social services department applied for care orders on all three children. These were easily obtained as the evidence of abuse presented to the court was overwhelming. Although the social worker's concerns about Rose's parenting abilities and her part in the abuse of her children diminished, there still remained considerable anxiety about her husband. Much to everyone's surprise and discomfort, when Mr James appeared at the magistrates' court, he was bailed to a probation hostel only five miles from home. Because of this, and the possible threat he offered, Mr Arkwright would not entertain the children's return home for, as he explained at the time, 'As far as I'm concerned he's [Mr James] still on the loose. I don't know what the magistrate was up to. Until he is put away, I must hang on to the kids.'

After a month at the children's home, a temporary foster home was found to care for all three children. The social worker had found it very difficult to find a family that would shoulder responsibility for three small children together. However, they remained there for a further three months until their father was found guilty of injuring Frances and sentenced to six months imprisonment. The following day, the children returned home to their mother who was immensely happy at having them back and celebrated the event by throwing a party for the family.

The story does not end here, for despite her husband's behaviour, Rose wrote to him regularly while he was at the hostel and visited him in prison. Although admiring Rose's loyalty, the social worker was worried by this turn of events as he had hoped that the marriage would end. All prospects of the children leaving care early were, therefore, shelved as there remained the distinct possibility that Mr James would return to live with his wife and children.

After four months in prison, Mr James was released. He did not, however, go back to Rose but went to live in a bedsitter and volunteered to undergo psychiatric treatment. Significantly, a week before his release, Rose asked her divorced sister to come and live with her with her baby. She had clearly used this as an excuse for not having Ted back. However, despite the failure to reconstitute the marriage, Rose's feelings towards her husband were still strong and she speaks occasionally of reconciliation. Needless to say, Mr Arkwright is not happy with this prospect, and is maintaining a careful watch on events.

Two years after the place of safety orders, the three children, now aged five, seven and nine years, are happily settled with their mother and seem to have recovered from their earlier experiences. However, a question-mark still hangs over their future if their step-father returns. In the words of their social worker,

'I'm afraid there are few happy endings in this game. There is always some loose end that makes the closing of files difficult. In this case, the loose end is the husband. Rose, as you know, is a soft touch and she just might invite him back.'

Although the three James children are still legally in care after two years, they were separated from their mother for only a little over four months. During the whole of this period, they were in regular contact with Rose who was encouraged and helped to visit them by her field worker, the staff at the assessment centre and the foster parents. Mr Arkwright had decided early in the case that, despite the considerable injuries to Frances and the miserable existence of all three children prior to their admission to care, Rose was a viable parent and her children should be returned home as soon as their safety could be assured.

**The Barton family at two years**

Few young people could have crammed into two short years as many changes of address, different partners and brief work experience schemes than has Gloria. We have seen in other contexts social workers' remarkable ability to forecast children's care careers. Gloria's social worker fully expected her to prove a nuisance and she has tried very hard to live up to these expectations.

After a month's stay at Sunnylands, Gloria moved to a children's home close to her old neighbourhood. She even returned briefly to St Paul's school, where she was given a guarded reception by her friends. There is nothing like discovery and a little ribaldry to check youthful ardour. Even a brief absence can disturb the social networks of adolescents and Gloria did not settle. As she commented,

'It wasn't the same. Everyone looked at me funny, particularly the teachers. Anyway, it was boring and useless, the same old stuff, day in and day out. Everyone knows there aren't any jobs and if there were, we wouldn't be getting them. So, why go?'

– a withering and perspicacious comment to which there seems little answer. Her school attendance became fitful and, in the few months before she was due to leave, she had virtually ceased to attend St Paul's.

However, if Gloria posed few problems at school, at her community home, things were different. She blithely disregarded their regulations on routine, on associates and, above all, on her nightly pleasures and routine. Gloria had no intention of compromising her hard-won liberty or her escape from Mum and the unappreciative, censorious audience of the wider family. As she commented, 'They say you're not to go to pubs or clubs – nothing. Even some discos and Silver Blades were out. What are you supposed to do, for God's sake? Sit and knit and wait for a moan from Auntie?' Thus, Gloria rapidly moved through a range of residential provision exhausting in rapid succession the patience of her children's homes, the Richmond Fellowship, the YWCA, the Sisters of the Resurrection, and the Children's Society. Her subsequent stays in sheltered lodgings usually lasted as long as the landlord's tolerance of unpaid rent arrears.

To brighten life's monotony, she would occasionally abscond to Cornwall with one of the more promising, inadequate and anomic young men living out similar careers either in or on the margins of care. These expeditions were more common in the summer when the funfairs took their soggy circuits of the half-empty resorts of the peninsular. Funfairs offer asylum to a wide range of adolescent refugees. They ask no questions, they provide work and meet the young's need for restless, instant excitement and fantasy potential.

However, all honeymoons are costly and usually a little delinquency helped to keep both the prodigals afloat. Gloria's look of sweet innocence and her boy friend's old world courtesy ensured that only he got the short sharp shock which they both richly deserved.

During brief lulls, and encouraged by her social worker, Gloria joined a variety of youth employment schemes. Opportunity knocked quite often for Gloria – and she rarely missed an opportunity to knock the schemes on which she found herself an unwilling participant. As Gloria commented,

'They call it youth training. Well, all I did was wash up at this local "caf". The only thing I learned was how to make them keep their hands to themselves. All these schemes are the same. You get a rotten job that no one wants and are supposed to look grateful into the bargain. Well they can stuff it.'

Similar fates befell attempts to interest her in the elderly, in supermarket work and many other, admittedly lack-lustre, opportunities.

Gloria's ambivalent attitudes to home remained unchanged. While she took little notice of the access limitations which were imposed to keep her clear of Derek (who, incidentally, received a suspended sentence) she visited her mother fitfully. The reunions were often stormy and acrimonious. Indeed, the visits had little expressive content. Gloria would arrive with a pile of washing and 'borrow' from the jar containing the rent money. Mother particularly disliked the freedom and independence which the girl now displayed. As Brenda commented,

'She's out all hours, swinging her handbag, made up like some tart on the beat. She's in more trouble now than she's ever been. When she was home, I knew where she was and she got a bloody good hiding if she wasn't back here by eleven. All the social says is, "We're the parents now, Mrs Barton." Well, they can bloody well get on with it. Gloria can take care of herself – she's as hard as nails – but I feel sorry for all those other kids the social looks after.'

Indeed, there is no disguising the fact that, generally, adolescents pose major problems for social services in those years immediately prior to their leaving care at eighteen – principally, problems of control. If they are in contact with home their relationships remain stormy and subject to crises, while if family links have withered, they are vulnerable and isolated on leaving care. Boys are frequently rejected by their parents because of minor delinquencies and lengthy unemployment while daughters are viewed as shameless and promiscuous. Unlike Gloria, many adolescents who have been long in care have few friends, little adult support and, sadly, they do not share Gloria's lust for life or survival skills. As her social worker accurately commented,

'We get an increasing number of these older teenagers, they spell havoc to the small children's homes, the CHEs aren't really suitable for them and many hostels are a bit like something out of Dickens. So, you just put them in bed-sitters and hope that the MSC [Manpower Services Commission] will keep them occupied. Thank God, the older they get, the less chance there is of a scandal. People just don't care about the seventeen and eighteen year olds.'

While Gloria avoided any conflict with the law, Dean, her charming brother, was less fortunate. After leaving school, he embarked on a Youth Training Scheme removing rubbish from the market, a job which combined endless prospects with no interest whatsoever. Several minor thefts were met with tolerance and fines, but he borrowed a van and was caught using the multi-storey carpark late one night as a race track. He spent three months in Haslar Detention Centre looking across to the city which had seen his dead father's happiest days.

Characteristically resolute, Brenda, his mother, refused to go and see him, although entreated by both social and probation workers to accompany them to her once familiar haunts. As she said,

'I don't care what they do. I'm far too old to go dancing off after any of them. When you get to my age, it's their place to visit me and I won't lose any sleep if they don't. When they do arrive, all they want is money or you have to do the washing. I'm tired. Kids? I brought up five of them, they're nice when they're little but that don't last long.'

## Summary

Our case studies have reinforced many of the issues raised in those preceding chapters which trace children's careers through care. While the heterogeneity of the care populations means that the problems Gloria Barton faces are very different from those of the Denbow or James children, some common features emerge.

It is quite clear that whether the client is satisfied or disenchanted with their children's care experience, they find referral to social services opens a Pandora's box. They lose control of outcomes and the more diffuse their children's problems and the lengthier their stays in care, the more parents adopt a passive stance. While they accept the ends of social work interventions, as time progresses they are less enthusiastic about the means.

Families change rapidly and it is difficult for social workers to gauge shifts in parental attitudes, the effects of arrivals and departures or the consequences of extraneous factors such as redundancy, imprisonment or illness. This task is complicated by the decline in social work visiting over time of parents, children and care-givers. In addition, social workers experience considerable discouragement in working with apparently indifferent and sometimes hostile mothers. It is not surprising that the maintenance of links between family and absent child fails to receive the emphasis that this study shows to be essential. Unlike adolescents, who have considerable ability in maintaining those relationships they consider important, younger children depend very largely on the efforts of social workers to keep them going. In addition, our case studies would suggest that the wider family is rarely involved and children's friendships in school and neighbourhood are virtually ignored.

It is also clear that in terms of placement stability and children's behaviour, the care situation does not 'solve' the problem. If links with home wither, then the child may have to face an adolescence in care, a time when all children undergo the stresses associated with transitions from child to young adult. At least we have seen that Gloria and Dean react to situations, although their strategies might excite our censure. Unfortunately, many other adolescents in care are more passive. They emerge at 18 poorly fitted for the considerable adjustment problems they must face in the community. It is also clear that social work resources generally are frequently insufficient for the tasks they face and that for some groups, such as adolescents in the community, creative thinking and innovation are markedly absent from thinking, planning and provision.

## Summary points

1. The case studies show how difficult it is to plan successfully for children in care. The families show unpredictable changes which make return home for children risky. Such vicissitudes preoccupy parents and diminish any priority that contact with their children might have.

2. As time passes, many parents increasingly adopt a passive stance. They find visiting difficult and some, particularly the parents of adolescents, argue that it is not their role to visit.

3. There is a clear need for social workers to inform parents, to involve them in the care task and to encourage their participation and regular visiting. This cannot be achieved with the low levels of contact between social workers, families, child and care-givers that we noted in Chapter 11.

4. The wider family still remains uninvolved in the care situation and, as at all stages in the child's care career, their participation should be engineered.

5. Adolescents in need of control and protection present social workers with considerable problems. To appear to give freedom to teenagers while exercising restraint and to guide and counsel the uncooperative is almost impossible. The task is made even more daunting by the lack of appropriate placements for adolescents and

little creative thinking in social services departments on what to do with them.

6. Adolescents form the majority of long-stay care cases. Three groups of adolescents should cause concern (a) those who present control and delinquency problems; (b) those who remain in care for failure to attend school. Some of these children are away from home, usually in residential care, and run all the risks of secondary problems accumulating while in care, particularly withering links with home; (c) those teenagers who have spent much of their childhood and adolescence in care, often spending their older years in residential settings because of frequent foster breakdowns.

7. Many adolescents leave care at 18 handicapped by poor educational attainments, lacking in social skills, and isolated from both social and family networks which can provide them with shelter and jobs. It is not satisfactory simply to hang on to adolescents until the statutory leaving age removes the 'problem'; these young people remain extremely vulnerable.

# 13. Conclusions

In preceding chapters, we have explored many of the issues that pose problems for maintaining links between children in care and their families. We have suggested that links between family and child absent in local authority care are part of a complex pattern of belonging: visiting, letters, the telephone and intermediaries are all significant in maintaining contact with home, but form only part of a wider membership 'package' for the child. Links have psychological, symbolic and power dimensions which are less tangible and therefore less considered by social workers in managing separation.

This study has demonstrated that the problems parents and wider families face in maintaining contact with the absent child cannot be comprehended in isolation; that is, understood through a scrutiny of visiting patterns, access restrictions and the distance, location and nature of children's placements in care. Barriers to links between parents and child are also inherent in the child-rescue orientation of much children's legislation, in the control obligations and public accountability of social work, and in the inheritance from the past of punitive and contaminating beliefs on families. A child-rescue perspective has also been encouraged by the case- rather than group-work orientation of many training courses which emphasise the individual rather than the context and wider structural issues. As a result, the development of a truly family-oriented service, as envisaged by Seebohm in 1968, is far from attainment.

In addition, we have also demonstrated the value of looking at outcomes over time. We have looked at child-care processes, the ways in which a sequence of events follow each other, often predictably, to influence a child's situation at any one moment in time and, as a result, the perspectives which participants adopt.

We have suggested that links with parents and the wider family are important to the child, not only because much research evidence indicates that the well-being of most absent children is enhanced by contact with home, but also because stable care placements and adequate substitute parenting cannot be guaranteed by local authorities. Obviously, child-care placements should be selected with more care and receive more support but, even then, it will remain difficult for social workers to be cognisant of the many factors encouraging placement breakdown. In addition, the majority of children who remain in care will be old enough to entertain several significant adults in their lives and, consequently, some will be very resistant to substitute parenting and the majority will wish to maintain family links. It is also clear that strong links with parents and/or wider family are associated with leaving care, while withering contacts with home imply long care careers for children.

In preceding chapters, we have demonstrated that, after two years, although the majority of children have left care and a number of adolescents are on the point of leaving, a quarter of the original 450 children are still in care and away from home. We have also seen that these children are likely to remain absent from home and in care for the foreseeable future; indeed, the situation of some children of junior school age is particularly problematic. In addition, a group of children move in and out of care, increasingly running the risk of a long sojourn away from home. These long-stay cases arouse many problems apart from those of family contact; they have educational, social and other behavioural concerns which have been highlighted in this and numerous other research studies. Yet, over time, it becomes increasingly difficult for parents and absent children to maintain contact, partly due to turbulent family circumstances and individual discouragements, partly due to aspects of the care process itself and social workers' decisions.

It would be useful, as a summary of much of the preceding material, to look at what this study says about processes in child care and the way in which they affect links, about the problems parents face in maintaining contact with their children, what messages the findings have for social workers and the consequences that withering relationships with their families have on the children.

## Child-care processes
The United Kingdom offers many opportunities for the study of processes simply because most of our welfare, penal, education and health services have long historical antecedents. We have seen in an earlier chapter the ways in which control and punishment of the poor, provision of minimum benefit, the exclusion of contaminating parents and, consequently, the separation of children from their families long characterised the state's intervention with children made visible by neglect and poverty. These beliefs are difficult to shrug off because they are inherent in much child-care legislation fashioned in the nineteenth century which survives little changed today.

Such influences also cling because nothing too cataclysmic ever seems to disrupt the gradual development and unfolding of our social and educational services. Whether or not this sequence is a logical development towards the best of all possible child care cannot be explored here, but child welfare has long antecedents and its processes are well established. While a sequence of events with powerful determining properties can be seen most clearly in our education system, recent studies of other organisations, such as those responsible for offenders, have also illustrated the value of research taking a career perspective. Findings suggest that the system itself can help to create the client. Such research has highlighted the long-term consequences of initial professional definitions of presenting problems and has charted the 'avenues' along which clients are directed as a result of these decisions.

We rapidly learned early in the 1960s that it was pointless to explore what was happening in educational and social services for children without taking into account the wider social and cultural contexts in which these services operate. For example, the lifestyles, childrearing patterns, values and aspirations of clients, whether in a public school or a state boarding school, were particularly influential on the outcome of the residential experience. Our subsequent glance at young offenders in community homes and secure units increased our interest in the processes which draw children into a system and keep them there. We hope that this scrutiny of the family links of children in care has also benefited from this theoretical approach. Whether or not social work shares the self-fulfilling tendencies of other systems has not been the focus of this study but, at least, sufficient evidence has been gathered to raise this disquieting issue.

The process approach has also allowed the study to take account of changes in definitions of the child's problems and relates these changed perceptions to the options actually available to social workers at any moment in time and the decisions they make. In addition, it highlights conflicts between the many different processes which simultaneously affect children in care – for example, how to ensure a stable educational environment while removal from home and moves between care placements mean several changes of school.

Clearly, the process model is not one which emphasises harmony and consensus. Processes take place at different rates and some will reach fruition earlier in the child's care career than others. For example, the onset of puberty or the age of consent are not negotiable for social workers, but they add piquancy to any girl's career in 'moral danger'. The unfolding of process is also complicated because the aims of different interventions are also irreconcilable. For example, concern over a child's need for protection and control may conflict with a desire for rehabilitation with the natural family. In the same way, the need to provide full-time education keeps many adolescents away from home and in residential care, a separation which, as we have seen, can have serious consequences for the child. Similarly, we have seen that the maintenance and tranquility of short-stay placements may take priority over issues more important for the child's future, such as frequent and enriching contact with natural parents.

In this respect, this study echoes much of our other work on the careers of delinquents where we found a preoccupation with control interfered with many other adolescent transitions. In addition, the intellectual, physical and emotional maturation of the child becomes more important as time passes. The older the child, the more confident he or she becomes in manipulating the system – by engineering breakdowns or transfer, by absconding, offending or by withdrawing cooperation with social workers. Increasingly, the passive client takes a hand in the process. Processes in child care, therefore, do not necessarily move towards the same ends. They are variable in speed, are multi-directional and, occasionally, conflicting.

In this study we have shown that the development of links between children in care and their families cannot be traced as a process in its own right. The ways that links are maintained, lost or regenerated are dependent on many other issues and different processes, each with different outcomes. For example, only in a few cases do major links decisions, such as the 'termination of access', become issues and directly affect contacts between children in care and their families. Many other barriers to contact, we have seen, are implicit in decisions made on placements, distance or a child's special needs.

This study has highlighted not only the instability of the child's care experience but also the significance of changes in the child's natural family while he or she is away in care. Processes in child care do not unfold in isolation. Children often leave care to go back to quite different family situations and neighbourhoods from those they knew before admission. Family processes of dislocation and reconstitution continue while the child is away, altering household compositions and demanding new roles and relationships from family members. Although we could not study the problems of a child's return in any systematic way, the frequency of children's re-entry to care and the evidence of some of our previous work would suggest that children and adolescents find return difficult.

While certain issues increased in significance over time, others declined. Legislation, for example, was at the outset especially important, as Packman has stressed, but over time we have seen that its influence on the care experiences of children decreases. As our study of place of safety orders confirms, several different care careers are possible despite a single legislative label.

We have seen that very influential in the maintenance of links between children and their families will be the access arrangements themselves. In this study, we have shown that only a minority of access arrangements are explicit, but contact between parent and child will reflect many other aspects of the care process and are implicit in many other decisions. As a strong link between parent and child has been shown in this study to be a major indicator of eventual rehabilitation, the implication for practice is clear. Much benefit would be obtained by giving more consideration to the ways in which other child-care processes affect links over time, and by establishing more explicit policies on family contact for every child. This becomes especially important when we see how dramatically other events can change original social worker expectations.

As aspects of child development and child-care processes can conflict, their reconciliation will seldom be harmonious and, as a result, social work with children in care will always be pragmatic, sometimes *ad hoc* and frequently very difficult. Nevertheless, this research has shown that some efforts with children in care are likely to be more effective than others and that the encouragement of the links enjoyed by parents with their absent children is one of these.

### Parents and the problems of maintaining contact

This study has shown how difficult some parents find maintaining contact with their long-absent children. While the majority of families experience barriers to contact, in only a few cases does this lead to the complete isolation of the children in long-term care. We shall shortly note that if mothers disappear, either the wider family or some other adult usually assumes the parenting role. Fathers, however, remain distinctly marginal in most care situations; they are rarely consulted or sought out, in strong contrast to their legal dominance in the late nineteenth century, when most child-care legislation was fashioned.

Maintaining contact with the absent child is difficult because families are poor, disrupted and continue to experience many of the pressures that precipitated their children into care in the first place. The recurrent crises of referral and reception of the child to care reflect long-standing structural problems in these families. Although all the families are at various stages of development, lone young mothers, absent fathers, unstable marriages and difficulties in step-parenting are among the most salient characteristics. Indeed, it is interesting to note how groups that haunted Victorian reformers, such as the indigent poor, the illegitimate, the lone mother, the chronically sick and the homeless and delinquent adolescent still surface in our child-care population. These enduring problems mean that many families are well known to social services; indeed, some have been for generations.

Very often children enter care because of the stresses associated with reconstituting families. This involves parents fashioning new identities, moving home, even excluding wider kin and friends. Indeed, as with parental visiting of absent children, it is often a change in established patterns that causes crises. We have also seen that the extended family usually exists locally but fails to assist children and mothers in crises. Relatives may have learned from bitter experience, they may disapprove of the current situation, they may, in fact, be kept in ignorance, unaware of the child's needs and the family's inability or unwillingness to cope.

It is also clear that adolescents, although their problems may be very severe, compounded by school, neighbourhood and limited opportunities, are viewed less sympathetically by the wider family. This has cultural, generational and social causes which we and many others have explored elsewhere. Therefore, it is not surprising that, as the number of asylums available to teenagers at risk shrink, young people begin to accumulate in local authority care. Neither is it remarkable that the secondary school, the police and youth services should be increasingly evident as referral agents to social services.

If the wider family is marginal when the child or adolescent enters care, it proves difficult to involve it later. Not only have relatives to overcome many of the barriers to contact that we have seen are inherent in any separation, but they have to neutralise the hostilities and reservations they previously entertained regarding the child and family.

This lack of involvement of the wider family, a source of support which remains largely untapped by social workers, means that children and young people enter care in crisis. The precipitating event may, in itself, be minor but juxtaposed with deeper problems, creates a pressing need; the crisis may crystallise in the minds of social workers an aspect of enduring, threatening family history or the referral may be dramatic, such as through injury or abandonment.

Although the parent may have sought out social services' help or the children have been in care before, nevertheless, a child's entry to care is usually traumatic for all. Mothers are anxious and guilty, children passive and disoriented. Indeed, previous care experiences seem only to heighten the family's anxiety. Naturally, the family's sense of violation is increased if referral to social services comes from outside, from neighbours, police and school as a result of risk, delinquency or school refusal. Parental outrage is exacerbated by some forms of legislation, such as place of safety orders, delinquency care orders and summonses for school non-attendance. For the family and child, the crisis, as it gathers, frequently assumes the air of a conspiracy which they are powerless to resist.

Referral may come from a variety of sources but, with most children and some adolescents, the problem is seen by all as the responsibility of social services. Other agencies define the problem, they may make clear their expectations, sometimes over-optimistically, and then they depart, their statutory duty done. Social workers are left to manage the hostility and anxiety of both families and children, to support the care-givers and to fashion care plans in the light of the likely duration of the situation. Nevertheless, the problem is perceived by social workers as a family issue, the focus is on mother, and the child is likely to have entered care with siblings. In fact, there is evidence that the less social workers view families as responsible or responsive, particularly with recalcitrant and delinquent adolescents, the more they assume punitive attitudes.

Social workers and others may have been alert to problems for some time but families seem ill-prepared for the actual shock of separation. Parents complain that they have been kept in ignorance and that they were ill informed of the possibilities and consequences attendant on certain referrals. All parents remained very confused about their rights and obligations under specific legislation.

Parents' confusion and ignorance may in part reflect social workers' desire to maintain control of a situation; it may also reflect parents' inability to comprehend information and its implication during a crisis, however carefully and repeatedly consulted parents may have been by social workers. Trauma blots out comprehension, particularly if the removal of the child has been precipitate, tearful and involuntary.

While parents usually were informed of the category of placement selected for their child, such as fostering or a community home, initially the actual address was frequently withheld from them. Indeed, one local authority in our study imposed a ban on all contact between parent and child during the first ten days to facilitate the child's settling-in. This accorded ill with mothers' considerable anxiety at the outset of the children's care experience, distress greatly increased by their inability to picture the children's actual situation. This initial freeze on contact also ignores the fact that most parental visiting patterns are set very early in the children's absence.

While there is often a general consensus between social workers and parents at the outset of a child's care career that some welfare or control intervention is needed, the actual strategy employed, particularly if it involves removal of the child, comes as a shock. We have seen how this sense of violation colours subsequent interactions between social workers and the parents for, over time, the consensus between them dissolves. Secondary problems created by the placements and enduring problems of control begin to loom while the initial difficulties which led to referral subside. Yet, parents are frustrated to find that their child or adolescent remains in care. It is also likely that social workers, mindful of the unsuitability of many of the actual placements in which children end up and the consequent high risk of breakdown, protect themselves from inevitable parental reproach by vagueness of plan and an air of general misplaced optimism. Hence, frequent movements of children between placements come to be viewed by parents as a demonstration of their child's difficulty and problematic state rather than a reflection on the inadequacy of the care offered. Indeed, with Packman, we have found that parents are happier with social services' intervention when they or their children present specific problems requiring precise interventions rather than when diffuse concerns are raised.

While parents are keenly aware that anxiety over their child's delinquency should not drive them to seek cosy chats with the police, they are initially more trusting of social services, although some, like Sally March, rapidly learn by their mistakes. They have a respect for professionals and are familiar with social workers in their wider welfare role, particularly helping the elderly, handicapped and sick who abound in their housing estates and high-rise flats. Parents are, initially, blissfully unaware of the power that professionals can wield *vis-à-vis* themselves and that, unlike children, other client groups, such as the elderly or handicapped, do not raise extreme issues of control, neglect or abuse. Neither is the visibility of their problems and public accountability such a pressing concern. However, once families with children in need of help surface for scrutiny, they find that they have begun a process which is quite beyond their control. They learn that help is conditional and issues which they had not bargained for at the outset, such as marital disharmony, their lifestyle or the behaviour of their other children, begin to assume prominence in social workers' concerns. Certainly it was not uncommon to find parents describing their social workers as 'wolves in sheep's clothing', in spite of the workers' valiant attempts to appear as sheep in sheep's clothing.

So, parents are usually ill-prepared for the sense of loss that the departure of their child brings and some nurse feelings of grievance and resentment. For the majority of mothers, the lifting of the onerous burden of looking after their children in discouraging circumstances brings guilt not relief. Mothers experience a sense of deep failure in a role that society holds in high esteem. Whether the mother is ill, abandoning or neglectful, even ill-treating, her sense is one of violation. Mothers' pain is not proportional to the quality of the relationship before separation but to their investment in it. Hate is as much an investment as love and mothers, particularly of adolescents, have had more than a decade of struggle to survive, to hang on to and protect their children.

Mothers respond as do the bereaved – they deny the hurt, they retreat into themselves and become preoccupied with trivia; they deny the reality of the situation. Thus, friends or the wider family on the margins of the crisis shrink away because they find their role in the unfolding drama ill-defined and the stage on which they have to perform gloomy and ill-lit. Indeed, this denial of a situation on the part of many mothers and their refusal to recognise the possible long-term nature of their separation from the child makes the formation of independent support groups very difficult. Unlike Gingerbread groups or self-help groups for the handicapped, the care situation covers a multitude of problems and displays just as many evasions of reality. Sadly, mothers of children in care rarely get together; neither do foster parents.

Fathers similarly feel a sense of violation and loss. If father is present in the household or even on its margins, the entry of the child to care is a reproach to his ability to provide for and protect his family. In the case of adolescents, he has failed to exercise sufficient guidance or control. Although the father can displace many of his frustrations onto his wife, arguing that she is responsible for the rearing of children, nevertheless he feels resentful. Entry of the child to care also arouses, once more, the father's guilt over previous scant care, his fitful parenting and voluntary separations from the family.

Guilt generates anger in parents which is displaced onto others, usually the social worker, who rapidly becomes seen as responsible for the whole situation, or on the substitute care-givers who are not doing things right and are seeking to appropriate the child. Eventually, parents' sense of violation and powerlessness encourages passivity and indifference. However skilled the social worker may be, this is an extremely difficult situation in which to assess parents' long-term viability to care and to construct regular, mutually enriching contact between parent and child, even in those situations where there are no cogent reasons for limiting access and scrutinising parental involvement. Indeed, the indifferent, ambivalent or aggressive behaviour of parents can serve merely to confirm social workers' fears of inadequate parenting.

While the placements that children in care experience may be suitable in theory, we have seen that in actual practice many of them leave much to be desired. Social workers find it extremely difficult to find suitable placements and, in their selection, links with home are not high on social workers' priorities. There are too few short-term foster situations and many residential homes are both insufficiently flexible and distant. In addition, the foster parents may come to entertain unrealistic expectations of sheltering the child in the long term and by an exclusive stance discourage parents. In the same way, the routine, size and totality of residential institutions may chill the exchanges between parent and child. Thus, barriers to contact between parent and child are inherent in many placements apart from the distance, inaccessibility, transport problems, lack of money and general insecurity which, we have seen, discourage parents from visiting.

We have noted how carefully regulated and normatively governed much visiting behaviour is. Denied a legitimate role, advancing alone into unknown territory and defined as inadequate, even detrimental to their children's welfare, parents shrink from making a visit. With younger children, although parents may entertain the distant prospect of their eventual return, the distress or indifference children frequently evince on the arrival of their parents is very discouraging. Parents are ill-prepared for these reactions and as they frequently visit alone, bereft of support and insight, they are deeply violated by their rejection. Foster parents also display unease at the children's reaction which can confirm their reservations about the natural parents' ability to care for and love the child. In the residential setting, much of the interaction between child and parent is public and displays of affection in such circumstances are difficult or even resisted by the child. We have seen parents feel that they are under examination, sitting a 'love test' for which preparation and correct performance are obscure.

Thus, parents feel deskilled and the parents of adolescents feel doubly deskilled. For not only is interaction with a liberated teenager rather difficult because there is not much to talk about, but the care situation robs parents of those residual roles that adolescents allow them – feeding, ironing, washing and occasionally counselling and lending. Even the brief weekend visits of adolescents to their parents are without satisfaction. Parents witness a blooming in their offspring, a flowering in which their tending has had no place. Neither can parents take comfort in the prospect that should an adolescent return home from care, he or she is likely to stay for any appreciable period. This, again, parents find rather discouraging.

In addition to these problems of maintaining links between themselves and absent child, some parents also experience limitations imposed by social workers on access to their children. Some of these restrictions parents find difficult to comprehend. While the exclusion of certain family members is usually clear and grudgingly accepted by parents, particularly in the case of injury or neglect, the wider conditions surrounding contact – for example, the use of neutral ground, the discouragement of children returning home for weekends and many of the non-specific barriers to contact – are particularly irksome. Parents feel unwanted and that they have nothing more to contribute to the well-being of their children. This feeling increases over time. As contact with the social workers declines, the children settle down and inertia steals over the child-care scene leaving parents feeling abandoned and angry.

Only at the breakdown of a care placement is there a momentary flurry of activity and sometimes efforts are made to resurrect family contact and encourage visits from and to parents and the wider family. Usually, this comes too late, for visiting and other patterns of contact are set early; indeed, the evidence would suggest that it is disturbance to an existing situation which considerably upsets the child. Unfortunately, we have seen that over time parents are visited less and less by social workers, there is little attempt to involve the wider family or seek out fathers and the blessings of stability, in fact, disguise the child's diminishing chances of reunion and increasing isolation.

As a conclusion, we shall shortly examine the situation and characteristics of those children who are completely isolated from their families at the end of two years. But, in spite of the barriers to maintaining links relentlessly explored in this study, we shall find that the majority of children and parents *do* manage to remain in contact. It says something for the resilience of the blood-tie that, in such unpropitious circumstances, links are maintained between family and absent child. Nevertheless, that some children, without due cause, find themselves isolated in care and without family contact as a direct consequence of social work intervention is surely to be deplored.

### Social workers and the management of links

In recent years, social work has attempted a generic focus, concentrating on the family as a whole and has tried to approach an individual's problems within this wider context. This strategy presents difficulties because of the complexity and widely differing nature of the families that seek social services help. We have seen that children's households vary in composition, in stages of development and in the cluster of problems that develop around a common core of poverty and vulnerability. Some families will have children who display neglect and abuse. Usually, these difficulties affect several children in the family. Other families will have problematic teenagers, girls out of control or boys reluctant to attend school or delinquent. These children tend to enter care alone. In addition, adults important to the child may be members of different households, each of which may be changing sometimes rapidly and will frequently have major problems of their own. It is also apparent that the network of kin and wider family, if it exists, fails to provide support in crises.

At the outset, social workers usually have inadequate or partial knowledge of families. Deeper insights develop only over time. Also, they have insufficient guidance from research and their training courses on what is significant in family dynamics and what can safely be ignored. It is also difficult, given the number of cases social workers usually have at one time, to maintain constant scrutiny of families, to be aware of change, and to fashion flexible support programmes and contingency plans for individual members. Indeed, a number of writers have suggested that many families, their children and care-givers receive insufficient support and this helps to account for the wearisome and repetitive picture of breakdowns and hasty palliatives that this study has illustrated. Quite clearly, social work activity declines over time, yet social workers are often severely circumscribed in their decisions, particularly in the range of appropriate placements available for children and in the amount of time they can give to families. Indeed, some families alone present a full-time job. In advocating, yet again, more social work effort with families and children, particularly focused on maintaining links between parent and absent child, we are well aware that resources are scarce and that any reallocation of social work priorities will most probably limit care for others.

We have seen that the gap between referral and reception of children into care is frequently very short, allowing little preparation of either mothers or children for the trauma of separation. Yet, the majority of children are known to social services, some will have been in care before, and all will have a potential for preventative work. While the actual decision to take the child into care was not scrutinised in this study, our impression is that those 450 children who did enter care received rather inadequate preparation for removal from home. This, of course, may be because we are only looking at those who finally enter care, by definition the failures of preventative work. It may also be because limited resources oblige social workers to take up a crisis orientation. However, it seems more likely that preventative work is insufficiently focused and dissipates itself by tackling insurmountable problems while those more amenable to improvement, such as parental participation, are forgotten.

But the difficulties that social workers face in taking the child into care lie deeper than aspects of family dynamics, pressing case loads and dissipated preventative work. Once the child is taken away from the parents, either voluntarily or forcibly, other issues come into play. In view of the stress in social work ideology on family support, on prevention, on the damage wrought by separation, inevitably, the removal of the child from home is viewed as a defeat for community care. Neither does the admission of children to care signal new initiatives from social workers; they merely repeat old strategies with less and less conviction. Social workers find themselves uneasy participants in child rescue which we have seen has considerable antecedents and an ideology all its own. They find themselves employing legislation which entertains in its language no whiff of shared care and which abounds in categories as quaint as they are pejorative, such as orders for place of safety, care and control and moral danger. Indeed, many of the instructions they receive for guidance from above encompass phrases reminiscent of the Sunday School.

Social workers rapidly find themselves unwilling and uneasy agents of social control – police officers in anoraks. While the prosperous have always had adequate defences to defeat interference in their child-rearing practices, the poor have been, and remain, very vulnerable to intervention. Beavering away in meetings and client care, attempting to meet a flood of needs even when these are filtered by the intake team, social workers are kept busy and deeply uneasy. They cannot remain unaware of structural issues and the ways in which deep inequalities in our society create vulnerability in their clients. But aspects of social workers' backgrounds, their training experiences and the 'welfare', 'service' and 'containment' inheritance of their social services departments hardly make them politically radical.

Social workers are keenly aware also, because of the frequency of placement breakdowns and the problems inherent in both foster and residential care, that the state's ability to parent is frequently in doubt. For many children, social workers are conscious that they cannot provide stable, adequate, substitute parenting and offer the partisan support and unconditional love that children need. Neither for adolescents can they meet adequately the conflicting demands of control and encouragement, provide care with freedom, which the developing young person requires. Frequently social workers question why school non-attendance or minor delinquency should exert a more cogent influence on the child's situation than the many problems which are created by the removal of a child from home. In addition to questions of class, social workers face race and gender questions. For example, why should a girl be defined as being in moral danger and ripe for removal from home while boys escape both the definition and its consequences?

Because the future circumstances of the child are very difficult to envisage, social work decisions are frequently extremely problematic. We have seen that often the child's best interests are not congruent, needs are different and conflicting. Even if plans for the child are fashioned which meet social workers' priorities, they are unlikely to be satisfactory on other criteria such as education, moral probity or control. Yet social workers, as a powerless professional group, are often called to account for deficiencies of care and control as perceived by external and vociferous critics in a way that stronger professional groups are not. For example, few criticise the police or the judiciary for the havoc wrought in wives' and children's lives by imprisoning husbands for minor property offences or maintenance arrears. Neither are the armed services strictured for the enforced and frequently quite unnecessary separations they impose on families and, consequently, the high levels of marriage breakdown. Yet, social services would be scourged by criticism for any failure to shoulder the consequences of such actions.

As a consequence, social workers approach the arena of child care rather like second-string gladiators, expecting thumbs down on their efforts. But, while ineffectual in some contexts, social workers should be reminded that in the lives of vulnerable families and children, they are very powerful. They define the families' problems, they determine whether a child will enter care and for how long. They can manipulate the choice of legislation to meet their definitions of the case and in some cases, such as by using place of safety orders, accord themselves considerable advantages in managing fraught situations or resolving contested interpretations of problems. Unlike the care-givers who have the daily tending task, the field social workers are responsible for the overall care strategy. They have wider oversight and greater power to decide on the child's care career. This gives them a weighty responsibility which should lead to careful and constant scrutiny of decisions. Were care-givers more professional or parents more informed, it could lead to more challenging of the field social workers' decisions and to considerable conflict. Finally, social workers can decide, with little risk of contradiction, on aspects of parental contact or family access and on children's links with their home and community – decisions which this study has shown have important consequences for the well-being of the child.

This makes field social workers very significant people in relation to their clients who are disadvantaged in a host of ways, ignorant of their rights, of procedures and of what the outcome might be. It is easy, when occupied with the daily demands of the care task, for social workers to forget their omnipotence when viewed from a client's position. It is also rather contradictory of social workers to complain about the ever-increasing control obligations thrust upon them while, simultaneously, enjoying power over clients' lives which is well in excess of many other child-care professionals such as teachers, doctors and youth workers.

Conscious of their power, social workers should be aware that some of their actions will have long-term consequences for families and children. While this study has not attempted to prove that self-fulfilling prophecies operate in social work in ways that they have been shown to influence children's educational or delinquent careers, there is sufficient evidence in preceding chapters to give social workers food for thought. To divide children largely between short-stay and long-stay cases and then to apportion heroic efforts to getting the short-stays out quickly while the long-stays convalesce has elements of self-fulfilment. This is reinforced by the slackening of social work activity with families, children and care-givers as time passes. We have also seen that children leave care in a way that does not correspond with their presenting problems. The line in the graph looks more like a precipice than a curve and once over the precipice, the child has a diminished chance of a return home. At least social workers should keep constantly in mind the tendency of systems to create their clients, for processes to maintain client visibility and thus constantly to redefine their problems and vulnerability.

This study has also highlighted with considerable precision a situation that has long been known – that unless the child leaves care quickly (that is, within six weeks) he or she has a very strong chance of still being in care in two years time. Yet, the administrative arrangements within social services and social work practice often do not reflect this acutely short timescale. We find periods immediately following a child's entry to care in which all parental or wider family contacts are discouraged or forbidden. We find case reviews, not daily for new entries, but at monthly or even six-monthly intervals, if then. We find that children remain the responsibility of intake teams and, bereft of a social worker to act as a protagonist and agent, the child's interests are displaced by other crises. We find balm and comfort applied to the wounds of separation when they should be kept open and salted. Above all, we find a time perspective entertained by social workers which is greatly at variance with the urgency experienced by the child, the family and which, as this study demonstrates, is in their best interests. Indeed, one of the most depressing and familiar social workers' responses to our six-monthly visits was, 'Good heavens, is it that long? It seems you were here only last week.'

It is also clear from this study that social work must give parental and wider family links high priority. They must develop adequate systems for scrutinising, recording and evaluating information on contact and be alert to significant changes in family visiting and other patterns. At the moment, many decisions, both explicit and implicit, on family contact are made subsidiary to other concerns. For example, contact is related to the suitability and tranquility of placements or to minimising distress in the children or to ensuring control or education. It is also noticeable that at case conferences on children in care, as the months pass, access arrangements and general family links are rarely critically examined. In the majority of cases, the wider social and family contacts of children receive perfunctory scrutiny, indeed for some they are not even considered. Many of the barriers to contact between parents and child are insufficiently appreciated by social workers and consequently pass unnoticed. Indeed, considering the brevity and spasmodic nature of many reviews, this is not surprising.

For example, Sinclair, looking at decision-making in statutory reviews of children in care, found that half of the reviews conducted in area offices took less than ten minutes and in 93 per cent of cases, only two people were present. Also, a DHSS study in 1982 of children in foster care showed that fewer than half of the local authorities examined regularly conducted reviews within the statutory time limits.[1]

We have also seen as the months pass that access limitations and overt barriers to contact are allowed to linger long after the initial reasons for their imposition have evaporated. Social workers move swiftly to impose restrictions on parental and family contact, both explicit and implicit, but are less zealous in minimising barriers to relationships once the need for caution and placement stability has disappeared. It is also clear that other aspects of belonging for the child, in visiting familiar neighbourhoods, in keeping home and school friendships, encouraging sibling contact and in involving the wider family and other networks seem to receive little emphasis from social workers. While it is true that many adolescents can maintain their relationships without help – indeed, some show scant regard for the caveats of social workers and care-givers – younger children cannot maintain links unless greatly encouraged. Naturally, the problems of distance, placement discouragement and stigma will affect all.

This and numerous other studies have suggested that social workers should not take the indifference, rejection and hostility of parents or children towards each other and their failure to seek *rapprochement* at face value. We have tried to illustrate that parents find visiting very stressful and that, bereft of a role, guilty, inarticulate and sometimes illiterate, linking on all dimensions will be difficult. In addition, we have also noted that many children find it difficult to visit home. Frequency of contact should not serve as a test of parents' depth of attachment to their children, an examination of the quality of relationships which parents pass or fail; where ill-prepared and without a syllabus, the family sit a 'love test' which is set and marked by social workers. Such an approach has all the deficiencies of examination by continuous assessment and none of its merits. Indeed, many children in independent schools and some of their parents would find such an examination failure as unfamiliar as it would be salutory. Recent studies of divorce show how complex and stressful contact between parents and absent child can be for all participants. A parent's care and love for the separated child does not necessarily correspond with conventional displays of feeling, with frequent visiting and other contacts. Nevertheless, maintaining links between parent and child absent in local authority care is one aspect of the care situation in which the interpersonal skills, so much emphasised in social work training, could achieve a great deal.

It is also clear that the withering of links with parents and the wider family is a gradual process. Although patterns of contact are set early and tend to endure, fitful parental visiting and gaps in contact are very significant. While all aspects of the child's care career should receive regular scrutiny, this is particularly true of links between parent and absent child because the consequences of withering links for the child are long stays in care, social isolation and poor functioning. Not only should specific restrictions on access be closely and regularly examined but all the barriers inherent in children's care placements and their family situation should be constantly analysed and reviewed.

This study joins those of Fanshel, Gambrill and Lasson in showing that the barriers to maintaining links between parent and child absent in care lie not in conscious decisions of parents, care-givers and social workers but in unconscious prejudices, in the inherent difficulties of separation and in the workings of bureaucratic organisations.

**The children**
As we have followed our 450 children through their experience of local authority care, the consequences have emerged of the difficulties parents face in maintaining links with absent children. We have noted that there has been a slow decline in parental contact with children away in either foster or community homes. In only a few cases is such a withering of parental links viewed as advisable but social workers, faced with many other pressing concerns, find it difficult to accord high priority to maintaining links between child and the family. But do children who face withering contacts with family make compensatory relationships with others? Do they enjoy stable and loving care which helps them fashion new lives for themselves and which will act as a springboard for an exit from care and a satisfactory young adult life?

At the end of two years in care, 54 of those 450 children who embarked on care careers have no contact with either parent, siblings or the wider family. While this may appear a low figure in comparison with the numbers who entered care originally, these isolated children form a considerable proportion of those still in care at two years – 54 out of 170 children. Indeed, these children with no family contacts form a still higher proportion of those viewed by social workers as likely to remain in care for the foreseeable future, that is 27 children out of 67 forecast as long-stay cases.

Naturally, some of these children will have forged new relationships with care-givers and, hopefully, will be in stable, rewarding placements; yet 22 of the children are not only isolated from their families but are also insecure in their current situations. This is because they have either experienced frequent breakdowns or because they are sheltered in temporary locations, such as short-stay foster homes or O and

A centres. Half of these children are under 12 years of age. Naturally, whether readers find such an outcome as cautiously encouraging or deeply distressing will depend on the perspectives and expectations they have of social work interventions, a point we shall return to shortly.

To conclude this study, it is useful to examine the situation of these isolated and footloose children for they highlight the consequences of declining parental contact which has been the focus of this study. Mindful of the clinical emphasis on the primacy of links between mother and absent child, let us look at children who had little or no contact with their natural mothers at the end of two years and see if alternative support has emerged.

Initially, let us look at the 14 children whose *mothers are dead*. Only one of these, an adolescent boy who has been in a CHE, was living with his natural father at the two-years stage and only two others, two young sisters, were in regular contact with their father. Seven children were fostered with other relatives and one other was able to see family members regularly, but visits to and from their natural fathers were very infrequent for all. Of the remaining three children – two girls and one boy – neither girl has any contact with her natural family, while the boy, now aged 17, has moved to live with his aunt and uncle. But his disruptive behaviour is causing so much trouble that this placement seems very unstable. Thus, for the majority of the 14 children whose mothers are dead, other relatives have assumed parental responsibilities.

Let us next look at the 47 children who had *no contact with their natural mothers, even though their mothers were alive*. Here, the pattern is much more varied and substitute care outside the extended family becomes more significant. Of these 47 children, six were able to enjoy regular contact with their natural fathers and three others saw close relatives occasionally. The remaining 38, however, were totally isolated from their natural families; the reasons for their mother's disappearance divided evenly between maternal indifference and social workers' restricting access.

Twelve children not only had no family contact but were also clearly unsettled in placements. These children were a varied group with two sets of young siblings stranded by placement breakdowns and a baby whose adoption plans had fallen through because of a change of heart by foster parents. Two other children, aged 10 and 12, are 'lingering' in care, almost the classic 'children who wait', and there are four older adolescent girls whose links with home have disintegrated. These young people continue to drift between temporary placements. It should also be noted that eight of these twelve isolated cases had their links with parents and wider family restricted by social workers.

While links with home may never have been strong, they were limited by specific restrictions on access.

Twenty of the 170 children still in care at two years were enjoying *some contact with their natural mothers*, but it was very intermittent and unpredictable. Although six of these children were seeing their natural fathers regularly, the other 14 experienced no other compensating family contact. Here, the causes of the children's isolation were almost all due to rejection on the part of mothers and in only one case was there a deliberate social work policy to restrict contact. For this group, the extended family played little part and adoption was not seen as an option. Half of these children experienced unsettled placements, mainly in residential care. Eight children were both unsettled in their care placements and almost completely isolated from their natural families, all but two of these were adolescents.

We would, therefore, estimate that out of the 170 children in care at two years, 22 (13 per cent) were experiencing considerable isolation while in care, in that they had little or no contact of any kind with their natural families and were unsettled in their current placements. Both Lasson's and Fanshel's studies show not only how closely these issues are interrelated but also that lack of parental contact leads to wider social isolation. Throughout their stay in care, these 22 children had very disrupted care careers, particularly in the number of placements experienced and in the extent to which these broke down. What is more, eight of these children were isolated as a result of social work decisions which have limited family links against parental wishes. Initially, these restrictions on parental contact sought to ease the establishment of permanent substitute parenting, but this hope had little prospect of fulfilment. While it was not our task to examine how effective limiting family contact can be in helping forge substitute parenting, Rowe's study of long-term fostering shows that even fostering which leads to adoption need not exclude the natural parents.

Therefore, it can be seen that 81 of the 170 children still in care after two years had elapsed had no or very little contact with their natural mothers. Fifty-four of these children have also lost touch with all other relatives, and fathers remain significant for only a very few children. Many of the children who remain will be long-stay cases, expected to remain in care for a considerable period of time; 35 of them at least a further year and 27 of them for two years or more. As a total of 96 of the 170 children in care at two years are expected to remain in care for at least another year and 67 for a further two years, these isolated children form 36 per cent and 40 per cent, respectively, of both long-stay groups. This means that two-fifths of all long-stay children in care – long-stay defined as being in care for at least three years – had no parental contacts after two years and the wider family was of little significance, yet in two-thirds of these cases, there was no social work reason for this exclusion.

Doubtless critics of social services will find such figures amply justify their criticism, while optimists will argue that this is a very small number of the original cohort of 450 who entered care. Nevertheless, it will be recollected that the five local authorities who cooperated in this study were carefully selected to provide insights into the national picture, both in terms of practice and outcome. If the processes described in this study characterise all of the local authorities in England and Wales – and there is every indication that they do – then we can conclude that as many as 7000 of the 40,000 children who enter care in England and Wales each year are destined for a long stay and withering links with their parents and wider family. It also means that at any one time at least 18,000 children in state care are without meaningful contact with their parents or with their wider family, a situation that is likely to impair their functioning and increase their general social isolation. Sadly, 7000 of these children are not only isolated but also do not enjoy a stable, alternative care placement and a third of this latter group are likely to be under the age of 11.

It is the function of research to present findings and draw tentative conclusions, thankfully leaving it to others both to dispute the implications and argue relevant policies. The isolation of some children in care and the problems that most face in maintaining family links may cause concern to those optimistic about social services intervention, be viewed with equanimity by those who expect less from state care, or merely confirm the strictures of those who view statutory welfare as cosmetic and controlling. These are not perspectives which we were asked to explore.

However, there is an obligation on social services to ensure that those children who are taken into care should receive an alternative experience which is less detrimental to them than the risks of staying at home. We can see that for some children these obligations are unfulfilled. In addition, considering the diminished life-chances of those children and adolescents who stay long in care, surely more vigorous efforts could be made to enhance their opportunities and increase their skills, if only to help them cope with the considerable demands they face on leaving care. For some, withering contact with home is compounded by general social isolation which deprives them of community support and job opportunities.

We were asked to investigate the problems parents face in maintaining links with their children absent in local authority care and, by adopting a process approach, we hope we have highlighted some of these difficulties and their consequences. In addition, the mass of data accumulated have cast light on some additional problems faced by social workers attempting to care for separated children.

It is clear that the isolation of a few children in care is inevitable not only because a minority of parents are either indifferent or damaging to their children but because stable, adequate substitute care is also difficult to ensure. In addition, we have seen that considerably more children suffer isolation while in care because of the barriers inherent in separation, the failure of social workers to appreciate the difficulties parents face in maintaining contact and an omission in social work planning to give children's family links much significance. A few more children suffer withering contact with home because of errors in social work practice, such as inappropriate and lingering access restrictions, unsuitable and unstable care placements or social workers' failure to scrutinise and maintain their efforts with families, absent children and care-givers. Admittedly, these omissions are always easier to see in retrospect and by remaining unaware of the many other demands made on social workers.

Yet this study does give grounds for optimism. With increased sensitivity to the problems parents face in maintaining links with their absent children, with increased knowledge of what to look for and what actions to take, social workers can nurture family contacts. Such efforts accord well with the training they have received and the ideology of social work. Compared with so many of the intractable problems that poor families face and which defy social work efforts, fanning parental and family concern is relatively straightforward. Just as the imperious questioning of Lady Bracknell rapidly created a family and wider social network for Ernest, so social workers, by questioning decisions, by insisting on appropriate placements and by giving parental links high priority, can enhance an absent child's sense of belonging.

# Notes

## Chapter 1

1. S. Millham, R. Bullock and P. Cherrett, *After Grace – Teeth* (London: Human Context Books), 1975; R. Lambert and S. Millham, *The Hothouse Society* (London: Weidenfeld & Nicolson), 1968; R. Lambert, S. Millham and R. Bullock, *The Chance of a Lifetime?* (London: Weidenfeld & Nicolson), 1975; S. Millham, R. Bullock and K. Hosie, *Locking Up Children* (Farnborough: Saxon House), 1978; *Research at Risley Hall, Research at North Downs, Research at Turners Court* (London: DHSS, Development Group), 1974–75; D. Berridge, *Children's Homes* (Oxford: Basil Blackwell), 1985.
2. J. Triseliotis (ed.), *New Developments in Foster Care and Adoption* (London: Routledge & Kegan Paul), 1980; J. Rowe, H. Cain, M. Hundleby and A. Keane, *Long-Term Foster Care* (London: Batsford), 1984.
3. Lambert and Millham, *The Hothouse Society*, op. cit.; Lambert, Millham and Bullock, *The Chance of a Lifetime?*, op. cit.; R. Lambert, J. Hipkin and S. Stagg, *New Wine in Old Bottles* (London: Bell), 1969.
4. Lambert and Millham, op. cit.; Lambert, Millham and Bullock, op. cit.; R. Lambert, *The State and Boarding* (London: Methuen), 1966.
5. Millham Bullock and Hosie, Research at Risley Hall, Research at North Downs, Research at Turners Court, op. cit.
6. S. Millham, R. Bullock and K. Hosie, *A Study of the Characteristics of Children in the Care of West Devon with Particular Reference to their Family Characteristics* (Dartington Social Research Unit), 1979; D. Fanshel and E. Shinn, *Children in Foster Care* (Columbia: Columbia University Press), 1978; J. Rowe and L. Lambert, *Children who Wait* (London, Association of British Adoption Agencies), 1973; Rowe, Cain, Hundleby and Keane, *Long-Term Foster Care*, op. cit.; I. Lasson, *Where's My Mum?* (Birmingham: Pepar Publications), 1981; Berridge, *Children's Homes*, op. cit.; B. Ackhurst, *Long-Term Residential Care* (London: Thomas Coram Research Unit, London University), 1974; B. Kahan, *Growing Up in Care* (Oxford: Blackwell), 1979; H. Maas and R. Engler, *Children in Need of Parents* (Columbia: Columbia University Press), 1979; S. Millham, R. Bullock, K. Hosie, M. Haak and L. Mitchell, *Give and Take* (London: Community Service Volunteers), 1980; R. Page and G. Clark (eds), *Who Cares?* (London: National Children's Bureau), 1977; Evidence of NAYPIC [National Association of Young People in Care] to House of Commons Social Services Committee, 1983; K. Blumenthal and A. Weinberg (eds), *Establishing Parent Involvement in Foster Care Agencies* (New York: Child Welfare League of America), 1984.
7. Millham, Bullock and Cherrett, *After Grace – Teeth*, op. cit.
8. R. Hood, *Homeless Borstal Boys* (London: Bell), 1966; D. Lowson, *City Lads in Borstal* (Liverpool: Liverpool University Press), 1970; A. Bottoms and F. McClintock, *Criminals Coming of Age* (London: Heinemann), 1973.
9. Kahan, *Growing Up in Care*, op. cit.; Page and Clark (eds), *Who Cares?*, op. cit.; NAYPIC, *Evidence to House of Commons Social Services Committee*, op. cit.; S. Millham, R. Bullock and K. Hosie, *Social Services for Adolescents in Croydon* (Croydon Consortium), 1984; G. James, *The Haringey Long-term Care Group* unpublished paper; P. Taylor and M. Stein, *Children Leaving Care* (Report to ESRC), 1985; House of Commons Social Services Committee, *Children in Care* (London: HMSO), 1984.
10. Rowe and Lambert, *Children Who Wait*, op. cit.; J. Goldstein, A. Freud and A. Solnit, *Beyond the Best Interests of the Child* (New York: Free Press) 1973; idem., *Before the Best Interests of the Child* (New York: Free Press), 1979.

11. Berridge, *Children's Homes*, op. cit.; Millham, Bullock and Cherrett, *After Grace – Teeth*, op. cit.; Millham, Bullock and Hosie, *Locking Up Children*, op. cit.; Rowe, Cain, Hundleby and Keane, *Long-Term Foster Care*, op. cit.; Triseliotis (ed.), *New Developments in Foster Care and Adoption*, op. cit.; R. Holman, 'The place of fostering in social work', *British Journal of Social Work*, V (1975), pp. 3–30; G. Trasler, *In Place of Parents* (London: Routledge & Kegan Paul), 1960; V. George, *Foster Care: Theory and Practice* (London: Routledge & Kegan Paul), 1970; R. Parker, *Decision in Child Care* (London: Allen & Unwin), 1966; H. Prosser, *Perspectives on Foster Care* (Slough: NFER), 1978; DHSS, *A Study of the Boarding Out of Children* (London: HMSO), 1981.

12. DHSS, *Code of Practice: Access to Children in Care* (London: HMSO), 1984.

13. J. Packman, *Child Care Needs and Numbers* (London: Allen & Unwin), 1968; B. Davies, *Variations in Children's Services among British Urban Authorities* (London: Bell), 1972; DHSS, *Children in Care in England and Wales* (London: HMSO), annual.

14. Rowe and Lambert, *Children Who Wait*, op. cit.; Fanshel and Shinn, *Children in Foster Care*, op. cit.; Lasson, *Where's My Mum?*, op. cit.; Page and Clark (eds), *Who Cares?*, op. cit.

15. Home Office/Ministry of Education and Science/Ministry of Housing and Local Government, *Report of the Committee on Local Authority and Allied Personal Social Services*, Cmd. 3703 (London: HMSO), 1968; O. Stevenson and P. Parsloe, *Social Service Teams: the Practitioners' View* (London: HMSO), 1978; R. Parker, *Caring for Separated Children* (London: Macmillan), 1980; J. Black, R. Bowl, D. Burns, C. Critcher, G. Grant and D. Stockford, *Social Work in Context* (London: Tavistock), 1983.

16. A. Morris, H. Giller, E. Szwed and H. Geach, *Justice for Children* (London: Macmillan), 1980; H. Geach and E. Szwed (eds), *Providing Civil Justice for Children* (London: Edward Arnold), 1983; NACRO, *School Reports in the Juvenile Court*, Report of a Working Party, 1984; L. Fox, 'Two value positions in recent child care law and practice', *British Journal of Social Work*, XII (1982), pp. 265–90; publications from the Children's Legal Centre and the Family Rights Group (London).

17. Morris, Giller, Szwed and Geach, *Justice for Children*, op. cit., A. Morris and H. Giller (eds), *Providing Criminal Justice for Children* (London: Edward Arnold), 1983; D. Thorpe, D. Smith, C. Green and J. Paley, *Out of Care* (London: Allen & Unwin), 1980.

18. *Expenditure Committee Report on the 1969 Act* (London: HMSO), 1975.

19. Evidence to the Expenditure Committee from Magistrates', Police and Youth Associations.

20. DHSS, *Children in Care in England and Wales*, annual publications; Reports from the National Child Development Studies at the National Children's Bureau (London); International Centre for Child Studies (Bristol) – the studies of J. W. B. Douglas and, for delinquents, the research of S. and E. Glueck, A. Dunlop and L. T. Wilkins.

21. J. Robertson, *Young Children in Hospital* (London: Tavistock), 1970; D. Hall and M. Stacey, *Beyond Separation* (London: Routledge & Kegan Paul), 1979; M. Oswin, *Children Living in Long-stay Hospitals* (London: Spastics International Medical Publications), 1978; R. King, N. Raynes and J. Tizard, *Patterns of Residential Care* (London: Routledge & Kegan Paul), 1971; M. Rutter, *Maternal Deprivation Reassessed* (Harmondsworth: Penguin), 1972.

22. Millham, Bullock and Hosie, *Locking Up Children*, op. cit.

23. Reports of inquiries into the care experiences of Maria Colwell, John George Auckland and Wayne Brewer; J. Goldstein, Freud and Solnit, *Before the Best Interests of the Child*, op. cit.; Rowe and Lambert, *Children Who Wait*, op. cit.

24. Social Science Research Council, *Children in Need of Care* (London), 1980.

25. D. Fruin and J. Vernon, *Social Work Decision-Making and its Effects on the Length of Time which Children Spend in Care* (London: National Children's Bureau), 1983;

J. Packman, J. Randall and N. Jacques, *Who Needs Care?* (Oxford: Basil Blackwell), 1986.

26. Millham, Bullock and Hosie, *Locking Up Children*, op. cit.; S. Millham, R. Bullock, K. Hosie and M. Haak, *Issues of Control in Residential Child Care* (London: HMSO), 1981; Berridge, *Children's Homes*, op. cit.

27. S. Millham, R. Bullock and K. Hosie, *Springboard: A Study of CSV's Job Creation Scheme in Sunderland* (London: Community Service Volunteers), 1977; Millham, Bullock and Cherrett, *After Grace – Teeth*, op. cit.; S. Millham, 'Processes in child care', in Met de Vakgroep Kinder-en Jeugdpsychiatrie, *Een Kink/d in de Kabel* (Groningen), 1983, pp. 30 – 43.

28. Goldstein, Freud and Solnit, *Before the Best Interests of the Child*, op. cit.

29. Dartington Social Research Unit, *Children Remanded to Care, Place of Safety Orders* and *Predicting Children's Length of Stay in Care and the Relevance of Family Links*, Research Reports, 1984.

## Chapter 2

1. R. Aron, *Main Currents in Sociological Thought* (London: Weidenfeld & Nicolson), 1965; T. Bottomore and R. Nisbet (eds), *History of Sociological Analysis* (London: Heinemann), 1979.

2. K. Popper, *The Logic of Scientific Discovery* (London: Hutchinson), 1961; J. Habermas, *Knowledge and Human Interests* (London: Heinemann), 1972; T. Luckmann (ed), *Phenomenonology and Sociology* (Harmondsworth: Penguin), 1978; H. Blumer, *Symbolic Interactionism: Perspective and Method* (Englewood Cliffs, N.J.: Prentice Hall), 1969.

3. Popper, *The Logic of Scientific Discovery*, op. cit.; K. Popper, *Objective Knowledge* (Oxford: Oxford University Press), 1972.

4. M. Rutter, 'Research into the prevention of psycho-social disorders in children', in J. Barnes and N. Connelly (eds), *Social Care Research* (London: Bedford Square Press), 1977, pp. 104–17.

5. Morris, Giller, Szwed and Geach, *Justice for Children*, op. cit.; H. Geach and E. Szwed (eds), *Providing Civil Justice for Children*, op. cit.; M. Freeman, *The Rights and Wrongs of Children* (London: Francis Pinter), 1983.

6. DHSS, *Code of Practice: Access to Children in Care*, op. cit.

7. D. Fruin and J. Vernon, *Social Work Decision-Making and its Effect on the Length of Time which Children Spend in Care*, op. cit.; Packman, Jacques and Randall, *Who Needs Care?*, op. cit.

8. Fanshel and Shinn, *Children in Foster Care*, op. cit.; Lasson, *Where's My Mum?*, op. cit.; T. Stein, E. Gambrill and K. Wiltse, *Children in Foster Homes* (New York: Praeger), 1978; R. Thorpe, 'Mum and Mrs So and So', *Social Work Today*, IV, no. 22, 1974.

9. Millham, 'Processes in Child Care', op. cit., pp. 30–43.

10. Millham, Bullock, Hosie and Haak, *A Study of the Characteristics of Children in the Care of West Devon with Particular Reference to their Family Circumstances*, op. cit.

11. D. Matza, *Delinquency and Drift* (New York: Wiley), 1964; D. Matza, *Becoming Deviant* (New Jersey: Prentice Hall), 1969; Oswin, *Children Living in Long-Stay Hospitals*, op. cit.; D. Robinson, *The Process of Becoming Ill* (London: Routledge & Kegan Paul), 1971; M. Hammersley and P. Woods (eds), *The Process of Schooling* (London: Routledge & Kegan Paul), 1976; J. McKinlay (ed.), *Processing People* (London: Holt, Rinehart & Winston), 1975.

12. Millham, Bullock and Hosie, *Locking Up Children*, op. cit.

13. J. Bowlby, *Maternal Care and Mental Health* (Geneva: WHO), 1952; A. and A. Clarke, *Early Experience: Myth and Evidence* (London: Open Books), 1976; Rutter, *Maternal Deprivation Reassessed*, op. cit.; Hall and Stacey (eds), *Beyond Separation*, op. cit.

14. Bowlby, *Maternal Care and Mental Health*, op. cit.; Clarke and Clarke, *Early*

*Experience: Myth and Evidence*, op. cit.; Rutter, *Maternal Deprivation Reassessed*, op. cit.; Hall and Stacey (eds), *Beyond Separation*, op. cit.

15. J. Robertson, *Young Children in Hospital*, op. cit.; Bowlby, *Maternal Care and Mental Health*, op. cit.; Ministry of Health, *The Welfare of Children in Hospital* (London: HMSO), 1959; W. Goldfarb, 'Variations in adolescent adjustment of institutionally reared children', *American Journal of Orthopsychiatry*, XVII (1947), p. 449.

16. Goldstein, Freud and Solnit, *Beyond the Best Interests of the Child*, op. cit.

17. Lambert, Millham and Bullock, *The Chance of a Lifetime?*, op. cit.

18. N. Timms (ed.), *Social Welfare: Why and How?* (London: Routledge & Kegan Paul), 1980; R. Rapoport, M. Frogarty and R. Rapoport, *Families in Britain* (London: Routledge & Kegan Paul), 1982, esp. section IV.

19. J. Packman, *The Child's Generation* (Oxford: Basil Blackwell), 1980.

20. R. Parker, *Caring for Separated Children* (London: Macmillan), 1980; Packman, *The Child's Generation*, op. cit.

21. Parker, *Caring for Separated Children*, op. cit.; Rowe and Lambert, *Children Who Wait*, op. cit.; S. Jackson, *The Education of Children in Care*, paper for Economic and Social Research Council (London), 1983.

22. Children placed 'at home on trial' remain legally in care but, depending on their legal status, may not be automatically removed from home without the social worker going through arranged procedures.

23. Packman, *Child Care Needs and Numbers*, op. cit.

24. R. and R. Rapoport, *Fathers, Mothers and Others* (London: Routledge & Kegan Paul), 1977; see also the unit of analysis in Census and *Family Expenditure Survey* publications.

25. Lambert, Millham and Bullock, *The Chance of a Lifetime?*, op. cit.

26. Ibid.

27. R. Merton, *Social Theory and Social Structure* (Glencoe, Illinois: Free Press), 1957.

28. Fanshel and Shinn, *Children in Foster Care*, op. cit.; J. Goldstein, Solnit and Freud, *Beyond the Best Interests of the Child* and *Before the Best Interests of the Child*, op. cit.; Stein, Gambrill and Wiltse, *Children in Foster Homes*, op. cit.; B. Tizard, *Adoption: A Second Chance* (London: Open Books), 1977; Hall and Stacey, *Beyond Separation*, op. cit.; Lasson, *Where's My Mum?*, op. cit.; M. Kellmer Pringle, *The Needs of Children* (London: Hutchinson), 1975; idem., *Early Child Care in Britain* (London: Gordon & Breach), 1975; R. Walton and M. Heywood, *The Forgotten Children* (Manchester: University of Manchester), 1971; A. Freud, *The Writings of Anna Freud* (New York: International Universities Press), 1969; Rowe and Lambert *Children Who Wait*, op. cit.; J. Wallerstein and J. Kelly, *Surviving the Breakup* (New York: Basic Books), 1980, A. Mitchell, *Children in the Middle* (London: Tavistock), 1985.

29. Millham, Bullock and Hosie, *A Study of the Characteristics of Children in West Devon with Particular Reference to the Family Characteristics*, op. cit.

30. DHSS, *A Classification of English Personal Social Services Authorities* (London: HMSO), 1977; DHSS, *Children in Care in England and Wales*, op. cit.

31. Dartington Social Research Unit, *Children Remanded to Care*, op. cit.

32. Dartington Social Research Unit, *Place of Safety Orders*, op. cit.

33. This group is discussed in Appendix II to this book.

34. Dartington Social Research Unit, *Children Remanded to Care*, *Place of Safety Orders*, *Predicting Children's Length of Stay in Care and the Relevance of Family Links*, *The Educational Experiences of Children in Care* and *Young Offenders in Care*, op. cit.

## Chapter 3

1. Parker, *Caring for Separated Children*, op. cit.

2. R. Parker, 'The gestation of reform: the Children Act 1948', in P. Bean and S. MacPherson (eds), *Approaches to Welfare* (London: Routledge & Kegan Paul), 1983, pp. 196–217.

3. Dartington Social Research Unit, *Children Remanded to Care*, op. cit.
4. Dartington Social Research Unit, *Place of Safety Orders*, op. cit.
5. DHSS, *Children in Care in England and Wales*, op. cit.
6. Dartington Social Research Unit, *Predicting Children's Length of Stay in Care and the Relevance of Family Links*, op. cit.
7. Dartington Social Research Unit, *Place of Safety Orders*, op. cit.
8. M. Rutter and H. Giller, *Juvenile Delinquency* (Harmondsworth: Penguin), 1983; M. Rutter, *Helping Troubled Children* (Harmondsworth: Penguin), 1975.
9. L. Hilgendorf, *Social Workers and Solicitors in Child Care Cases* (London: HMSO), 1981.
10. Packman, Randall and Jacques, *Who Needs Care*, op. cit.
11. I. Pinchbeck and M. Hewitt, *Children in English Society* (London: Routledge & Kegan Paul), 1973.
12. Ibid.
13. Ibid.
14. Morris, H. Giller, E. Szwed and H. Geach, *Justice for Children*, op. cit.; Geach and Szwed (eds), *Providing Civil Justice for Children*, op. cit.; House of Commons Social Services Committee, *Children in Care*, op. cit.
15. Pinchbeck and Hewitt, *Children in English Society*, op. cit.
16. Dartington Social Research Unit, *Place of Safety Orders*, op. cit.
17. Quoted in Pinchbeck and Hewitt, *Children in English Society*, op. cit.
18. Ibid.
19. K. White, *Residential Child Care Past and Present*, M.Sc. thesis (University of Edinburgh), 1973.
20. Millham, Bullock and Cherrett, *After Grace – Teeth*, op. cit.
21. Pinchbeck and Hewitt, *Children in English Society*, op. cit.
22. Ibid.
23. *The Times*, 25 January 1983.
24. DHSS, *Code of Practice: Access to Children in Care*, op. cit.
25. M. Craft, J. Raynor and L. Cohen, *Linking Home and School* (London: Longman), 1967.

## Chapter 4

1. See review by L. Taylor of D. West and D. Farrington, 'The Delinquent Way of Life', *New Society*, no. 756 (31 March 1977), p. 667.
2. DHSS, *Children in Care in England and Wales*, March 1982. More recent statistics for March 31st 1983 show a fall for numbers in care to 86,600, 44% of whom are fostered and 24% are in local authority residential care. Because of changes in recording repeated admissions, comparisons of entries to care cannot be made with earlier years. Thus, for consistency, 1982 figures are used throughout the text.
3. Ibid.
4. Ibid.
5. Ibid.
6. DHSS, *Children in Care in England and Wales*, March 1974.
7. This finding is also confirmed by the research of F. Loughran, University of Bristol, Dartington/Bristol research seminar, 1983.
8. DHSS, *Children in Care in England and Wales*, March 1982.
9. Ibid.
10. *Report of the Care of Children Committee*, Cmnd. 6922 (London: HMSO), 1946.
11. HO/DES/Ministry of Health/Ministry of Housing and Local Government, Cmnd. 3703, op. cit.
12. O. Stevenson and P. Parsloe, *Social Services Teams: The Practitioner's View* (London: HMSO), 1978.
13. R. Parker, 'The gestation of reform: the Children Act 1948', op. cit.

## Chapter 5

1. Packman, Randall and Jacques, *Who Needs Care?*, op. cit.
2. W. Jordan, 'Families and personal social services', in Rapoport, Fogarty and Rapoport, *Families in Britain*, op. cit., pp. 447–58.
3. Dartington Social Research Unit, *Predicting Children's Length of Stay in Care and the Relevance of Family Links*, op. cit.
4. Packman, Randall and Jacques, *Who Needs Care?*, op. cit.
5. J. Burgoyne and D. Clark, 'Reconstituted families', in Rapoport, Fogarty and Rapoport, *Families in Britain*, op. cit., pp. 286–302.
6. DHSS, *Children in Care in England and Wales*, March 1982.

## Chapter 6

1. Dartington Social Research Unit, *Predicting Children's Length of Stay in Care and the Relevance of Family Links*, op. cit.
2. Packman, Randall and Jacques, *Who Needs Care?*, op. cit.
3. See similar patterns for juvenile re-offending in M. Power, R. Benn and J. Morris, 'Neighbourhood, school and juveniles before the courts', *British Journal of Criminology*, XII (1972), pp. 111–32.
4. Rowe, *et al.*, *Long-Term Foster Care*, op. cit.
5. Dartington Social Research Unit, *Predicting Children's Length of Stay in Care and the Relevance of Family Links*, op. cit.
6. Ibid.
7. Dartington Social Research Unit, *Place of Safety Orders*, op. cit.
8. Ibid.
9. Packman, *Child Care Needs and Numbers*, op. cit.
10. DHSS, *Code of Practice – Access to Children in Care*, op. cit.
11. P. Marris, *Loss and Change* (London: Routledge & Kegan Paul), 1974; Hall and Stacey, *Beyond Separation* (eds) op. cit.; E. Kubler-Ross, *On Death and Dying* (London: Tavistock), 1970.
12. Hall and Stacey (eds), *Beyond Separation*, op. cit.
13. S. Jenkins and E. Norman, *Filial Deprivation and Foster Care* (Columbia: Columbia University Press), 1972.
14. J. Aldgate, 'Identification of factors influencing children's length of stay in care', in J. Triseliotis (ed.), op. cit., pp. 22–40.
15. J. Thoburn, *Captive Clients* (London: Routledge & Kegan Paul), 1980.
16. Ibid.

## Chapter 7

1. J. Wallerstein and J. Kelly, *Surviving the Breakup*, op. cit., p. 130.
2. Burgoyne and Clark, in Rapoport, Fogarty and Rapoport, *Families in Britain*, op. cit., pp. 286–303.
3. Lambert and Millham, *The Hothouse Society* op. cit.; Lambert, Millham and Bullock, *The Chance of a Lifetime?*, op. cit.
4. Lambert and Millham, *The Hothouse Society*, op. cit.; Lambert, Millham and Bullock, *The Chance of a Lifetime?*, op. cit.
5. Hall and Stacey (eds), *Beyond Separation*, op. cit.
6. Rowe and Lambert, *Children Who Wait*, op. cit.; Goldstein, Freud and Solnit, *Beyond the Best Interests of the Child*, op. cit.; D. Pilling and M. Kellmer Pringle, *Controversial Issues in Child Development* (London: Elek), 1978; Fanshel and Shinn, *Children in Foster Care*, op. cit.; Maas and Engler, *Children in Need of Care*, op. cit.; Lasson, *Where's My Mum?*, op. cit.; see also publications of the Family Rights Group and the Children's Legal Centre.
7. Committee of Inquiry into The Care and Supervision Provided in Relation to Maria Colwell (London: HMSO), 1974.

8. Bowlby, *Maternal Care and Mental Health*, op. cit.; D. Winnicott, *The Family and Individual Development* (London: Tavistock), 1965; A. Freud and D. Burlingham, 'Infants without families', in *The Writings of Anna Freud* (New York: International University Press), 1973.

9. Rutter, *Maternal Deprivation Reassessed*, op. cit.; M. Kellmer Pringle, *The Needs of Children*, op. cit.

10. Pilling and Kellmer Pringle, *Controversial Issues in Child Development*, op. cit., p. 112.

11. J. Robertson, *Young Children in Hospital*, op. cit.; H. Schaffer and W. Callender, 'Psychologic effects of hospitalisation in infancy', *Pediatrics*, XXIV (1959), pp. 528–39; J. Douglas, 'Early hospital admissions and later disturbances of behaviour and learning', *Developmental Medicine and Child Neurology*, XVII (1975), pp. 456–80.

12. Hall and Stacey, *Beyond Separation*, op. cit.; L. Yarrow, 'Separation from parents during early childhood', in M. and L. Hoffman (eds), *Review of Child Development Research* (New York: Russell Sage), 1964.

13. Lambert, Millham and Bullock, *The Chance of a Lifetime?*, op. cit.

14. Rowe and Lambert, *Children Who Wait*, op. cit.

15. Walton and Heywood, *The Forgotten Children*, op. cit.; P. Boss, *Exploration into Child Care* (London: Routledge & Kegan Paul), 1971; R. Parker, *Decision in Child Care*, op. cit.

16. Kellmer Pringle, *The Needs of Children*, op. cit.

17. G. Trasler, *In Place of Parents* (London: Routledge & Kegan Paul), 1960; Parker, op. cit.

18. *Report on the Committee on Children and Young Persons* (London: HMSO), 1960.

19. Millham, Bullock and Cherrett, *After Grace – Teeth*, op. cit.; J. Carlebach, *Caring for Children in Trouble* (London: Routledge & Kegan Paul), 1970; N. Tutt, *Care or Custody* (London: Darton, Longman and Todd), 1974.

20. J. Packman, *The Child's Generation*, op. cit.

21. R. Parker, *Caring for Separated Children*, op. cit.

22. E. Miller and G. Gwynne, *A Life Apart* (London: Tavistock), 1972.

23. Parker, *Caring for Separated Children*, op. cit.

24. R. Rapoport, R. Rapoport and Z. Strelitz, *Fathers, Mothers and Others* (London: Routledge & Kegan Paul), 1977, p. 87.

25. Goldstein, Freud and Solnit, *Beyond the Best Interests of the Child*, op. cit.

26. Rowe and Lambert *Children Who Wait*, op. cit.; B. Tizard, *Adoption: a second chance*, op. cit. See Appendix III.

27. Rutter, *Maternal Deprivation Reassessed*, op. cit.

28. George, *Foster Care: Theory and Practice*, op. cit.

29. P. Righton, 'Parental and other roles in residential care', Report of National Children's Bureau Conference, 1972.

30. R. Holman, 'The foster child and self knowledge', *Case Conference*, XII (1966), pp. 295–98.

31. E. Weinstein, *Self-Image of the Foster Child* (New York: Russell Sage), 1960.

32. R. Thorpe, *The Social and Psychological Situation of the Long-Term Foster Child with Regard to his Natural Parents*, Ph.D. thesis, University of Nottingham, 1974.

33. Rowe, Cain, Hundleby and Keane, *Long-Term Foster Care*, op. cit.

34. O. Stevenson, 'Reception into care – its meaning for all concerned', in R. Tod (ed.), *Children in Care* (London: Longman), 1968, pp. 8–17.

35. J. Berry, *Social Work with Children* (London: Routledge & Kegan Paul), 1972.

36. C. Holtom, *Staff Stress in Residential Work with Adolescents*, lecture to Annual Conference of Association for the Psychiatric Study of Adolescents, 1972; Righton, 'Parental and other roles in residential care', op. cit.; M. Mason, 'The importance to a child of his family', in Tod (ed.), *Children in Care*, op. cit., pp. 1–7; Thorpe, 'Mum and Mrs So and So', op. cit.

37. Maas, *Children in Need of Parents*, op. cit.

38. Fanshel and Shinn, *Children in Foster Care*, op. cit., p. 487; D. Fanshel and E. Shinn, *On the Road to Permanency* (Columbia: University Press), 1982.
39. T. Stein, *et al.*, *Children in Foster Homes*, op. cit.
40. Wallerstein and Kelly, *Surviving the Breakup*, op. cit., pp. 307, 311. See also, A. Mitchell, *Children in the Middle* (London: Tavistock), 1985.
41. I. Lasson, *The Family Links of Children in Residential Care*, MSc., University of Nottingham, 1979, p. 336.
42. Hall and Stacey (eds), *Beyond Separation*, op. cit.
43. Dartington Social Research Unit, *Predicting Children's Length of Stay in Care and the Relevance of Family Links* in S. Millham, R. Bullock and K. Hosie, *Processes in Child Care* (Aldershot: Gower), forthcoming.
44. Goldstein, Freud and Solnit, *Before the Best Interests of the Child*, op. cit.
45. Jenkins and Norman, *Filial Deprivation and Foster Care*, op. cit.; Thorpe, 'Mum and Mrs So and So', op. cit.; J. Aldgate, 'Identification of factors influencing children's length of stay in care', in J. Triseliotis (ed.), *New Developments in Foster Care and Adoption*, op. cit., pp. 22–40; Rowe, Cain, Hundleby and Keane, *Long-Term Foster Care*, op. cit.
46. Rowe, Cain, Hundleby and Keane, *Long-Term Foster Care*, op. cit.
47. R. Parker, *The Future of the Tending Professions*, Lecture for the 10th Anniversary of Seebohm, University of Bath, 1978.
48. Berridge, *Children's Homes*, op. cit.; Rowe, Cain, Hundleby and Keane, *Long-Term Fostering*, op. cit.; Lasson, *Where's My Mum?*, op. cit.; Fanshel and Shinn, *Children in Foster Care*, op. cit.
49. Rowe, *et al.*, *Long-Term Fostering*, op. cit.

## Chapter 8

1. Dartington Social Research Unit, *Predicting Children's Length of Stay in Care and the Relevance of Family Links*, op. cit.
2. J. Aldgate, 'Identification of factors influencing children's length of stay in care', in J. Triseliotis (ed.), op. cit., pp. 22–40.
3. DHSS, Social Work Service, Scotland, *A Longitudinal Study of Children in Care*, 1983.
4. Children readmitted to care are dealt with in Appendix II.
5. P. Gibson and P. Parsloe, 'What stops parental access to children in care?', *Adoption and Fostering*, VIII (1984), pp. 18–24.
6. Rowe, Cain, Hundleby and Keane, *Long-Term Foster Care*, op. cit.
7. Packman, Randall and Jacques, *Who Needs Care?*, op. cit.
8. Packman, *Child Care Needs and Numbers*, op. cit.

## Chapter 9

1. C. Lowenstein, 'An intake team in action in a social services department', *British Journal of Social Work*, IV (1974), pp. 115–41; J. Buckle, *Intake Teams* (London: Tavistock), 1981; A. Hall, *The Point of Entry* (London: Allen & Unwin), 1974; C. Addison, 'A defence against the public? Aspects of intake in a social services department', *British Journal of Social Work*, XII (1982), pp. 605–18.
2. Dartington Social Research Unit, *Predicting Children's Length of Stay in Care and the Relevance of Family Links*, op. cit.
3. DHSS, *A Study of the Boarding Out of Children*, op. cit.
4. D. Fruin and J. Vernon, *Social Work Decision-Making and its Effects on the Length of Time which Children Spend in Care*, op. cit.
5. M. Rutter, *Changing Youth in a Changing Society*, The Nuffield Provincial Hospitals Trust, 1979; S. Millham, *The Dependent Adolescent*, Dartington Social Research Unit, 1978.
6. Lasson, *Where's My Mum?* op. cit.

7. M. Hoghughi, *Assessing Problem Children* (London: Burnett), 1980.
8. Dartington Social Research Unit, *Predicting Children's Length of Stay in Care and the Relevance of Family Links*, op. cit.
9. Lasson, *Where's My Mum?*, op. cit.; Oswin, op. cit.; Hall and Stacey, *Beyond Separation*, op. cit.
10. E. Weinstein, *The Self-Image of the Foster Child* (New York: Russell Sage), 1960; R. Thorpe, *The Social and Psychological Situation of the Long-term Foster Child with Regard to His Natural Parents*, op. cit.
11. Lasson, *Where's My Mum?*, op. cit.; Wallerstein and Kelly, *Surviving the Breakup*, op. cit.; Fanshel and Shinn, *Children in Foster Care*, op. cit.
12. S. Wolkind, *The Mental Health of Children in Care*, Paper to the Economic and Social Research Council, 1983.

## Chapter 10

1. S. Millham, 'Processes in child care', op. cit.
2. B. Kahan, *Growing Up in Care*, op. cit.; R. Page and G. Clarke, *Who Cares?*, op. cit.; NAYPIC, *Evidence of the House of Commons Social Services Committee*, op. cit.
3. Weinstein, *The Self-Image of the Foster Child*, op. cit.; Thorpe, *The Social and Psychological Situation of the Long-Term Foster Child with Regard to his Natural Parents*, op. cit.; R. Holman, 'The place of fostering in social work', op. cit.

## Chapter 11

1. Dartington Social Research Unit, *Predicting Children's Length of Stay in Care and the Relevance of Family Links*, op. cit.; Aldgate, 'Identification of factors influencing children's length of stay in care', in Triseliotis (ed.), op. cit.
2. S. Jackson, *The Education of Children in Care*, op. cit.
3. Lasson, *Where's My Mum?*, op. cit.
4. Fruin and Vernon, *Social Work Decision-Making and its Effects on the Length of Time which Children Spend in Care*, op. cit.
5. Wallerstein and Kelly, *Surviving the Breakup*, op. cit.

## Chapter 13

1. R. Sinclair, *Decision Making in Statutory Reviews on Children in Care* (Aldershot: Gower), 1984; DHSS, *A Study of the Boarding Out of Children* (London: HMSO), 1982.

# Appendix I.  Later leavers

We saw in Chapter 8 that the majority of children who entered care were able to leave quickly. Indeed, half of our 450 entry went home before six months had elapsed. Most of these children had entered care because of temporary breakdowns in mother's ability to care and the families were known to social services beforehand. We saw that the children who left care early were able to do so largely because of improvements in the family situation, such as a mother's recovery from illness or the resolution of accommodation problems, rather than because of significant changes in parental attitude or child behaviour.

We noted that by six months and more clearly at twelve months older children were beginning to accumulate in care. For those who stay in care, child-focused rather than family problems become more significant. School problems, being out of control and minor delinquency characterise those who stay and many of their difficulties are aggravated by being in care itself – the secondary problems of adjusting to separation that we have described.

We have also noticed in this research the increasing stability of the care situation and that changes in placement, legislation and access arrangements decline over time. Once six months in care had elapsed, there was a slow trickle of departures from care so that 27 of the 222 children in care at six months had left by the twelve-months stage and a further 25 by the end of the two years.

These 52 children who left care after six months show many of the characteristics of early leavers but also share certain features with those who stay long. Half of them were over eleven years of age but many were voluntary receptions. Usually, contact with home or the wider family had been maintained and, although difficulties in their behaviour often persisted, there were no pressing reasons for them to remain in care.

Thirty-two of the 52 children were boys, eight were infants under the age of two at the time of admission to care and just under half were adolescents. At first glance, these children seem somewhat straightforward compared with those who remain long in care. Twenty-two of the 52 children had originally come into care because of a breakdown in their family's ability to provide for them and 14 others were adolescents whose behaviour was causing concern. Thirty-eight originally came into care voluntarily and ten others were on care orders (three for delinquency and four for full-time education). Serious rejection, neglect and abuse were, therefore, uncommon among this group – a feature noticeable among many of the children who were able to leave care before six months.

However, unlike the early leavers, these later departures were more likely to present behaviour problems and the reasons why the 52 children were able to leave care were by no means simple. For example, not all (15) of these later leavers left care to return to their natural families, although this partly reflects the increasing age of children. For those that did, return was frequently difficult. In addition, 20 returned to a household which was different from the one they were inhabiting before admission to care. Even for those who went back to the same household, 16 of the 32 families had undergone a structural change while the child had been away. There is, therefore, considerable change among the families of these later leavers.

## Social work oversight
Thirty-seven of the 52 children who left care between six and 24 months had the same field social worker throughout their stay. However, the experience of these later leavers was similar to that of children who remain long in care in that they received less social work input during the early months than did children who left care quickly. Unlike the early leavers, many of these children were able to go out of care because of administrative changes or unexpected improvements in their family situation rather than because of intensive rehabilitative work by their social workers.

## Legal status
A quarter of the 52 children changed their legal status while in care. Six of these were voluntary receptions, two of whom became wards of court, one a care order for delinquency and three others for whom place of safety orders had to be taken. One of these was subsequently followed by a care order for being 'beyond control', another by an interim care order, and in the third case, voluntary care was repeated. Seven others of the later leavers first came into care via place of safety orders, five of which were followed by care orders for neglect, one voluntary care and another a ward of court (followed subsequently by an interim care order). Legislative histories were, therefore, relatively uncomplicated.

## Placements
We have already noted the propensity of some children to transfer placements while in care and to have very disrupted care experiences. As this pattern continues with the placements of this group of later leavers, this should cause some concern. The 52 children experienced 108 placements in all, 21 of which broke down prematurely. Initially,

five were placed at home, 15 in foster care and 32 in residential care and these proportions persisted for most of their time in care. As most of the children were in voluntary care, placements at home are uncommon and this contrasts sharply with those still in care at two years, the majority of whom are on care orders and some one-third of whom are able to live at home. Yet, 33 of the 52 children changed placement while in care indicating continued fluctuation and instability in the care experience, especially as placement breakdowns affected 21 of this group. There was also considerable movement for short-term, administrative reasons, especially among the various residential settings.

### Family links

While in care, patterns of family links enjoyed by these children were varied. While specific restrictions on parental contact were applied in only 22 of the 52 cases, 14 of them as a result of social work decisions, contact between children and parents was severely circumscribed. Only half of the children were able to see their natural mothers regularly (more than once per fortnight) during their stays in care, and very few children had frequent contact with their natural father. However, changes to these patterns of contact while the child was in care were common, far more so than for those who stay long. For example, some absent mothers renewed contact with their children and periods of silence alternated with frequent visiting. In some cases, it was the wider family or older siblings who kept contacts going. It was the maintenance or renewal of contact with the natural family that enabled the majority of these children to leave care. Non-specific restrictions to contact, however, continued to press heavily on this group and 80 per cent were still experiencing barriers to contact from difficulties intrinsic to their placements.

### Conclusion

The 52 children leaving care between six months and two years presented few administrative problems. There were few complications of legal status or fraught social work decisions about access. However, their family circumstances and future careers are by no means certain and in this they mirror many of the long-stay cases. Nevertheless, the care careers experienced by these later leavers reinforces the significance of maintaining links between parents and children absent in care, for it was this that, for the majority, made exit from care possible.

# Appendix II. Readmissions to care

In looking at children's care careers, we stressed at the point of reception the significance of previous involvements with social services. Three-quarters of the children in our study cohort were already known to social services and 29 per cent had been in care before. We have suggested that this influences social workers' definitions of the child's care needs. An accumulation of problems, it seems, precipitates children into care.

Similarly, we noted later that social workers were not optimistic about the future of many children who left care quickly and that 45 per cent of the 228 who had gone out of care by six months were expected to return to care again in the near future. A follow-up study showed that these gloomy forecasts were largely borne out, although social workers err on the side of caution and are unduly pessimistic. For example, of the 105 children expected to come into care again in the near future, 38 did so within a period of two years after the reception we originally studied. In contrast, only eight of the 68 who were not expected to re-enter care actually did so. Of the children who left care and on whom the social workers were undecided about their chances of subsequent return, 13 out of 55 came back. In contrast, only three of the 52 children leaving care between 6 and 24 months after reception were readmitted during the two-year follow-up period and, generally, social workers were far more optimistic about these children's viability to cope in the community.

If we follow up the 228 children who left care before six months for a period of two years after their initial reception, we find that 59 of them (26 per cent) came into care again at some point. For 39 of them, the duration of their stay in care was short but for the remaining 20 it was for more than six months. Three of the 52 who left care later in our study (after six months) were also subsequently readmitted, making 62 readmissions in all. Seventeen of these readmissions came back again for a third stay during the follow-up period, four of them for a long sojourn on this subsequent occasion.

The majority of these readmissions, therefore, were for a short period and were usually voluntary receptions following a recurrence of family breakdown, parental illness or, for adolescents, a resumption of difficult behaviour at home or school. Groups of siblings were often involved and the placements selected were already known by the children. However, for a third of the children readmitted at each stage, re-entry to care resulted from a serious deterioration in the home situation and on this next occasion they were not able to leave care quickly.

It is also clear from the follow-up study that the children who oscillate in and out of care present considerable behaviour problems of control, school refusal and minor delinquency both while at home and on re-entry to care. They were often assessed by social workers, foster parents and residential staff as presenting behaviour problems in their placements.

While it was the recurrence of home problems that led social workers to readmit these children to care, in a third of cases, there were accompanying moves to gain greater legal control by obtaining care orders or assuming parental rights and to seek long-term placements for the children. Specific restrictions over access to the natural family were applied by social workers to six of the 18 cases and, at the two-year stage, three of these children had lost all contact with their natural families.

In the light of this evidence about readmissions, our overall picture of the children's care careers will need minor modification. For example, we saw that at the six-months stage, 228 of the original 450 children had left care. However, 24 of these soon came back, this time for a stay of more than six months. This increases the total number of children in the original cohort who have experienced a stay in care exceeding six months to 246. Similarly, we noted that 170 of the original cohort were still in care after two years. However, 18 of the readmissions were also back in care at this point, so increasing to 188 the number in the original cohort who were in care at the time of the two-year follow-up.

# Appendix III. Our results compared with other relevant child-care studies

i) *David Fanshel: Children in foster care*

Some interesting comparisons emerge when our study group at reception and at two years is compared with that used by Fanshel and Shinn in their follow-up of 624 children in the care of New York State. We have already noted that comparisons are made difficult by the fact that, whereas our study population includes all children coming into care for whatever reason, Fanshel and Shinn have made many exclusions.

In fact, only 57 of the 450 children covered by our research (that is, 13 per cent) would have qualified for inclusion in the New York study. When the duration of the child's stay in care is taken into consideration to equate with Fanshel's criterion, this leaves us with a minority of only 31 children (18 per cent) in care at two years who meet Fanshel's criteria.

It is important when making comparisons between child-care studies to note any selectivity in the study populations because such differences could significantly alter any findings. The cohort on which this research is based is extremely wide, representing all children in local authority care, whereas Fanshel's study population focuses more on young children coming into care for long periods after family breakdowns. Children in his study also seemed to stay longer than in our cohort. For example, three-quarters of his 624 children were still in care at Fanshel's second investigation point, that is between 18 and 23 months, whereas we find 31 comparable children out of 57 (54 per cent) at the two-year point.

Nevertheless, it is encouraging to find many similarities in the general patterns of family links experienced by separated children in both studies. It does seem that despite differences in research emphasis the general problems of managing separation are very similar in Britain and North America. Approximately two years after reception to care, Fanshel found that 31 per cent of his study population had no family contacts at all and that 11 per cent enjoyed only the most irregular of links with their natural families. In comparison at our two-year stage, eight of the comparable 31 children in our study population (26 per cent) had lost contact with their relatives and four others (13 per cent) had very infrequent contact. In both studies, therefore, after two years the frequency of family contact enjoyed by children who stay long in care, mostly young long-stay cases, is similar – at around 40 per cent. This is particularly interesting because of very different care situations, welfare organisations and placement options between the two countries. It suggests that withering links between parents and child are affected by common problems in managing separation as well as by the idiosyncratic features of two different welfare systems.

ii) *Barbara Tizard: Adoption, A Second Chance* (1977)
The use of long-stay residential placements for very young children who remain in care is now rare, whatever the situation may have been at the time of Barbara Tizard's study. In our study, 83 out of the 450 children entering care were aged under two years on admission and this group of very young children are the most vulnerable to care reception. However, the majority of these young entrants left care quickly, for example 56 children were out of care by six months. Although a residential placement was not uncommon on reception for these young children (ie. nine children went first to a community home and 12 to hospital) residence did not last long. Thus, for the 19 children who were still in care at two years out of the 83 who originally entered care, *none* had lingered in a residential home. All had either been fostered or were living at home. This applies equally to young children as well as to infants, that is children under five. Children's long sojourn in residential care usually starts at the age of 7, 8 or 9, after several breakdowns in fostering, abortive rehabilitations or oscillations in and out of care.

iii) *Rowe and Lambert: Children Who Wait* (1973)
Rowe and Lambert scrutinised 2812 children in the care of 33 voluntary and statutory agencies in Britain. They asked the agencies to estimate out of all children who were fostered or placed in residential care, those who were in need of a family placement. The study excluded those children in care living with their own parents, children who had been in care for less than six months and young people over the age of 11. From this 'snapshot' view of 2812 children, Rowe and Lambert concluded that 626 (22 per cent) were thought by social workers to need a substitute family. In our study, 88 children out of the 450 met the criteria applied by Rowe and Lambert, 9 (10 per cent) of whom were 'waiting' for a family placement two years after their entry to care.

Such findings demonstrate that there have been significant changes in recent years in the care experience of infants and younger children. There has been a marked decline in the use of residential care and fewer children 'wait' for alternative family placements. In any case, such children represent a small minority of care admissions and even a minority of longer-term cases. To base blanket local authority child care policies on minority needs, however pressing these may be, could be detrimental to other groups of children, particularly adolescents and short-stay cases.

# Index